WORLD INDUSTRY STUDIES   2

The Global Textile Industry

WORLD INDUSTRY STUDIES

Edited by Professor Ingo Walter,
Graduate School of Business Administration,
New York University

1   COLLAPSE AND SURVIVAL: INDUSTRY STRATEGIES IN A
CHANGING WORLD
Robert H. Ballance and Stuart W. Sinclair

2   THE GLOBAL TEXTILE INDUSTRY
Brian Toyne, Jeffrey S. Arpan, Andy H. Barnett,
David A. Ricks, Terence A. Shimp

3   BLUE GOLD: THE POLITICAL ECONOMY OF NATURAL GAS
J. D. Davis

Forthcoming

THE CHEMICAL INDUSTRY IN THE WORLD ECONOMY
Thomas J. Ilgen

POLITICS VS. ECONOMICS IN THE WORLD STEEL TRADE
Kent Jones

MICROELECTRONICS: BUSINESS STRATEGY, GOVERNMENT POLICY
AND INTERNATIONAL COMPETITION
Thomas A. Pugel

THE WORLD MINING INDUSTRY: INVESTMENT, STRATEGY AND
PUBLIC POLICY
Raymond Mikesell

The Global Textile Industry

Brian Toyne, *University of South Carolina*
Jeffrey S. Arpan, *University of South Carolina*
Andy H. Barnett, *Auburn University*
David A. Ricks, *University of South Carolina*
Terence A. Shimp, *University of South Carolina*

and

Joseph E. Andrews, *University of South Carolina*
J. Carl Clamp, *University of South Carolina*
Clarence D. Rogers, *Clemson University*
Geoffrey Shepherd, *The University of Sussex, England*
Tran Van Tho, *International Business Information, K.K., Tokyo, Japan*
Edward A. Vaughn, *Clemson University*
Steven Woolcock, *Royal Institute for International Affairs, England*

London
GEORGE ALLEN & UNWIN
Boston   Sydney

George Allen & Unwin (Publishers) Ltd,
40 Museum Street, London WC1A 1LU, UK

George Allen & Unwin (Publishers) Ltd,
Park Lane, Hemel Hempstead, Herts HP2 4TE, UK

Allen & Unwin, Inc.,
9 Winchester Terrace, Winchester, Mass. 01890, USA

George Allen & Unwin Australia Pty Ltd,
8 Napier Street, North Sydney, NSW 2060, Australia

First published in 1984

British Library Cataloguing in Publication Data

The Global textile industry.—(World industry studies; no. 2)
1. Textile industry
I. Toyne, B.   II. Series
338.4'7677   HD9850.5
ISBN 0-04-338110-3

Library of Congress Cataloging in Publication Data applied for

Set in 10 on 11 point Times by Phoenix Photosetting, Chatham
and printed in Great Britain by Billing and Sons Ltd,
London and Worcester

Contents

Textile Industry Advisory Board

Preface

abstract

In a time of rapid change, and increasing uncertainty, it is a formidable challenge to anticipate future problems and arrive at solutions that will increase the international competitiveness of national industries. This book is the result of the Center for Industry Policy and Strategy's effort to help the textile mill products industry meet this challenge. It provides national industries with an international perspective that will become increasingly necessary for an understanding of its strategic alternatives in a world that is increasingly interdependent. It presents a worldwide analysis of the textile mill products industry and identifies policy and strategy alternatives for the industries of both developed and developing countries.

The book represents the cooperative efforts and perspectives of a research team comprised of researchers from the University of South Carolina (USA), Clemson University (USA), the University of Sussex (United Kingdom), the Royal Institute for International Affairs (United Kingdom) and International Business Information, K.K. (Japan). To insure that the research and the resulting policy and strategy recommendations are of pragmatic value to textile mill products companies, the research team was advised and assisted by an industry Advisory Board consisting of twelve senior operating executives of some of the US industry's leading public and private corporations, and its suppliers of textile machinery and man-made fibers.

While the book represents a team effort, and reflects the free exchange and blending of a variety of viewpoints and contributions, each member of the team had initial responsibilities for certain elements as follows:

Chapter 1 – Brian Toyne
Chapter 2 – Jeffrey S. Arpan; Brian Toyne
Chapter 3 – Clarence D. Rogers; Edward A. Vaughn
Chapter 4 – Joseph E. Andrews
Chapter 5 – Andy H. Barnett
Chapter 6 – David A. Ricks
Chapter 7 – Terence A. Shimp
Chapter 8 – Brian Toyne
Chapter 9 – Brian Toyne

Dr Geoffrey Shepherd, University of Sussex, contributed to the economic analyses of the European industries and case studies on the current and future strategies of three European textile mill products companies. These contributions are included in Chapters 5 and 7. Mr

Steven Woolcock, Royal Institute for International Affairs, contributed to the political analysis of the European industries which appears in Chapter 6. Mr Tran Van Tho, International Business Information, K.K., contributed the case studies on the current and future strategies of three Japanese textile mill products companies (Chapter 7), and information for the economic and political analyses of the Asian industries (Chapters 5 and 6). Mr J. Carl Clamp, Distinguished Lecturer in Management, University of South Carolina, acted as a consultant and provided pragmatic and insightful comments on the drafting of all nine chapters. Prior to joining the University of South Carolina's faculty, he was president of United States Filter Corporation and an executive of International Telephone and Telegraph, Allis-Chalmers, and General Mills.

We are indebted to all who contributed to this study in many ways. The James C. Self Foundation's financial contribution to the Center for Industry Policy and Strategy enabled us to conduct *on-site* investigations in Asia and Europe, as well as some domestic travel and other expenses related to the study. Dean James F. Kane of the College of Business Administration, University of South Carolina, contributed significantly to the study by his encouragement and by releasing us from many of our other responsibilities as faculty members of the College. We are also most appreciative of the executives of the Asian, European and United States textile mill products companies who participated so willingly and openly in the fourteen company case studies included in this study. Equally, the members of the textile industry Advisory Board were most generous of their time and expertise. We are in their debt.

Finally, there are numerous staff who make contributions to any effort such as this one. The drafting and redrafting of the chapters, and the keeping of records and documents could easily overwhelm the most seasoned of persons. Of special note are the efforts of Patti Bearden of the Divison of Research, College of Business Administration, University of South Carolina. In addition, several graduate research assistants put in many hours of work on the project, particularly Kathrine Huelster, Sam Koh, Martin Peterson and Charles Zlock.

While we are indebted to all those who assisted the project team on this study, the conclusions and recommendations remain the sole responsibility of the project team.

Columbia, South Carolina   Brian Toyne (Project Director)
April 1983   Jeffrey S. Arpan
                                        Andy H. Barnett
                                        David A. Ricks
                                        Terence A. Shimp

1

The Focus and Purpose of The Study

Introduction

Many industries vital to the economic well-being of developed nations are being seriously challenged, even threatened, by foreign competitors and the economic and political actions of the competitors' governments. Although this increasing intensity in the competitiveness of 'global' industries spans several decades, the situation became particularly evident and critical in the 1970s. Apparel, automobiles, chemicals, steel, electronics, apparel and textile machinery are just a few of the industries that have seen the dynamics of their domestic and overseas competitive environments change and intensify.

The principal reasons put forward to explain this intensification in competitiveness reflect the complexity of the problems confronting these industries. They include charges of 'unfair competition' initiated and supported by foreign governments; the restructuring of entire industries; escalations in the cost of energy; trends toward worldwide oligopolistic competitive structures; and, in some cases, inconsistencies in the domestic and foreign commercial policies of governments.

Regardless of the single or combined accuracies of these and other explanations, what appears necessary to improve the international competitiveness of these industries is a more 'global' understanding of the forces that result in change in the dynamics of international competitiveness. More specifically, industries need to acquire more comprehensive and international perspectives of their individual industries, their competitors and the international dynamics of competition.

In an era of rapid economic, political and technological changes, and the increase in uncertainty that these changes bring about, it is a formidable challenge to anticipate problems, identify key issues and arrive at solutions that will enhance the domestic and international competitiveness of particular industries. This book is the product of the Center for Industry Policy and Strategy's effort to meet this challenge for the global textile mill products industry. It presents an analysis of the major worldwide changes that are occurring in the economic, political and technological forces that directly affect this industry and the competitiveness of national industries and concludes with an analysis of policy and strategy alternatives designed to enhance the competitiveness of textile mill companies in their home and overseas markets.

The Scope and Purpose of the Study

The main purpose of this research was to gain a better understanding of the global competitive dynamics of the *textile mill products* industry (see definition in Appendix 1), and its competitive structure. Such an understanding was considered important and necessary for the formulation of future policy and strategy alternatives for companies in the textile mill products industry. In general, the study was designed to identify and analyze (1) the critical changes occurring in the forces that directly and indirectly affect the global and domestic competitive environments of the textile mill products industry, (2) the policies and strategies that US, European and Asian companies, and their governments, are using or developing, (3) the policies and strategies that are likely to be successful in the future, and (4) the strategic choices textile mill companies should consider adopting if their international competitiveness is to be enhanced. Government policy initiatives supportive of the strategic choices recommended will also be discussed.

Limited project funds necessitated restricting the regional industries of the world for the research effort. While data on the global textile mill products industry were collected, the US, European and Asia Pacific textile mill products industries received the major focus in terms of on-site investigation in this study.

The Asia Pacific industries were selected for on-site investigation because of their phenomenal growth and recognized international importance *vis-à-vis* the European and South American industries. For example, Japan is the second largest producer of textile yarn, only exceeded by the United States. In addition, South Korea and Taiwan have become leading fabric producers and exporters, following Japan's pattern.

The European industries were selected for on-site investigation because they had to make considerably more rapid adjustments as a result of the formation of the European Community (EC). Consequently, the adjustments that European industries made, and the political options considered and finally implemented by their governments, provide a set of tested policy and strategy scenarios. The actual outcomes of these scenarios, although strongly influenced by local cultural, social and political factors, contain information on what policies and strategies have and have not been successful, and why.

The US industry was selected because of the size of its domestic market and its leadership role in productivity. Its government also played a major and significant role in the formulation and implementation of the Long Term Arrangement Regarding International Trade in Cotton Textiles (LTA) and the Multi-fiber Arrangement Regarding International Trade in Cotton Textiles (MFA).

Major Research Questions

If textile mill products companies are to enhance their international competitiveness in the 1980s, they must be able to respond flexibly to a wide range of domestic and international political and economic changes. Central to this study was the identification and analysis of those changes critical to the competitiveness and flexibility of textile mill companies, and the question of how to respond to the favorable and unfavorable effects of changes.

The issues addressed in this study were of two distinct types: (1) those *fundamental forces* that, from a practical perspective, cannot be altered but need to be taken into account in any policy planning, and (2) those *problem areas* that can be addressed and resolved, at least in part, through proper decisions and that need timely policy attention.

Among the fundamental forces is the set of demographic, labor force and social changes. For instance, examples in the US include the aging of the US population, the increasing participation and heightening expectations of women in the labor force, and the prospects of shortages in the supply of some types of skills. Changes such as these are of sufficient magnitude to alter US society and cause fundamental changes in its institutions.

A second force is the continued growth in international economic interdependence. Economic policies of individual nations in a variety of areas once regarded as purely domestic can be expected to exert an increasingly significant influence on economic developments in other countries, including, for example, national industrial policy. A European example was the formation of the European Community, which resulted in increased competition among the industries of member nations.

Another force is the continued growth in competitiveness of

foreign competitors in the form of trade and direct investment in the European and US economies. The US and European fabric and apparel industries are particularly vulnerable to import competition and competition in other national markets because of the industry's structural characteristics and the fact that textiles is one of the first internationally competitive industries generally developed by developing countries.

Against this backdrop of rapid fundamental changes in the domestic and international competitive environments of the industry, there are many problem areas requiring resolution. What political, cultural, social and economic factors adversely affect the US, European and Asian industries' development and response? What policy changes could be made by their governments to remove competitive obstacles and to enhance their industries' ability to respond? What constitute practical responses by textile mill products companies?

Specifically, the major research questions addressed in this study included the following:

1   What fundamental changes occurred to the global textile mill products industry during the last two decades that directly and/or indirectly affected the competitiveness of the US, European and Asian industries?
2   What factors currently restrict and/or impede the various textile mill products industries' abilities to respond to the fundamental changes that are occurring?
3   What policy role could the various governments play in removing current obstacles in order to enhance the competitiveness of their industries?
4   What effective policy and strategy adjustments can and should be undertaken by textile mill products companies?

The study consisted of three parts. The first part examined the trends in structural factors and market forces that determine the intensity and dynamics of the competition in each national industry. In general, these structural factors and market forces are the same in all national industries. Competition in an industry is the result of the dynamic interplay of five basic competitive forces: (1) the relative bargaining power of the industry and its suppliers; (2) the relative bargaining power of the industry and its buyers; (3) the threat of new entrants; (4) the threat of substitute products or services; and (5) the level of rivalry among existing firms. Further, the strength of these forces, individually and combined, is determined by the structural features of the industry, which include such things as entry and exit barriers, economies of centralization of functional activities, capital requirements, switching costs (from one industrial sector to another, from one product line to another), access to distribution channels, the pervasive and fundamental influence of production and product technologies, government policies, rules and regulations, and so forth.

The second part examined the differences in selected factors and forces of national industries that determine the intensity and dynamics of international competition within the global textile mill products industry. These differences included: (1) factor cost differences among countries (such as wage rates, costs of other inputs, capital–labor combinations and productivity); (2) differing circumstances in the national markets such as supplier relations, customer relations, market sizes and socio-cultural factors; (3) different roles that national governments play (such as incentives, subsidies and degree of protection); (4) differences in the rates at which new production and product technologies are introduced; and (5) differences in the goals, strategies and resources of national and international competitors, and their ability to monitor and react to foreign competitors and changes in the environment.

The first two parts of the study depended heavily on the analysis of secondary data and information, and used such traditional techniques as trend analysis, comparative analysis and the interpretative abilities of the researchers and practitioners.

The third part of the study examined the domestic and international strategies of major competitors that make up the global textile mill products industry. Both successful and unsuccessful competitors and strategies were examined. The varying abilities of the competitors to adapt to, take advantage of or otherwise influence the competitive milieu of their industries, and the factors that distinguish successful and unsuccessful competitors were of critical importance. Eventual success is directly linked to the understanding competitors have of their industry's market forces and structural factors, the changes that are occurring in them, and the strategic alternatives they are prepared to consider and select from in order to compete.

The third part depended primarily on the analysis of data and information collected as a result of in-depth interviews with executive operating officers of eight US, three Japanese and three European textile mill products companies. In order to understand the process by which firms react to their environments and competitive conditions, it is necessary to examine behavior as close as possible to the competitors.

In selecting these fourteen companies, every effort was made to insure that they were representative of the types of textile mill products companies to be found in the United States, Japan and Europe.

The main criterion was, however, a willingness to cooperate and frankly discuss their current operations and future plans. Clearly, the sample of companies is not representative in any statistically rigorous sense. The findings and conclusions derived from a study of corporate strategies must be interpreted within the broader environmental conditions prevailing in the international industry, in light of other studies and the experience of the readership.

In each chapter more detailed information is provided about the specific research methodologies employed.

Organization of the Book

Chapters 2–9 present the findings, conclusions and recommendations arrived at as a result of this study. Chapter 2 presents a brief overview of what constitutes a textile complex; its major segments and markets and their interdependencies are highlighted. This is followed by discussion of how complexes differ internationally.

Chapter 3 presents an overview of the technology used by textile industries in the manufacture and treatment of yarns and fabrics. The rapid changes that have occurred or are occurring in this area are of signal importance to the international competitiveness of national textile complexes.

Chapter 4 presents an analysis of international fiber and textile mill products trade data from the 1960s. An analysis of world production, consumption and trade patterns is followed by a study of regional patterns. The changing roles and significances of the US, European and Asian complexes in world markets conclude this chapter. Notwithstanding the influence of trade barriers on trade patterns, such an analysis provides valuable insights into the relative and changing competitiveness of textile complexes. It also provides a necessary backdrop to the more detailed analyses presented in subsequent chapters.

The economic and political factors that affect national textile industries and that determine their international competitiveness are analyzed in Chapters 5 and 6. Chapter 5 is devoted to a study of the economic structures of the textile industries to be found in Asian and European countries and the United States. Chapter 6 describes and comparatively discusses the influence that these countries' governments have on the international competitiveness of their textile industries.

The results of the corporate interviews are presented and comparatively analyzed in Chapter 7. The presentation includes an analytical discussion of the executives' perceptions of the threats and opportunities that changes in the economic, political and technological dimensions hold for their industry and the adjustments and strategies they are implementing, by country and then comparatively.

Chapter 8 draws together the findings and conclusions presented in the previous chapters to analyze the three regional industries of Asia, Europe and the United States. The major purpose of this chapter was to identify and then comparatively analyze the major strategies adopted by these industries.

Chapter 9 concludes this study by presenting and analyzing a series of short-term and long-term recommendations for textile mill companies and national industries. These recommendations reflect the cultural, social, economic and political settings of these industries, and our interpretations of global economic, technological and political trends. When necessary, the types of government policies required to support these recommendations are addressed.

2

The Textile Complex and the Textile Mill Products Industry[1]

Introduction

The textile complex is involved in the production of natural and man-made fibers and their conversion into apparel, home furnishings and industrial goods. Figure 2.1 identifies the major segments of the complex, their linkages and the three major end markets served by the complex, from the point of view of the textile mill products industry.

Natural and man-made fibers, chemicals and textile machinery are essential inputs in the making of textile products. These inputs are produced by other industrial complexes, which often have specialized segments dedicated to and dependent upon the textile mill products and apparel industries for their economic prosperity.

The textile mill products and apparel industries are the employment nucleus of the complex. They manufacture the yarns, threads, fabrics and end products sold by the complex, and are directly dependent upon the complex's end markets for their prosperity.

Although most countries manufacture textile products, most lack the supply and demand conditions necessary to support entire textile complexes. For example, not all countries are endowed with the land or climatic conditions necessary for the production of agricultural products such as cotton and wool. Some countries do not have the indigenous technological or financial capabilities to develop and support chemical complexes capable of producing man-made fibers, or textile machinery. Others lack the necessary internal markets required to achieve economies of scale in the production of man-made fibers, chemicals and 'mature' textile fabrics. As a result, there is considerable variation between countries in their textile manufacturing industries, their dependence upon foreign inputs and/or markets, and their abilities to compete internationally.

The remainder of this chapter presents an overview of textile complexes necessary for understanding the problems confronting the tex-

2.1 The Textile Complex

tile mill products industries of the world. It is divided into two major sections. It first presents a brief description and comparison of the major segments in a textile complex, then proceeds with a discussion of major international differences in textile complexes and the textile business cycle.

The Major Segments of a Textile Complex

As a consumer of materials and services and producer of products, the textile complex may be considered as consisting of three major segments: fibers; fabric formation and finishing; and end-use manufactured products. The complex is also dependent upon several related industries: textile machinery, chemicals and agriculture.

Fibers
Fibers are generally classified into two principal groups: natural and man-made fibers. Man-made fibers are further broken down into regenerated or cellulosic fibers and synthetic or non-cellulosic fibers.

Natural fibers such as cotton, linen, jute and wool are products of agriculture and are a significant factor in international agribusiness. Regenerated fibers such as rayon, acetate and triacetate are products of naturally occurring cellulose, usually cotton and wood, and are hence related to both forestry and agriculture. Synthetic fibers such as polyester, nylon, acrylic and polypropylene are petrochemical derivatives. Other chemically based textile materials are dyestuffs, often related via technological organization to pharmaceuticals; resins for durable-press, soil-release and fluid repellency, often related to polymer/plastics technology; and fundamental elements and compounds such as chlorine, urea and formaldehyde, which form the basis for many auxiliaries used in textile wet-processing.

While there are thousands of natural-fiber producers throughout the world, there are relatively few major producers of man-made fibers (less than thirty). The main reason is that man-made fiber production is very capital and knowledge intensive and has significant manufacturing economies of scale. The major producers of man-made fibers are based in developed countries, and are typically part of large diversified multinational chemical companies operating in an oligopolistic market. In the USA, DuPont, Celanese, Eastman and Monsanto are the largest firms, while outside the USA the largest firms are Italy's ENI and Montedison; Germany's Hoechst, Bayer and BASF; Britain's ICI; France's Rhone-Poulenc; the Netherlands' Akzo; and Japan's Mitsubishi Rayon, Asahi Chemical, Mitsui Chemical, Toray Industries and Teijin.

Compared to the other major segments of the textile complex, developed countries still dominate production of man-made fibers. However, production technologies of certain man-made fibers are considered 'mature': well established, well known and produced in many developing countries. As a result, fibers made from these mature process technologies are more price competitive and less restricted in terms of production location. On the other hand, the technologies for specialty, higher value and more complex fibers are newer, more complicated, less price competitive and more restricted to developed country firms.

Fabric Formation and Finishing
The intermediate segment of the textile complex (essentially the textile mill products industry) can be broken down into three relatively distinct operations: yarn spinning; fabric forming; and fabric finishing. Although numerous small and independent companies specialize in these operations, most textile mill companies have integrated operations from yarns through fabric forming to fabric finishing.

Textile yarn, for the most part, is an intermediate in the production of fabric. Strand products such as craft yarns, cords, cables and braids are manufactured in considerable poundage; but the major use for yarn is to weave or knit fabric or to tuft carpeting. Generically, yarn is categorized as being one of two types: staple-fiber yarn and continuous filament yarn. Staple-fiber yarn is manufactured by the spinning process from discontinuous fibers one to several inches in length; continuous filament yarn is a product of the extrusion process in which chemical solutions are solidified and stretched after passing through millimeter-sized spinnerets. After formation, continuous filament yarn is often modified to provide bulk, stretch or texture. Depending on ultimate use, yarn may be further twisted, plied, dyed, surface treated or packaged. As an industry segment, processors of staple-fiber yarns are referred to as spinners, while processors of filament yarn are termed throwsters or texturizers. Spinners and throwsters selling packaged yarn are the nucleus for the yarn sales market. Yarn is sold by the pound or kilo; its value is determined by fiber content, thickness or count, amount of twist, and extent of after treatment. In vertically integrated companies, the yarn production element takes the form of a department or division.

Yarn spinning has become a highly capital-intensive process, requiring textile machinery and equipment designed to separate and disentangle fibers, to spin yarns and to treat them chemically. The spinning of several different kinds of fibers into a single yarn requires additional know-how and equipment.

Fabric is the fundamental product of the textile industry. Three principal methods of producing fabric are by weaving, knitting and non-woven technologies. In weaving, the most versatile and extensively utilized technology for manufacturing flat goods, sets of yarns are interlaced at right angles on a loom. In knitting, yarns are interlooped by latched or spring needles arranged in a circular or linear array. Non-woven technology involves interlocking fibers or yarns by mechanical, chemical or thermal means.

Woven fabric market segments can be identified according to fabric width, surface texture, yarn composition or fiber content. Examples include narrow fabrics and broad woven goods; dobby (fancy) and jacquard fabrics; blended and filament fabrics; cotton and worsted goods. Each is frequently considered an industry sub-segment and often defined by a separate market structure. Knitted fabrics are commonly described and marketed according to their technology of formation. Circular or jersey, tricot, raschel, and double-knit are examples. Women's hosiery and men's half hose are related formation technologies, but are also considered separate segments, as are knitted gloves, caps and sweaters. Non-woven structures, which technically include tufted carpets, are most frequently associated with end-use applications such as floor coverings, disposables, or fabrics for civil engineering. When sold in rolls from the forming machine, fabric is termed greige or grey and as such is the basis of the greige goods market. In vertical operations, greige mills provide input for finishing, or wet-processing, plants.

Until the 1950s, weaving was the major fabric forming process. Knitting was a specialized process used to form apparel fabrics for such products as sweaters, stockings and some underwear. In the 1950s, tufting began to displace weaving as the dominant process in the manufacture of carpets. By 1975, tufting accounted for over 95 per cent of all carpet manufactured in the United States and was of growing importance in the manufacture of apparel fabrics. Beginning in the middle 1960s, knitted fabrics, in the form of double knits, made serious inroads into apparel fabrics. However, the major output of the fabric segment in most countries is broadwoven fabric, although narrow and knit fabrics are also produced in sizeable quantities.

Some non-woven fabrics have displaced traditionally formed fabrics in the manufacture of such products as disposable diapers, coated fabrics for furniture, wall coverings, luggage and car roofs, discardable medical and surgical products (drapes, gowns, masks), carpet underlayings, apparel inner-linings, household and industrial wipes, sanitary napkins, and many packaging materials. The importance of non-wovens is not only their substitutability for wovens, but in new applications. While the total production of non-wovens has remained well below that of wovens and knits, non-wovens have experienced faster growth rates (188 per cent from 1971 to 1977; INDA, 1978).

The finishing process is both knowledge and capital intensive. Finishing provides comfort, ease of care, durability and aesthetic properties that can significantly affect final goods' competitiveness in the market place – and, in many cases, result in a mature product beginning a new product life cycle. For example, permanent press treatment of basic shirts and slacks essentially created a new line of garments. The predominant method of finishing involves wet-processing.

Textile wet-processing involves the treatment of fiber, yarn or fabric structures with chemicals that are carried by a fluid. Most often the carrier fluid is water; and very frequently wet-processes are carried out in a dyehouse, bleachery or finishing plant. Fiber wet-processes include degreasing and scouring of wool and raw stock dyeing or dyeing in fiber form. Yarn wet-processes include bleaching and/or dyeing in yarn form. Fabric wet-processing encompasses cleaning or preparing fabrics for subsequent treatment, providing fabric coloration by dyeing or printing, and enhancing functional properties by applying chemical finishes. Like other textile operations, wet-processing technology evolved through experiences gained in the handling of one of three traditional materials: cotton, wool or silk. As each of these materials has been handled differently and independently due to differences in chemical and physical properties, distinct wet-processing technologies have resulted.

Generally, fabrics manufactured for traditional cotton end-uses, such as shirtings and sheetings (polyester/cotton blends, for example), are wet-processed according to cotton finishing technology, while fabrics for wool or worsted end-uses, such as suiting goods (polyester/wools or double knits, for example), are finished using wool technology, and fabrics for silk end-uses, such as nylon for blouses, are finished using silk technology. Further, woven and knitted fabrics as well as floor coverings are very often finished in separate plants. Reasons for this segregation include fabric structural differences and chemical, machinery and processing requirements. In addition, mechanical surface modification such as sanding, brushing or napping is frequently carried out in the fabric finishing sector.

Most wet-processing organizations can be categorized as being either commission finishing houses or finishing divisions of vertically integrated firms. Commission finishers process greige fabric, often purchased on the greige market by converters, under contract. Finished fabric is sold in rolls, folds or bolts to outlets, converters or fabricators. In vertical organizations this fabric is processed further for specific end-use applications.

The key factors in the textile mill products sector in the forming of fabrics are the textile machinery and equipment used, the skills of the technical staffs to service the machinery and equipment, the capital necessary to buy machinery, and quick access to new fibers introduced to the market. In most countries, an increased emphasis on fabric quality and productivity had emerged as critical factors in the competitiveness of this segment of the complex.

In general, apparel fabric is produced by larger firms, which typically require large minimum orders of one color or design. Firms also tend to specialize by type of fabric: heavy, medium or light weight fabric; woven vs. knit fabric; man-made fiber fabric vs. natural fiber fabric; and intricately patterned fabric vs. simple fabric. The basic reasons for this specialization are the different equipment and the number and complexity of steps required to make each type of fabric.

The fabric segment is in the middle segment of the complex in terms not only of the manufacturing flow but also of capital and knowledge intensity, industry life cycle and degree of competition. This segment is also considerably less concentrated than the man-made fiber production segment.

Even though there are many more firms producing fabric than man-made fibers, the majority of them produce a relatively small percentage of total output. However, the bulk of fabric is produced by a small number of large firms. Thus the fabric sector in most textile complexes has a dualistic nature: thousands of small- and medium-size firms each producing a limited range of products and accounting for a comparatively small percentage of total output, and a much smaller number of large firms each producing a wider variety of products and, as a group, accounting for a disproportionate share of total output.[2]

The largest firms in the USA are Burlington, J. P. Stevens, Milliken, West Point-Pepperell, Springs Mills and about a half dozen others. Outside the USA, the largest producers are Britain's Courtaulds, Coats Patons, Tootal and Carrington; Japan's Kanebo, Toyobo, Mitsubishi Rayon and Unitaka; South Korea's Daewoo and Sunkyoung; and France's Dollfus-Mieg. However, both inside and outside the USA, there are major differences among the largest firms in terms of their production by end-use categories (see Table 2.1 for an example of US firms). In terms of product life cycle, complex specialty fabrics are considered to be in earlier stages, while basic woven fabrics are in the mature stage.

Manufacture of End-Use Products
Principal end-use applications for textile products are apparel, home

Table 2.1 *Market Dependence of Major US Textile Mill Companies (Percent of Total Sales)*

| | Market Sectors | | | | | |
| | Apparel sector | | | Home | | |
Company	Bottom weight	Top weight	Total	furnishings sector	Industrial sector	Other
Burlington Industries	✓			34	8	
Cannon Mills				90		
Collins & Aikman			26	44	30	
Cone Mills	✓		85			
Dan River	✓	✓	79			
Fieldcrest				90		
Graniteville	✓		85			
Lowenstein (M.)		✓	47	31	22	
Reeves Bros.	✓		35		42	
Riegel Textiles	✓		50	20		22[a]
Spring Mills		✓	44	43		19[b]
Stevens (J. P.)	✓		47	29	13	8[c]
United Merchants		✓	51		14	
West Point-Pepperell	✓		30	60	10	

[a] Diapers
[b] Frozen Foods
[c] Printing

Source: 'Textiles: Current Analysis', *Industry Surveys* (New York, NY: Standard & Poors), July 1980, p. T-56, Section 2.

furnishings and industrial. Sometimes referred to as the 'cut and sew' segments, companies engaged in these businesses transform two-dimensional roll goods into three-dimensional utility items. In addition to fabric, other textile components such as thread and interlining are basic input materials. Fundamental operations include marketing; dimension determination; cutting; sewing; pressing; and packaging.

The largest of the three final production stages in the textile complex is the manufacturing of apparel. The manufacturing process begins with the design of the garment to be made, based on forecasts of fashion, style and needs of consumers. The design is next made into patterns, which are used to cut the fabric purchased from fabric companies. The cut fabric is normally then sewn into garments,[3] tagged, and shipped through the distribution channels. In reality, however, most apparel companies do not perform all these functions; much contracting exists. Cutting and/or sewing contractors and sub-contractors rely on designs and pre-cut fabrics supplied to them by retailers, jobbers[4] or larger manufacturers.

Traditionally, apparel has been a creative, family, and price-competitive industry comprized of tens of thousands of small companies averaging less than 100 employees and producing an extremely narrow product line. It has also been an industry where production changes have come very slowly – fabric is laid, cut and sewn much as it was forty years ago. However, the apparel industries of many countries have recently experienced a major restructuring that is expected to continue in the future.[5] The larger firms' share of total output has increased, the capital and knowledge intensity of the industry have increased, and the product lines produced by many apparel firms have widened and been upgraded.

The apparel segment of the textile complex is the most labor intensive, fragmented and price competitive. Of all major segments, it has the lowest entry barriers in terms of capital and technical knowledge requirements. Only the larger firms typically produce garments in more than one category (e.g. men's outerwear, women's dresses, children's sleepwear), and most firms produce garments only in a specific price and fashion range (e.g. high fashion women's dresses, inexpensive children's pants, etc.). The largest firms in the USA are Levi Strauss, Blue Bell and Interco (each with sales over $3 billion and $1 billion, respectively), followed by Cluett Peabody, Hart Schaffner and Marx, Kayser-Roth, V. F. Corp., Kellwood, Warnaco, and Jonathan Logan (each with sales over $400 million). Outside the USA, the largest firms are: Kashiyama, Renown, Courtaulds, Triumph and Bidermann.

The home furnishing sector is essentially comprized of domestic items such as floor coverings (carpets and rugs), upholstery, sheets, pillowcases, blankets, drapes, washcloths and towels. These products are frequently made in fully integrated firms which often package the goods for retail distribution. In general, floor coverings made from man-made fibers involve the most capital-intensive process, and in the USA production is located primarily in the Southeastern United States (especially Georgia).

The carpet industry relies heavily on man-made fiber producers for R&D, which has manifested itself in the form of new fibers or fiber blends with better wear, color or cleaning properties. The product and process technologies for most types of sheets, pillowcases, blankets, towels and drapes are considered mature, and hence not restricted to developed country production locations. However, there are some production economies of scale that result in both product and industrial concentration and a trend toward greater automation. Like their counterparts in the apparel segment, large US producers of home furnishings rely heavily on equipment manufacturers for R&D and on a marketing strategy of product differentiation.

The industrial goods sector is highly diverse in terms of inputs and outputs, but *not* companies. The vast majority of industrial fabrics are made by divisions of the largest integrated textile mill companies, such as Stevens, West Point-Pepperell and Burlington, although some industrial fabrics made from non-wovens are produced by non-textile firms. Examples of industrial fabric products are dryer felts, filter bags, tents, awnings, automotive interior components, sandpaper backings and mail bags. Due to this diversity of output, the related product and process technologies are also mixed, and difficult to generalize. It is also difficult to generalize about the market growth of industrial fabrics, although some estimates indicate that it will be a major growth area in the United States and Europe in the 1980s and beyond.

Related Sectors and Activities
While not considered technically a part of the textile complex, several other economic sectors play an important role in textile complex activities. What basically distinguishes them is the fact that they do not necessarily have to exist domestically in order to have a full textile complex, as long as their output (goods or services) can be imported or utilized by domestic firms.

The agricultural sector basically provides the raw material for natural fibers: primarily cotton, wool, flax and silk.[6] Price, availability and quality are all important, but consumer demand and preferences largely dictate their relative importance in fiber production.

Petrochemicals are the basic feedstock for most man-made fibers (excluding cellulosics) and dyeing and fabric treatments. The existence of a domestic chemical industry is generally helpful to a country's textile complex development, as most large man-made fiber producers are divisions of large chemical companies. However, as is the case with natural-fiber inputs, the most important and basic chemicals are available worldwide for importation.

The textile machinery and equipment industry is a sub-sector of machinery manufacture. It can be further differentiated into machinery for forming yarns; handling, treating or modifying yarns; forming fabrics; mechanically or chemically treating fabrics; and forming garments or other fabric structures.

Most of the manufacturing breakthroughs in the textile complex have occurred because of technological improvements introduced by textile machinery firms. Generally, the newer equipment is more labor saving and efficient than its predecessors. These developments have increased the international competitiveness of higher labor-cost countries as they substitute capital for labor. In addition to reducing production costs and improving on the quality of fabrics, the newer technology also permits the manufacture of more complicated products, another competitive advantage for firms in the textile complex.

Due to the substantial and increasing costs of purchasing new technology/equipment, however, its utilization has been greater in the financially stronger fiber and fabric sectors, and in the financially strongest firms in all sectors. In addition, the fact that most new equipment is developed by equipment firms rather than firms in the textile complex has resulted in new equipment being made available worldwide fairly quickly – i.e., the equipment firms have an incentive to sell their equipment to as many textile complex firms as possible, no matter in what country they are located.

The beginning dependency of the US textile complex on foreign textile technology can be seen from the data presented in Table 2.2. Until the late 1960s, the United States had a trade surplus in textile machinery. This was the result of US leadership in the use of man-made fibers in the manufacture of textile, and the earlier acceptance of these products by US end markets. Since the early 1970s, however, the USA has experienced a worsening trade deficit as foreign

Table 2.2 *US Trade in Textile Machinery (SIC 3552) (US $m.)*

Year	Imports for consumption	Exports	Trade position
1980	597	355	(242)
1979	518	355	(163)
1978	555	328	(227)
1977	367	239	(128)
1976	368	202	(166)
1975	304	254	(50)
1974	356	304	(52)
1973	381	340	(41)
1972	426	228	(198)
1971	333	158	(175)
1970	221	179	(42)
1969	167	142	(25)
1968	161	132	(29)
1967	131	135	4
1966	128	157	29
1965	78	136	58
1964	59	140	81

Source: US Department of Commerce, *US Imports/Consumption and General, SIC Based Products by World Areas*, and *US Exports/Domestic Merchandise, SIC Based Products by World Area*, Washington, DC: US Government Printing Office, various issues 1964–1982.

textile machinery manufacturers wrested technological leadership from US textile machinery producers. Foreign manufacturers were quicker to grasp the important role that increases in fabric quality and productivity would play in the 1970s and 1980s.

Finally, in any highly competitive industry, timely and appropriate distribution of the product is a critical determinant of success. This is certainly true for the apparel segment, given its higher competitive state and more frequent changes in style and fashion. In the distribution of apparel, a larger role is being assumed by large retailers at the expense of historically dominant family-owned department stores and manufacturers. In addition, fashion forecasting and market research related to apparel and fabrics are being increasingly done at the retail level, and the largest retailers are more and more involved in direct contracting – domestically and internationally. The large retailers often assume the designer role, contract for the garment, the fabric and even the fiber to be used, provide financing, and specify all the related logistics.

Whether these large retailers buy extensively from domestic or foreign sources clearly affects the domestic textile complex: the more they buy abroad, the greater is the competitive pressure placed on domestic producers, and the greater is the assistance given to foreign producers. The latter point is important because selling in a foreign market is more difficult than selling in one's own domestic market: consumer preferences are different, distribution and pricing practices are different, and there are a number of other barriers to be overcome such as tariff and non-tariff barriers, warehousing, transportation, etc. A retailer can help a foreign producer overcome many of these problems. Therefore, the relationship between retailers and manufacturers (foreign and domestic) is very important, and an often neglected area of consideration in analyzing what changes are taking place in the global textile complex.

International Differences in Textile Complexes

The basic function and general characteristics of each segment of the textile complex are similar in most countries. That is, a typical sewing plant in Sri Lanka performs essentially the same operations as its counterpart in West Germany or in the USA; the man-made fiber industry in all countries is more capital intensive than the fabric industry, and the fabric industry is more capital intensive than the apparel industry. However, in the fabric and apparel segments, there appears to be a fairly wide range of substitutability of capital and labor. Textile firms in one country may be more capital intensive than their counterparts in other countries. Differences are also evident, for example, in the complexity of products produced in each country, the skill, sophistication and wages of labor employed, the degrees of vertical integration, the industry concentration levels, the number of segments in existence in each country, the importance of the textile complex to the countries, and the degree of their international activities and competitiveness. Thus all textile complexes are not identical.

In terms of the degree of textile complex development, there is a continuum ranging from embryonic to declining. The embryonic stage is typically found in the least developed countries, and is primarily oriented toward producing simple fabrics and garments made from natural fibers for domestic consumption. These countries typically are net importers of fiber, fabric and apparel, and their textile complexes resemble an amalgamation of cottage industries. A second stage of development involves the export of apparel, largely restricted to low end, mature varieties, 'native' apparel, or apparel requiring elaborate hand-work such as embroidery. Many of the ASEAN (Association of Southeast Asian Nations) countries fit into this category. A third stage evolves when domestic production of fabric increases sharply in terms of quantity, quality and sophistication. In addition to rapidly expanding and upgrading apparel exports, these countries also begin exporting fabric, and may subsequently develop their own fiber sector. Their textile complexes become larger, more diversified, more concentrated and more internationally active. South Korea recently passed through this stage, and some of the more advanced ASEAN countries and Eastern European countries are well into this stage of development. Mainland China, on the other hand, is entering this stage.

Assistance by large manufacturers and retailers in more developed countries often plays an important role in this process. They provide assistance through foreign investment, contracting or the provision of other forms of assistance (managerial, marketing, etc.). Movement from stage 2 to stage 3 is also typically spurred by local government policies of import substitution and export development.

A fourth stage of development can be called 'The Golden Age': apparel and fabric production become even more sophisticated, and huge trade surpluses result. Man-made fiber production is also more extensive and sophisticated, even though imports of certain complex fibers may be increasing. The textile complex continues to consolidate, to diversify in product mix and to spread internationally via foreign direct investments and contractual arrangements of its own firms. Taiwan is clearly in this stage of development, followed recently by Korea. Hong Kong's geographical limitations made it difficult for it to develop its own man-made fiber sector, but its apparel and fabric sectors are at the most advanced level of this fourth development stage.

A fifth stage of development is full maturity. Overall employment in the complex declines (and particularly in the apparel sector), even though total output may be increasing. Industrial concentration continues, product and process sophistication reach very high levels and capital intensity increases significantly (primarily due to the necessity of substituting capital for labor and for producing more complex products). Japan, the USA and Italy are clearly in this mature stage, although significant differences remain among them. The most notable differences are Japan's more vertically integrated structure and much greater use of offshore production and contracting, and the Italian government's assistance to its domestic complex.

The sixth and final stage of development is one of significant decline. Employment and the number of firms are reduced substantially, and significant trade deficits appear in many sectors (especially in apparel and fabric). Many segments appear to be dying or beyond revitalization, even though some specialized segments may be still healthy and offshore production increase significantly. The UK, Germany, France, Belgium and the Netherlands are all basically in this stage of textile complex decline, although to varying degrees.

Throughout this entire process of development, the international flow of technology, capital and know-how is very important. The faster and wider it spreads, the more rapid the development process becomes. The largest producers and retailers in the developed countries, along with equipment manufacturers, have been largely responsible for such flows and are expected to continue to be so in the future. These increased flows, combined with the constantly shifting comparative advantage in production and changes in government policies, make for a truly dynamic and competitive global textile environment. For example, a firm can design a sophisticated garment for export to another country made from fibers it produces in several countries being spun and woven into fabric in another country, perhaps being dyed and finished in its own or still another country, then sewn in still another country for export to the ultimate consuming country. The controlling company can profit from each process (if its own subsidiaries are involved) or from the entire process (either the final profit or the final profit plus 'service income' from the other companies involved for having masterminded the whole scheme). And if one of the intermediate stage countries or the final stage country encounters some problem (e.g. their quota is used up), the firm can shift the process to another country. Such flexibility can be critical to the success of a company competing in textiles on a global basis.

Other major differences among countries' textile complexes are the degrees of vertical integration within the complexes, degrees of offshore investment/production, and the extent of government involvement. In general, firms in Asian textile complexes are more vertically integrated than those of the USA, and have more foreign production facilities (vertical integration meaning fiber firms owning fabric and/or apparel firms, or fabric firms owning apparel firms, etc.). For example, one of Japan's largest fiber companies, Toray Industries, wholly or partially owns numerous fabric and apparel companies in Japan. It also owns fabric companies in Korea (1), Taiwan (2), Hong Kong (3), Indonesia (7), Thailand (6), Malaysia (4) and Singapore (1), and numerous apparel companies throughout Southeast Asia either directly or jointly with Textile Alliance Ltd, a Hong Kong based firm now 67 per cent owned by Toray. In fact, by the mid-1970s, Toray had established vertically integrated textile operations in Taiwan, Thailand, Indonesia and Malaysia. And, by establishing fiber plants in Korea and the Philippines with local firms that had already vertically integrated forward from fabric into apparel, Toray essentially established vertically integrated operations in these countries as well.[7]

But Toray was not the only company to pursue such a vertical integration strategy domestically or internationally. Its main Japanese competitor, Teijin, followed a similar strategy in Southeast Asia. In Malaysia and the Philippines for example, these two Japanese fiber firms control most of these nations' man-made fiber textile complex via equity participation, loans and/or other contractual arrangements.[8] Other firms that followed similar but less extensive internationally vertical integration strategies were Textile Alliance Ltd and Yangzekan of Hong Kong, which both established vertical integration from spinning through apparel in Hong Kong and several Southeast Asian countries, and most of Japan's large spinning companies (such as Toyobo and Kanebo), which vertically integrated backward into natural fiber yarns in Latin America (during the 1950s) and forward into fabric and apparel in Japan and the Asia Pacific area (to a lesser extent).

Offshore manufacturing[9] refers to the practice of exporting finished (component parts) or semi-finished manufactures to lower-cost countries for completion. The finished products are then re-exported for distribution.

There are several factors that bear on the decision to use this particular manufacturing strategy. Among the most important are the relative tariff levels in the home country and the host country, which determine effective protection rates; whether the production process is continuous or consists of detachable sub-processes that can be transferred abroad without loss of scale economies at home; the relative impact of the 'change of nature' and similar restrictive clauses that governments impose on the transferability of the production process; the bargaining power of the particular labor(s) involved; the level and growth of foreign competition necessitating a corporate response; the level of maturity of the industry and the product; differences in the legal environments of the home and host countries for particular industries; and the relative labor skills required.

In general, this manufacturing practice has not been used extensively by the world's textile complexes. However, there has been more offshore manufacturing in apparel than in fabrics, and virtually none in fiber. There has also been more extensive use of offshore manufacturing by textile complexes of some countries than by others: the complexes of West Germany, the Netherlands and Belgium have used this production-cost-reducing technique more extensively than the complexes of other European countries and the United States. In particular, the governments of the United Kingdom and France have opposed it because of its employment implications, and have introduced means to control this form of trade and its growth.

Most industrialized countries permit the return of products assembled or processed abroad. However, there are considerable differences in the regulations and restrictions imposed by governments on this form of manufacturing. (See Chapter 6 for a more detailed discussion on these differences.)

Most US offshore manufacturing is done under Item 807 of the Tariff Schedules of the United States. This tariff item permits US manufacturers to export US component parts and materials for additional work, and pay duty only on the value added upon re-entry into the United States. However, the exported parts and materials must be ready for assembly without further fabrication, do not lose their physical identity, and are not advanced in value or improve in condition except by being assembled. As a result of these restrictions, only the US apparel industry has been in a position to take advantage of the regulation. The restrictions effectively limit the export of textiles destined for eventual consumption in the US to cut fabrics. In contrast, the European textile mill industries are permitted to export uncut fabric overseas for additional work, thereby gaining a considerable advantage *vis-à-vis* the USA in the sale of their outputs.

Government involvement and assistance in the textile complex are considerable in developing countries. Import substitution policies, industrial development assistance and export assistance are among the many policies and activities of developing country governments. In the developed countries, while levels of trade protection have increased substantially over the past two decades, governments have not been as supportive of their domestic textile complex, with the notable exception of the United Kingdom and France.[10] The public sector of the Italian industry has also been provided considerable

Table 2.3   *Shares of the Textile and Clothing Industries in Total Manufacturing Employment (%)*

Country	Textile industry			Clothing industry		
	1963	1973	1976	1963	1973	1976
Belgium	12.7	9.9	9.1	7.3	8.0	7.1
Denmark	6.4	5.0	4.6	5.6	4.1	3.9
France	9.9	7.3	6.4	7.1	5.4	5.0
West Germany	7.4	5.4	4.8	5.0	4.5	3.8
Ireland	13.0	11.3	9.9	9.8	8.1	7.1
Italy	17.9	10.6	9.5	6.2	6.1	5.7
Luxembourg	0.8	0.5	0.2	1.1	1.4	1.2
Netherlands	7.8	5.5	4.7	10.1	4.5	3.1
United Kingdom	9.1	7.4	6.8	5.0	4.7	4.7
EC	9.9	7.2	6.5	5.9	5.1	4.7
Austria	13.8	9.5	8.0	6.0	5.8	5.7
Finland	8.4	5.8	5.0	6.2	6.8	6.7
Greece	13.3	—	14.1	9.0	—	8.1
Norway	6.1	3.7	3.3	5.6	3.1	2.5
Portugal	37.9	23.4	21.0	0.3	4.6	4.9
Spain	13.7	8.7	8.6	2.6	4.7	4.7
Sweden	5.0	3.2	2.8	5.6	3.0	2.4
Switzerland	10.9	7.5	7.2	5.3	3.7	3.3
Turkey	31.8	22.3	22.9	0.2	1.0	1.3
Other OECD Europe	13.5	10.4	10.1	4.5	4.2	4.3
Total OECD Europe	10.5	7.8	7.3	5.7	4.9	4.6
Canada	6.4	6.1	5.4	6.6	6.0	5.9
USA	6.3	6.3	5.9	7.0	6.5	6.3
Japan	14.3	10.5	9.4	2.8	3.6	4.3
Australia	7.2	5.6	5.0	6.6	5.7	4.9
New Zealand	7.0	7.0	6.4	10.9	8.4	7.2
Total OECD	9.8	7.8	7.2	5.6	5.2	5.1

Sources: United Nations, *Yearbook of Industrial Statistics*, New York, NY: United Nations, various issues 1964–1979; Organization for Economic Cooperation and Development, *Textile Industry in OECD Countries*, Paris: OECD, various issues 1963–1979.

government support. However, as noted in Chapter 8, the public sector is small, and this intervention has not had a pronounced influence on the way the Italian industry has developed.

Table 2.4 *Shares of the Textile and Clothing Industries in Total Manufacturing Production (Value-Added) (%)*

Country	Textile industry			Clothing industry		
	1963	1973	1976	1963	1973	1976
Belgium	9.8	7.0	5.9	3.6	3.5	3.5
Denmark	5.5	4.2	3.8	4.1	2.4	2.1
France	8.6	5.5	4.6	3.9	2.2	2.0
West Germany	4.8	3.3	2.9	5.2	3.6	3.2
Ireland	10.4	9.1	8.7	5.2	4.2	3.9
Italy	9.2	7.5	7.2	3.4	3.3	3.2
Luxembourg	0.5	0.1	0.1	0.4	0.4	0.4
Netherlands	6.5	3.4	3.0	5.8	1.7	1.2
United Kingdom	6.5	5.5	4.4	2.6	2.3	1.9
EC	6.7	4.8	4.2	4.0	2.9	2.6
Austria	10.4	6.7	5.0	4.1	3.5	3.1
Finland	5.7	4.2	3.8	4.2	3.9	3.9
Greece	15.2	—	15.6	5.1	—	5.2
Norway	5.0	2.7	2.5	3.9	1.9	1.4
Portugal	20.2	18.1	16.0	2.3	2.3	3.2
Spain	14.2	7.0	6.7	2.6	3.1	3.8
Sweden	3.9	2.6	2.2	3.5	1.7	1.4
Switzerland	4.7	3.9	4.0	5.9	4.9	4.3
Turkey	22.0	15.1	15.4	0.1	0.5	0.7
Other OECD Europe	8.2	6.0	5.8	4.0	3.0	2.9
Total OECD Europe	6.9	5.0	4.5	4.0	2.9	2.6
Canada	4.7	4.3	3.7	3.4	3.0	3.1
USA	3.8	3.9	3.5	3.6	3.0	2.8
Japan	9.0	6.8	5.7	1.3	1.5	1.8
Australia	5.7	4.6	4.3	3.9	3.2	3.1
New Zealand	5.3	6.3	5.1	5.4	4.4	4.1
Total OECD	5.3	4.8	4.2	3.6	2.8	2.6

Sources: United Nations, *Yearbook of Industrial Statistics*, New York, NY: United Nations, various issues 1964–1979; Organization for Economic Cooperation and Development, *Textile Industry in OECD Countries*, Paris: OECD, various issues 1963–1979.

Table 2.5 Labor Cost Comparisons, Summer 1981

	Average cost per operator hour (3-shift basis)						
	Without charges (local currency)	Charges paid to worker (local currency)	Other charges (local currency)	Total cost per hour (local currency)	Rate of exchange (US $1 =)	Total cost (US $)	Ratio to US cost (%)
NORTH AMERICA							
USA	5.45	0.43	1.15	7.03	—	7.03	100
Canada	6.30	0.65	1.02	7.97	1.20	6.64	94
Mexico	48.95	13.17	14.04	76.16	24.84	3.06	44
EUROPEAN ECONOMIC COMMUNITY							
Belgium	211	78	83	372	39.83	9.34	133
Denmark	53.18	7.45	6.37	67.00	7.61	8.80	125
France (N.)	20.01	3.94	13.34	37.29	5.83	6.40	91
France (E.)	19.20	2.49	11.92	33.61	5.83	5.77	82
W. Germany (N.)	12.14	4.00	3.71	19.85	2.43	8.17	116
W. Germany (S.)	11.20	2.94	4.24	18.38	2.43	7.56	108
Greece (N.)	119	29	31	179	59.55	3.00	42
The Netherlands	16.00	2.96	5.69	24.65	2.69	9.16	130
Ireland	2.21	0.45	0.27	2.93	0.67	4.37	62
Italy	4,366	1,965	2,469	8,800	12.17	7.23	103
United Kingdom	2.44	0.31	0.37	3.12	0.56	5.57	79
OTHER WEST EUROPEAN COUNTRIES							
Austria	47.91	6.93	31.26	86.10	17.09	5.04	72
Norway	38.04	4.74	13.47	56.25	6.07	9.26	132
Portugal	80.43	25.53	17.70	123.66	65.95	1.88	27

Spain	207	93	140	440	96.3	4.48	64
Sweden	30.96	5.05	14.04	50.05	5.24	955	136
Switzerland	13.27	1.39	2.59	17.25	2.11	8.18	116
NORTH AFRICA							
Egypt	0.25	0.06	0.04	0.35	0.82	0.43	6
Morocco	2.76	0.25	1.17	4.18	5.56	0.75	11
Tunisia	0.585	0.097	0.142	0.824	0.53	1.55	22
SOUTH AMERICA							
Argentina	10,260.	2,320.	2,820.	15,400.	7,575	2.03	29
Brazil (N.)	73.2	22.3	37.0	132.5	102.5	1.29	18
Brazil (S.P.)	135.1	41.0	69.1	245.2	102.5	2.39	34
Brazil (S.)	107.4	32.7	54.2	194.3	102.5	1.90	27
Chile	61.58	6.04	32.54	100.16	39.00	2.57	37
Columbia	62.8	7.4	28.0	96.2	55.84	1.76	25
Venezuela	12.08	5.02	7.05	24.15	4.29	5.63	80
NEAR EAST							
Iraq	0.30	0.04	0.17	0.51	0.30	1.70	24
Syria	4.81	0.44	0.95	6.20	3.93	1.58	22
Turkey	80	33	17	130	121.5	1.07	15
ASIA							
Hong Kong	7.20	1.05	0.25	8.50	6.00	1.42	20
India	4.62	1.07	0.70	6.39	9.22	0.69	10
Indonesia	335.3	42.3	18.9	396.5	630	0.63	9
Japan	778	239	122	1,139	232.7	4.90	70
Pakistan	2.59	0.90	0.63	4.12	9.84	0.42	6
Philippines	2.91	0.37	0.16	3.44	7.98	0.43	6
Singapore	1.99	0.29	0.16	2.44	2.17	1.12	16
South Korea	624	247	56	927	688	1.35	19
Sri Lanka	3.12	0.10	0.10	3.32	20.37	0.16	2
Taiwan	40.3	5.0	2.5	47.8	36.30	1.32	19
Thailand	7.5	0.3	NIL	7.8	23.00	0.34	5

Source: Werner Associates Inc., *Newsletter* (Brussels), June 1981.

Still another difference among various nations' textile complexes is their relative importance to their nations in terms of employment, gross national product and export earnings. For example, textile products are the largest export of Hong Kong (roughly 40 per cent of its total exports), South Korea (about 30 per cent) and Taiwan (20 per cent) but a very small percentage of total US and German exports.[11] Tables 2.3 and 2.4 provide comparative data on various countries' employment in textiles and apparel as a percentage of their total manufacturing labor force, and their textile output as a percentage of total manufacturing output. These tables show that the fabric and apparel segments vary considerably in terms of their relative importance to each country.

Finally, there are significant differences in productivity and wage rates. As shown in Table 2.5, the average total cost per operator hour is considerably lower outside the USA: Sri Lanka's cost is only 2 per cent of the US costs, Thailand's 5 per cent, the Philippines' 6 per cent, India's and Indonesia's 10 per cent, Singapore's 16 per cent, Korea's and Hong Kong's 20 per cent, and those in Latin America range from 18 per cent to 80 per cent. On the other hand, Belgium, the Netherlands, West Germany, Italy and a few other European countries have rates *higher* than the USA.

There are also significant international differences in productivity. In spinning and weaving, for example, the USA has the highest level of productivity of all major producers, while Japan is the only Asian nation with a productivity level greater than one-half of the US level, as shown in Table 2.6.

In sum, the global textile complex is a composite of many highly different national textile complexes. It is these differences that make global competition so intense and complicated, and equally complicated to analyze.

Table 2.6   *International Productivity Comparison Index (Spinning & Weaving) (USA = 100)*

USA	100
West Germany	87–95
Italy	75
Japan	74
France	70
UK	55
Hong Kong	50–51
Taiwan	45
South Korea	44
Pakistan	10

Source: Werner Associates Inc., *Newsletter* (Brussels), June 1981.

The Textile Business Cycle

The textile business cycle is usually measured by output or textile production. Changes in production levels form cycles of varying amplitudes and duration. Cycles in textile production are usually accompanied by similar cycles in fiber consumption, active spindle hours, textile employment, textile payrolls, mill margins and profits.

The textile cycle differs from most industrial cycles, which normally have four phases: expansion, recession, depression and revival. However the textile cycle appears to consist of only two distinct phases: (1) the expansion phase, during which sales are heavy, unfilled orders are accumulated, mill inventories are depleted, and prices and output increase; and, (2) the recession phase, during which sales decline, and prices and production decrease (Vaughn, 1964).

During the expansion phase of the textile cycle, sales are relatively active and profits are generally high. Additionally, there is little pressure to reduce prices since inventories are not a major problem. However, as the recession phase emerges, trade slows and inventories accumulate. When inventories increase, more capital becomes idle because of the investment in materials. The loss from capital earnings is only one of the costs related to inventory accumulation. Additional costs are incurred because of more handling, warehousing and insurance.

The level of inventory has always been a significant factor in textile business indicators. To reduce inventories and the cost of carrying inventory firms are pressured to lowering prices. Adjustments are made in production to reduce output, and unemployment increases.

Notes

1   This chapter is oriented primarily to persons who are not extremely knowledgeable about the textile complex and the textile mill products industry in both domestic and international contexts. Persons who already possess such knowledge may choose to skip Chapter 2 and proceed directly to Chapter 3.
2   In the USA, there are approximately 5,000 textile firms (SIC 22), of which the largest 50 account for 50% of the industry's total output and the largest 35 for roughly 35% of the industry's total output (Source: American Textile Manufacturers Institute).
3   Apparel can also be made from leather, plastics and 'non-wovens', and instead of being 'sewn' can be cemented or fused. However, most apparel is sewn from woven fabrics.
4   Jobbers perform all the functions of an entrepreneur, including frequently cutting the material, but leave the assembling and pressing of the garments to contractors.
5   There are roughly 15,000 apparel firms in the USA, the largest 50 of which account for 27–86% of industry sales, depending on product line.

6   The agriculture sector in a broad context also provides leather (from animals) and wood and other cellulosics for some man-made fibers.

7   For more detail on Toray's operation, see Arpan, Barry and Tho (forthcoming).

8   Ibid.

9   Europeans call this manufacturing practice 'outward processing'.

10   For more details on government policies affecting the apparel and fabric industries, see Arpan, de la Torre, Toyne, *et al.* (1982), Chapters 4, 5 and 6; and the US Department of Commerce publication on overseas restraints to textile and apparel import (1981a).

11   *The Economist*, 12 December 1981, p. 71. In Japan's case, textile exports during the 1940s and 1950s accounted for nearly 50% of her total exports, but now account for less than 10%.

3

Technological Developments in the Textile Mill Products Industry[1]

Managers in the textile industry are under tremendous pressure to increase productivity, to improve manufacturing performance, to improve product quality and at the same time to protect the environment. They are keenly aware of these demands, and have made considerable effort to determine the most cost-effective approach at each stage of processing. These pressures on management are resulting in changes at all stages of processing. In some cases the changes are occurring so rapidly and are so extensive that there is talk of a technological revolution in textile production. In this chapter a summary of changes in each processing stage is discussed.

Opening and Cleaning

Bales of fiber arrive at the textile mill from a number of sources. Cotton from a selected number of bales is opened and placed in a mix laydown. From each bale, fibers are blended to produce a clean, uniform quality of material for further processing.

The purpose of the opening room machinery is to loosen up and break the cotton layers taken from the bales into smaller pieces and deliver this pre-opened stock to the cleaning machines for further opening and cleaning. This opening/cleaning process is one of the most important processes in the textile manufacturing operation. This reasoning is summed up by the axiom 'in the end it is the beginning that counts'. Manufacturing of textile products begins in the opening room. If the fibers are not properly selected and properly fed at this first stage of processing, production efficiency will be decreased and the product produced may not have the expected quality characteristics.

The traditional attitude seemed to be that laying down the mix and feeding the fiber could be accomplished by anyone. The bales in the mix could be laid out and the layers of fibers could be fed to the hopper. This seems easy enough, but the fact is that precision blending did not occur in most instances. However, the reduction in product quality and processing efficiencies that could be traced to the opening/cleaning process did not appear to be of vital importance prior to the 1960s. This may have resulted from low-speed carding, spinning and weaving and the fact that there were no dust regulations.

Technological changes in the opening/cleaning process occurred slowly until about 1960 when they began to catch on more rapidly. Several of the factors that provided the impetus for change in this process were: consumers were complaining about product quality, management was concerned about import competition, and man-made fibers were used more in blends. Although these were significant factors, the strongest motivating force probably came from the stringent clear air standards set by the Occupational Safety and Health Administration (OSHA) of the United States. These factors, along with technological advances in the carding, spinning and weaving processes, which have significantly increased speeds and productivity, have necessitated optimizing machine efficiencies in the opening room.

Changes to improve and automate the opening/cleaning process have moved at a rapid rate in recent years. Developmental work has resulted in several refinements, and a large variety of new machines is available. Automation and computer technology provided the necessary tool for optimizing fiber utilization. Computer methods are available for selecting the best combination of bales for a mix laydown to produce a specific end-use product. The bale selection criterion can be based on how each fiber quality contributes to the manufacturing performance and product attributes. Bale pluckers and automatic feeds can be programmed to feed a specific amount from bales in the laydown. These programmed machines can feed in excess of 1,000 pounds per hour and at the same time assure homogeneous blending. This precision blending minimizes the within bale variation and the between bale variation. Such precision is too often lacking or unattainable in manual feeding. Thus, human error associated with feeding and blending is removed by these automated machines. In fact the human element is removed from the opening room, except for preparing the mix laydown. Proper blending results in reduced and evenly distributed variations in fiber characteristics, uniform processing, improved yarn quality, lower raw material cost, and savings in labor cost.

Properly opened tufts of fiber are required for efficient cleaning. The opening and cleaning machines work together to clean the fiber. Cotton taken from the bale is a tangled mass of closely packed fibers that contains varying amounts of foreign matter – dirt, dust, sand, leaf, bract, motes and seed particles. The opening machine beats, loosens and separates the fibers into small tufts. These opened tufts are thrown against grid bars that retain the clean fibers and allow impurities to fall through.

Automated equipment in the opening room that is completely controlled by microprocessors can deliver a well-opened stock to the cards through the introduction of the chute-feed system. This system eliminates the making of picker laps and the transporting of picker laps. This type of automated system is very near ideal for the opening/cleaning process, since the masses of fibers are gradually and gently opened to smaller and smaller tufts without being repeatedly compressed. Although the chute-feed system by-passes the picker, the picker is not dead: the modern picker is fully automated. The loading and doffing of the picker lap has been automated. Recent developments in picker design have changed the hopper-feed techniques and the transport of stock through the system. These innovations resulted in a better quality picker lap along with increased productivity.

Carding

The card remained virtually unchanged until the early 1960s when new technology produced the forerunners of the present-day high-production card. The only major changes prior to the 1960s were the development in 1834 of the self-cleaning revolving flat card, which replaced the stationary flats that had to be removed for cleaning periodically, and the introduction of metallic clothing wire. The cards of today still use the same operating principles as the earlier cards and possess the same working elements: licker-in, main cylinder, flats, doffer, doffercomb and web detaching rollers. These original (standard) cards operated at a rate of 4–18 pounds per hour depending on the type and quality of the fiber used as well as the desired purity and nep (one or more entangled fibers) count. In the late 1960s and early 1970s, new technology was used in the modification of existing cards and the development of new machines such as the designs of Bettoni and Carminati-Zinser. These modified and new cards obtained speeds of approximately 50 pounds per hour. Bettoni used one set of flats above and below the cylinder and increased cylinder size, while his 'monocard' coordinated three small cards in tandem. In the Carminati-Zinser card, small clothed rollers replaced the flats. In five to eight years, high-production cards from many countries had replaced their earlier prototypes and were obtaining speeds of 100–250 pounds per hour. An estimated 32,000 cards are now being used in mills in the United States. Of course not all of this number are high-production cards, but their number increases as they replace the older and slower machines.

The development of new card clothing and the use of chute feeding and electronics have greatly contributed to carding speed increases. Although its introduction was somewhat controversial, the direct feeding of the cotton sheet to the card through chutes is generally recognized as being a major factor in increasing card speed and the automation of the cardroom. Advantages of chute-fed cards over lap-fed cards are elimination of run-out problems such as clothing damage from the lap ends by the jerking of the feed roll, a more constant feed, higher efficiency, a sliver uniformity approximately equal to that of a conventional lap-fed sliver, a more uniform yard-to-yard weight, as well as reduced labor costs and error. A known disadvantage to chute feeding is less blending capability, but this can be overcome by using blending machinery. Metallic card wire is one of the most important of the technological improvements that allowed high production cards to attain their present speeds. It is now recognized as an essential component. The stiff, metallic card wire replaced flexible clothing and has the advantages of decreasing labor and material costs as well as increasing the time period between required stripping.

The use of electronic clutches, solid state circuitry, microprocessors, DC motors and mini-computers have provided greater control and higher efficiency for cards as well as contributing to automation. Other advantages of high production cards are improved dust and trash removal, lower maintenance and production costs, and less space requirements.

Combing, Drawing and Roving

To prepare card sliver for spinning it must be further processed at drawing and roving. If a higher quality product is to be delivered at spinning it may in addition be necessary to process the card sliver at combing.

Card sliver contains dust, dirt, leaf particles, bract, neps, short fiber, fiber hooks and a non-parallel fiber arrangement. The function of the comber is: to separate the long fibers from the short and immature fibers, which go into noils; to straighten the longer fibers and increase fiber parallelization; to remove the noils, which consist of neps, short fibers and foreign matter; and to impart a sheen or luster to the combed sliver.

The combing process is unique in that it is the only open-end process from carding to spinning in the yarn manufacturing process. This open-end or fiber separation is necessary for the comber to perform its function. Fibers in the incoming raw stock (card sliver) are reduced to an individual fiber state, which allows the combing action to perform its function efficiently.

The importance of combing depends on the demand for higher-quality and finer yarns. If demand swings towards finer yarns, fiber blends and higher-quality specifications, then an efficient combing operation is necessary. Combed sliver with fibers of a more uniform length and of a longer average staple will produce a stronger and more even yarn. The yarn from a combed sliver, with straight and parallel fibers, will have a distinct sheen or luster.

The first high-speed comber ran at 150 nips (combings) per minute. For some time it was believed that 250 nips per minute constituted an upper limit, simply because of the mechanical design of the comber. Recent improvements in machine design, elimination of uncontrolled acceleration, weight reduction, balancing of the swinging masses, and stronger rocker shafts made higher speeds possible. Developing a new nipper also led to increased speeds and improved efficiencies. The current modern high-production combers run at 240 nips per minute.

The combing process has been further automated by automatic can changers and mechanical feeding of the lap. The operation is further simplified by a lap transport system, which automatically returns the empty lap spools.

The drawing frame performs the function of drafting and doubling of slivers from the carding or combing process. Its objectives are: to straighten and parallel the fibers in the sliver; to improve the uniformity of the slivers; to blend the fibers by feeding several slivers through the drawframe; and to deliver a sliver of a specified weight.

During the 1950s, the drawframe was improved by constructing a heavier and more precisely engineered piece of machinery. These improvements and the introduction of the two-zone drafting system permitted speeds to increase gradually without a detrimental effect on sliver quality. The increase in speed raised much discussion about the need of going from 100 feet per minute to 300 feet per minute and then 400 feet per minute. The questions slowly disappeared and delivery speeds gradually increased to 600 feet per minute in 1960. About this time, the number of deliveries was reduced to four. In a short period of time a two-delivery drawframe was introduced with a speed of 800 feet per minute. Today, the two-delivery drawframe has the capacity to run at 1,640 feet per minute, and one-delivery machines are available with delivery speeds around 2,000 feet per minute. The following refinements have also been made in the modern high-speed drawframe: antifriction bearings to support the coiler;

stop motions to stop the frame automatically when the sliver breaks; automatic can changers; larger cans; power driven creels; and leveling (or evening) devices.

Delivery speeds have thus more than tripled since 1960. This means that fewer machines are required in the manufacturing process and the process has become less labor intensive. A reasonable objective may be to have fewer machines but this can be a disadvantage. When high-performance machines such as these are used in production, it only takes one mechanical failure to cause serious disruptions in the manufacturing process.

The roving frame is the machine that processes the drawing sliver prior to spinning. At this stage the drawing sliver possesses uniform, parallel fibers that have been blended to meet the specifications set in yarn manufacturing. The purpose of the roving operation is to attenuate the thick drawframe sliver into a roving that is suitable for the spinning frame. Roving is a continuous, slightly twisted strand of fibers. The roving is wound onto a specially designed package for later use on the spinning frame.

The roving frame is not designed to contribute to the blending, opening and cleaning of the raw material; however, it must consolidate the fibers and impart the twist required for further processing. The specific functions of the roving frame are: to reduce the drawing sliver to a smaller size by drafting; to insert twist in the drafted strand to give it strength; to lay the coils of roving accurately and uniformly onto the bobbin; to wind the layers of roving on the bobbin at a rate to give the correct tension; and to build a tapered bobbin by decreasing the number of coils per layer of roving.

During the 1950s and early 1960s many attempts were made to eliminate the roving operation. One reason for these attempts was the number of passages used to reduce the drawing sliver – at one time up to five passages were applied on the roving frame. Another reason was the susceptibility of the machine to misdraft. Attempts were also being made to spin drawframe sliver directly on the ring spinning frame. The possibility of by-passing the roving frame slowed its development during this period.

Nevertheless, a newly designed frame was introduced in 1960. The 'Rovermatic' frame incorporated new technologies that resulted in faster speeds and automation. By 1965 the speed of the frame had increased to 1,200 rpm for a 14 × 7 inch delivery package.

The introduction of open-end spinning in 1965 renewed the possibility of by-passing the roving frame. Some thought that with open-end spinning there was no longer a real need for roving. However, it was soon recognized that open-end spinning had its limitations. Only in the medium and coarse yarn counts could this new technology compete with ring spinning. This new competing technology provided the impetus for additional research and development in ring spinning, which resulted in productivity and automation gains. The continued use and development of ring spinning has had a positive effect on the development of the roving frame. New roving frames have been designed with higher speeds, improved efficiency, labor-saving devices and partial or full automation. By 1980 the speeds on these new machines had increased to 1,800 rpm for the 14×7 inch bobbin. Frames with automatic doffing are available and some frames provide innovative techniques for the removal of dust and fly.

Yarn Spinning

Until a few years ago, the textile industry used the same basic principles of forming fibers into yarns as were used for several hundred years – drafting, twisting with a traveller and a spindle, and winding. In drafting, the fibers are attenuated to make the output material longer and thinner than the input material. Twisting provides the force that interlocks the fibers together in a strand of yarn with the strength that is required for further processing and end-use qualities. The twisted fiber takes a curl shape or a spiral position in the yarn. In the winding process the yarn is wound onto a bobbin.

On early ring spinning frames the drafting, twisting and winding processes were interdependent processes linked by the fiber flow. The productivity of the ring spinning system is thus directly related to the most restrictive process. Technological progress has been made in reducing the links between processes. The introduction of the roller drafting system made it possible to separate drafting from the twisting and winding processes. However, the link between twisting and winding on the modern conventional ring spinning system has not been resolved. The performance of the system has improved with advances in technology, but it is still somewhat restricted. The primary factor limiting the productivity of the modern system is the rate at which the yarn package can be rotated. The specific limitations are: the mechanical limitation of the traveller; the yarn strength necessary to withstand high yarn tensions in the balloon; package size, which is restricted by the size of the yarn balloon; the power required to rotate the yarn package; and higher speeds, which require more frequent doffing. Within the bounds of these limitations, innovative technological advances have allowed spindle speeds to increase greatly over the last twenty years, advancing from about 12,000 rpm in 1960 to about 20,000 rpm in 1980. As speeds increase, output increases. Consequently, fewer machines are required in new or modernized spinning rooms for a given level of output than with the older machines.

Although many advances have occurred in ring spinning outputs, most of the newer developments have been in the area of open-end spinning. This system of forming fibers into yarns employs the principle of centrifugal action instead of a spindle to form the yarns. Drafting, twisting and winding are completely independent processes in this system. From the drafting stage the fibers are transferred separately across the break to a collecting point at which they become attached to the open end of the yarn. As the fibers arrive, the open end is twisted as the yarn is withdrawn and wound onto a takeup package. The rate at which the yarn is withdrawn determines the yarn count. For example, a coarse yarn would require a slower rate of withdrawal than a fine yarn.

In 1967, open-end spinning was touted as the salvation of the spinning industry. Many believed that it would soon capture a major share of the market. It was promoted as being able to use a low-quality fiber and produce almost any yarn. Mill experiences have shown that this is not true. The initial open-end spinning machines had several problems that slowed acceptance by the textile industry. For example slivers with an excessive amount of trash and dust would not run efficiently in open-end spinning. Trash and dust particles accumulated in the rotor groove, causing yarn quality to deteriorate and excessive ends-down, which in turn lowered production efficiency. Also the yarn strength was lower than that from a comparable ring spun yarn. The biggest problem was that open-end spinning was not entirely adequate for producing fine yarns. For this reason open-end spinning is not a new technology that replaces ring spinning, but a system that competes with ring spinning in the coarse yarn markets.

Continued research by machinery manufacturers and others has reduced or eliminated many of the problems associated with open-end spinning. Most of the new generation machines have automatic trash and dust removal, automatic knotting, improved rotor design to produce finer yarns and higher speeds of operation. It has also been determined that processing performance and product quality can be improved by matching fiber quality characteristics to the proper rotor spinning system.

Weaving

The last two decades have seen more refinement than invention in basic weaving technology. While shuttleless looms have experienced an upsurge in popularity since 1970, all of the basic shuttleless systems were available by 1960. Sulzer Brothers began commercial production of its missile machine in 1953. The Maxbo air-jet loom was being used for commercial fabric production in Sweden in 1950, and the first water-jet machine was exhibited by the Czechoslovakian state corporation, Elitex, in Brussels in 1955. As early as 1878, rigid rapier looms of a primitive sort were used in the production of carpets. Draper Corporation provided considerable impetus for the production of modern flexible rapier machines with the introduction of its DSL model in 1957.

The primary thrust of research and development in weaving technology has been toward increasing the productive capacity of the machines. This has been accomplished largely with the faster and more reliable weft insertion systems and with wider machines. Most missile and rapier machines operate at 300+ picks per minute (ppm), while jet machines have speeds in excess of 500 ppm, with some water-jet looms reaching 800 ppm. Most shuttleless looms weave fabrics in excess of 51 inches wide, with newer machines having width capabilities in excess of 100 inches.

Indeed, the push for productivity has been the strongest reason for the shift toward shuttleless machines by US textile mills. The number of shuttleless looms in the USA rose from just under 18,000 in 1972 to 33,400 in 1978. In 1972, 335,200 looms produced 11.1 billion linear yards of fabric, while in 1978, 262,000 looms produced 10.7 billion yards, which translates into 7,725 more yards per loom in 1978. Given that most of the shuttleless looms are wider than conventional shuttle looms, the increase in productivity per loom in terms of square yards is even greater.

Another characteristic of modern weaving machines is greater use of electronics. Many have electronic monitoring systems that alert weavers and technicians to the cause of stops. The telemechanique system on the Saurer 400 not only distinguishes between weft, warp and mechanical stops, but identifies whether mechanical stops are due to low oil pressure or inadequate rapier belt tension. Sulzer Brothers has developed an electronically controlled tappet motion, SEM, which allows patterns to be changed by simply changing a program cassette. Push-button control and electronic weft-stop motions have become almost standard features on modern looms.

Electronic monitoring systems on weaving machines have led to expanded use of computer control systems in weave mills. These systems provide nearly instantaneous efficiency information broken down by department, shift, weaver and fixer sets, style sets, and machine. With memory, the need to read pick clocks at the end of each shift is eliminated. Total stops are also recorded and may be broken down into weft, warp and mechanical categories, allowing managers and technicians to pinpoint where efficiency is being lost. The systems may also be programmed with new warp yardage to produce daily warp run-out forecasts.

Environmental quality has been significantly improved by modern weaving machines. Due to the absence of the checking motion of conventional shuttle looms, shuttleless looms are naturally quieter. Noise levels have been further reduced on some machines, such as the SACM MAV-DN rapier loom, by the use of insulated covers. Most shuttleless looms are safer and less intimidating, since the possibility of being struck by a flying shuttle is eliminated.

Besides higher productivity, US textile firms cite reduced labor costs and better product quality as advantages of shuttleless looms. The machines use large weft packages that are creeled in by the weaver, eliminating the need for Unifil or magazine tenders.[2] Features on some machines, such as automatic pick finders, make repairing stops much faster. Most shuttleless machines are self-lubricating, which reduces wear on parts and required downtime for maintenance. With regard to quality, some mills are discovering that fabrics with 12–14 per cent seconds on shuttle looms may be run with 2–3 per cent defects on shuttleless machines.

In the USA, rapier looms currently enjoy the greatest popularity, with 23,503 machines in place or on order as of May 1980. Rapier machines can be less expensive than air-jet and missile machines, providing for shorter return on capital. They are also more versatile than air- or water-jet looms. Rapier looms can handle a wide range of average quality weft yarns and most have multi-color weft capabilities. These advantages make them ideal replacements for ageing box-type shuttle looms.

Draper Corporation leads in US rapier loom sales with more than 16,000 of its DLG model in place. Draper believes that the DLG can do anything the Sulzer missile can do for a much lower price. Dornier, one of the earliest makers of rapier machines, continues to do well with 2,500 machines sold in the USA. Picanol's PGW machine is also very popular.

One of the disadvantages commonly associated with rigid rapier machines is the floor space required. The Saurer 400 machine cuts space requirements in half by using two telescoping rapiers. The Saurer 500 two-phase machine uses a single rapier to insert yarn into two widths of cloth. Insertion occurs in one width while beat-up is occurring in the other. The amount of floor space required by double-width machines is further reduced with the SACM MAV-DN model, which uses two sets of rapiers to produce two superimposed fabrics.

Following the rapier machines in popularity are the missile

machines, with over 18,000 machines, the vast majority of which are by Sulzer Brothers, in place or on order in the USA. Sulzer Brothers has steadily improved on its basic, and very solid, design. Some of the improvements on its newest model, PU, include a shortened beat-up for greater speed, more compact design and self-adjusting projective brakes. Crompton and Knowles is currently developing an air missile loom, a prototype of which was on display at the American Textile Machinery Exhibition (ATME) in 1980.

While air-jet machines are currently in fourth place in US shuttle-less loom sales, they are expected to take about one-third of the market by 1985. Acceptance of air-jet machines has been hindered by several problems, some of which have been resolved in recent years. The use of relay nozzles has overcome the width limitations encountered by single-nozzle machines. While once limited to spun yarns, air-jets were displayed at ATME (1980) weaving fine filament yarns as well. Two problems remain, however, The cost of air-jet machines makes them suitable only for mass-produced fabrics that can be run at high speeds. Further, the speed of air-jet machines requires use of only the highest quality yarns.

The fastest type of shuttleless machine is the water-jet loom, which is currently third in popularity. Water-jet machines were displayed at ATME (1980) operating at up to 850 ppm. In 1975, at an exhibit in Milan, Nissan displayed one of its machines operating at 1,000 ppm. Despite the advantage of speed, water-jets have the disadvantage of being severely limited in the types of yarns they can weave. It is believed that they are suited primarily to smooth filament yarns.

A review of modern shuttleless weaving machines would not be complete without mention of one peripheral device commonly associated with their use. The weft insertion speeds of shuttleless machines can create a problem with weft breaks as the weft yarn is unwound from the package. One solution is a precision-wound flat cheese type of weft package. Most commonly, weft accumulators are used to unwind a length of yarn from the weft package before picking. The yarn is taken from the accumulator by the picking motion under a minimum of tension. This reduces the quality requirements for weft packages and allows weaker yarns to be used. For rapier and missile machines, variable speed accumulators controlled by a photoelectric cell, such as the SAVI, are most popular. Since the picking force provided by jet machines is insufficient to unwind yarn from the weft package, accumulators are essential on such machines. Jet machines are generally equipped with measuring drums that unwind the amount of yarn needed for the pick length.

Wet-Processing

Technological advances in wet-processing over the past decade have centered on reduced energy consumption and lower requirements for water. The incentives for these advances were provided by sharply increased energy costs and the more stringent government regulations on water pollution. Research in these areas also led to other improvements in wet-processing: shorter dyeing cycles, better color control, and reduced labor requirements.

The typical wet-processing chain of events, whatever the fabric concerned, is preparation, dyeing and finishing. Preparation involves taking greige fabric from the loom or fabric straight off the knitting machine, complete with all its natural and man-made contaminants, and removing all these contaminants, to a level at which the fabric will be receptive to the dyeing operation. In the dyeing operation, several techniques are used to apply coloration to the fabric. In the finishing process, some of the special qualities of fabric are added. These include durable press, water repellency, moth proofing, stability, soft hand, appearance and resistance to soil and flame.

It is not necessary for all fabrics to be processed through these three processes. Some materials, such as surgical goods, may receive a high degree of preparation and no dyeing and finishing. Only preparation and finishing may be necessary for yarn-dyed goods. The possible combinations in the wet-processing sequence are enormous, and depend on the fiber qualities, the manufacturing process and the desired end-use characteristics.

Most of the wet-processing machines developed during the past decade have been modifications of existing equipment. These modifications in design and operation of the machines or processes have centered on lower energy consumption, efficient use of plant floor space, reducing time in processing and production, increasing machine and process versatility, protecting the environment, and increasing automation and electronic microprocessor control of textile manufacturing sequences. There were few completely new technological advances.

With high energy cost and high consumption it is not surprising that energy is a primary concern of the textile industry, particularly the wet-processing area. The textile industry ranks high on the list of the most energy consumptive industries in the United States. Two manufacturing processes, dyeing and finishing, use more than three-fourths of all the energy consumed in the production of fabric or yarn. Most of this is used in evaporating water or solvent from the material. It is thus hardly surprising that the entire wet-processing and, indeed, the entire textile production machinery scene is dominated by concern to conserve in various ways. It is impossible to cover recent production machinery without constant reference to energy-saving innovations that have taken place in the past several years.

A second area of primary concern to the wet-processing sector is government regulations. The regulations impose a cost on the industry and they are considered non-productive. In the United States for example, some of the regulations that the wet-processing sector must deal with include: the Toxic Substances Control Act, the Safe Drinking Water Act, the Resource Conservation and Recovery Act, the Clean Water Act, the Clean Air Act, the Flammable Fabrics Act, the Consumer Products Safety Act, the Occupational Safety and Health Act, and the Federal Insecticide, Fungicide and Rodenticide Act.

New machines, with energy-saving features, are being used in almost every area of wet-processing. Washers have been designed with counter-current water flows to reduce both energy consumption and chemical usage. Incorporated in many of these designs are systems capable of water re-use and heat recovery. Solvent scouring equipment has been modified to eliminate wetting and drying steps, thus reducing energy consumption. Heat recovery and heat re-use designs have also been incorporated in dryers. Dyeing machines have been designed to operate at low liquor ratios. Low liquor ratios allow rapid dyeing times, which results in lower energy and chemical consumption. Finishing machines have been designed to increase speed and provide for very low pickup levels using hard roll pads or foam applications. New tenter frames have been developed to be more energy efficient. Several of these frames are shorter in length, but cloth can be processed at higher speeds due to improved air flows.

The Global Textile Industry and Textile Technology

Developments in the technologies of spinning and fabric forming can be subdivided into three stages. The first stage extended from the 18th century to the pre World War II era, and started as a result of English-based spinning and weaving technologies associated with the manufacture of natural-fiber textiles. These technologies spread rapidly to Europe, then to the United States, and finally to developing countries. The technologies were labor intensive and improvements came slowly. The second stage lasted from the mid-1930s to about the 1960s and was dominated by US-based technologies developed for the manufacture of synthetic- and blended-fiber textiles. These technologies were also relatively labor intensive when compared to the technologies of other industries, and spread rapidly to other countries. The third stage, dominated by European and Japanese technologies, extended from the mid-1960s to the present.

Unlike the first two stages, which had their impetus from the manufacture of textiles made first from natural and then natural/synthetic fibers in sufficient quantities to meet demand (e.g. long production runs of standardized fabrics), the impetus underlying the third stage was competition within and among countries. Since a basis of this competition is product differentiation and costs (e.g. shorter runs of specialized fabrics), substantial and rapid improvements occurred in productivity, productive versatility and product quality. In addition, significant reductions in manpower requirements also occurred, accompanied by some upgrading in occupational skills.

Textile mill companies in Asia, Europe and the United States were not slow in adjusting to the competitive requirements of the third stage. While expansion of capacity has been limited in recent years, substantial outlays have been made for new plants and equipment designed to increase manufacturing efficiency and versatility. Large investments have been made to automate chute feeders of fibers, to increase spinning speeds, and for the automatic doffer. Installation of open-end spinning equipment was expanded during the 1970s, since it offered reduced labor costs, greater machine speeds, improved yarn quality and better uniformity. The acceptance of the shuttleless loom also accelerated in recent years. These looms are faster, and provide a degree of flexibility and have capabilities not available in shuttle looms.

As a result of this modernization, many industry experts still consider the US textile industry the most productive and cost efficient in the world. However, this upgrading of technology and modernization by the US industry has made it more dependent on foreign textile machinery manufacturers. Furthermore, the industries of Europe and Japan have increased productivity at a faster rate than the United States, and are closing the productivity gap of the 1960s and 1970s.

As shown in Table 3.1, US shipments of textile machinery did not keep pace with apparent consumption. While the average annual growth in US shipments between 1964 and 1980 was 5.0 per cent, the average annual growth in apparent consumption was 7.4 per cent. The slack between domestic demand and supply was filled by imports.

However, the increasing dependency of the US textile mill products industry on foreign textile machinery sources is considerably greater than the 2.4 per cent difference between shipments and apparent consumption would suggest. As already discussed, most major innovations in textile machinery in recent years originated in other countries. The significance of this foreign leadership in textile

Table 3.1 US Trade in Textile Machinery

Year	Value of shipments US $m.	Value of exports US $m.	Value of imports US $m.	Apparent consumption[a] US $m.	Imports as a % of apparent consumption	Exports as a % of shipments
1980	1,105	355	597	1,347	44.3	32.1
1979	1,055	355	518	1,218	42.5	33.6
1978	949	328	555	1,176	47.2	34.6
1977	857	239	367	985	37.3	27.9
1976	918	202	368	1,084	33.9	22.0
1975	861	254	304	911	33.4	29.5
1974	987	304	356	1,039	34.3	30.8
1973	821	340	381	862	44.2	41.4
1972	738	228	426	936	45.5	30.9
1971	728	158	333	903	36.9	21.7
1970	712	179	221	754	29.3	25.1
1969	672	142	167	697	23.9	21.1
1968	592	132	161	621	27.2	22.2
1967	623	135	131	619	21.2	21.6
1966	777	157	128	748	17.1	20.2
1965	664	136	78	606	12.9	20.5
1964	559	140	59	478	12.4	25.1
Average annual growth rate %	5.0	8.6	18.7	7.4	9.9	4.0

[a] Apparent consumption is defined as domestic shipments plus imports less exports.

Sources: US Department of Commerce, *Annual Survey of Manufacturers*; *US Foreign Trade: Exports*; *US Foreign Trade: Imports*; *US Imports/Consumption and General, SIC Based Products by World Areas*; and *US Exports/ Domestic Merchandise, SIC Based Products by World Areas*, Washington, DC: US Government Printing Office, various issues 1964–1982.

machinery innovation can be seen in the additional data presented in Table 3.1 and also in Table 3.2. From 1964 to 1980, US exports of textile machinery grew at an average annual rate of 8.6 per cent. However, US imports grew at more than twice this rate, or 18.7 per cent. More important, perhaps, are the figures on imports as a percentage of apparent consumption and exports as a percentage of shipments. These data suggest that during the early 1960s US textile machinery manufacturers were world technological leaders across a broad spectrum of textile machines. Until 1967, exports as a percentage of shipments exceeded imports as a percentage of apparent consumption. Starting in 1968 however, imports as a percentage of apparent consumption have persistently exceeded exports as a percentage of shipments. In 1980, imports represented 44.3 per cent of apparent consumption, and exports represented 32.1 per cent of shipments.

US textile machinery manufacturers are still exporting a considerable share of their shipments each year, and may be technological leaders, but in narrower product lines (e.g. rapier looms). The data presented in Table 3.2 tend to support this conclusion. It is significant

Table 3.2   *US Trade in Textile Machinery by Region, 1980*

Region	US exports		US imports		Trade balance
	Value US $m.	% of total value	Value US $m.	% of total value	Value US $m.
Total trade	355.1	100.0	597.2	100.0	(242.1)
Western hemisphere	160.2	45.1	6.0	1.0	154.2
Western Europe	110.8	31.2	526.2	88.1	(415.4)
Communist areas in Europe	4.0	1.1	5.5	0.9	(1.5)
Asia	46.9	13.2	53.5	9.0	(6.6)
Australia & Oceania	9.1	2.6	6.0	1.0	3.1
Africa	24.0	6.8	Neg.[a]	—	24.0

[a] Negligible

Sources: US Department of Commerce, *US Imports/Consumption and General, SIC Based Products by World Areas*, FT 210, Annual 1980, and *US Exports/Domestic Merchandise, SIC Based Products by World Areas*, FT 610, Annual 1980, Washington, DC: US Government Printing Office.

to note, however, that the US trade balance was in a surplus position only for the Western hemisphere (Canada), Australia and Oceania, and Africa. It was in a deficit position with those regions of the world that had advanced textile machinery industries. In addition, most exports in 1980 were in spare parts for already installed equipment.

It is evident from the data that the US textile mill products industry continues to look to overseas textile machinery manufacturers for assistance. To remain internationally competitive, the US industry has become highly dependent upon these manufacturers for improvements in productivity and product quality.

The Impact of Technological Change and Diffusion on Competitiveness

It is extraordinarily difficult to quantify the impact of technological change and diffusion on a country's international competitiveness, or that of any specific company. While some efforts have been made for national economies and their balance of payments, virtually no research is publicly available at the level of the firm. Yet there does appear to be consensus in the literature that new technology adoption is a critical component in increasing competitiveness, especially for high labor cost countries, and perhaps for most firms regardless of location. There also appears to be consensus that (a) the faster technology diffuses, the shorter is the competitive edge gained by early adopters, and (b) the rate of technology diffusion has increased sharply during the last two decades, both domestically and internationally.

It is beyond the scope of this book to assess precisely what has been the impact of technological change and diffusion on the international competitiveness of national textile mill products industries. However a few general observations can be made.

(1) Most of the larger companies have increased their spending on R&D, either by themselves directly, or by purchasing new equipment embodied with new technology. These expenditures have contributed favorably to the companies' international competitiveness.

(2) The cost of new technology (development, acquisition and utilization) has increased sharply since the 1960s, limiting it to larger and/or financially stronger firms. This point, combined with point (1), has resulted in increased concentration of national textile industries. However, the effect on the international competitiveness of national industries has been mixed (see Chapter 8).

(3) The increasingly rapid diffusion of technology internationally has resulted in increased foreign competition for firms in both domestic and foreign markets. This has been due primarily to the aggressive international sales activity of textile machinery companies based inside and outside the USA.

(4) While many developing-country textile firms have not yet been able to purchase or technologically absorb the most recent

technologies, their use of less recent forms in combination with their significantly lower wage levels has steadily increased their international competitiveness. As they continue to upgrade their technological ability, their competitiveness will increase further unless firms in developed countries such as the USA continue to develop and utilize still newer technologies.

(5) Given point (3), a key competitive strategy for firms is to slow the diffusion of new technology in order to maintain a technological and competitive edge. However, this can be accomplished only if such technology is developed by them ('in-house', proprietary technology), rather than by textile equipment companies or by firms in other segments of the textile complex (e.g. man-made fibers). Otherwise, textile firms will not be able to control the diffusion process.

While staying ahead in the technology area will continue to weigh heavily in the future competitiveness of national textile industries, it will not be sufficient, for reasons discussed in subsequent chapters.

Notes

1   This chapter summarizes the major production technologies in each processing stage of the textile mill products industry and the changes in the technologies that have taken place over time. Readers with strong technical backgrounds may choose to skip this chapter and go directly to Chapter 4.
2   Some textile mills feel that this practice is not a prudent use of highly skilled labor.

4

International Trade Patterns

Introduction

The purpose of this chapter is to provide information on the world production, consumption and trade of textile mill products. This information is pertinent to the identification and understanding of the external and internal forces described in Chapter 1. To accomplish this purpose, data are arranged in table form in which the world's textile industry is compared and contrasted with other industries and with itself over time.

The chapter is divided into four parts to present a systematic flow of description from the global level down to the regional level. Accordingly, the first part focuses on world production and consumption of textile products. The second part describes world trade in textile mill products, while part three identifies the major participating regions. Part four centers on currency exchange rate movements as an impetus to interregional trade. In this section the USA is used as an example and its textile trade is correlated with the foreign exchange value of the dollar. The final section summarizes the findings of the chapter and addresses strategic issues facing the global textile industry.

In general, each of the three parts dealing with measurement presents data in two forms: absolute levels of weight or value, and relative levels (percentages). The two types of measurement are used to complement each other since neither type alone would yield useful information to anyone not thoroughly familiar with the item being measured. Additionally, care was taken to avoid the choosing of a unit of measurement that would unnecessarily bias conclusions.

The World Textile Industry

Food, shelter and clothing are the universal problems of over 4 billion world inhabitants. The attempts to solve these problems have created some of the largest industries in existence. The textile industry, in solving the problem of clothing and many of the shelter needs as well, is important to the welfare of the world population in two ways. First, it provides goods for consumption and, second, it creates large numbers of jobs that provide the means of consuming to a significant proportion of the population.

A look at Figure 4.1 confirms the importance of textiles in world consumption. The chart is intended to illustrate typical growth patterns in manufacturing industries, but it can also be interpreted to

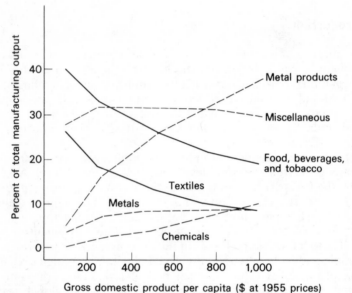

Gross domestic product per capita ($ at 1955 prices)

Figure **4.1**   Typical Patterns of Growth in Manufacturing Industries
(based on time-series analysis for selected years, 1899–1957)

Source: Alfred Maizels, *Industrial Growth and World Trade*, Cambridge, England: Cambridge University Press, 1963, p. 55.

illustrate the importance of the industries shown. For example, when gross domestic product is very low, indicating a less developed country or a very small economy, textiles typically rank highly as a percentage of manufacturing output. In fact, virtually every country has a textile industry, and textiles is one of the first industries developed by a country. Many of the world's countries fall into this category. For instance, Taiwan's textile industry employs 16 per cent of the country's manufacturing labor and produces 19 per cent of its manufactured goods. Of approximately 160 countries in the world, all must either produce or import textile products. Consequently, any event affecting the textile industry has wide-ranging impact and merits close study and thorough understanding.

World Textile Production

To continue the description of the world textile industry, Table 4.1

Table 4.1 *World Production and Per Capita Consumption of Selected Fibers*

| | World fiber production | | | | |
Year	Man-made [a] '000 MT	Natural[b] '000 MT	Total '000 MT	World population (millions)	Fiber consumption per capita (pounds)
1960	3,310	11,607	14,917	3,027	10.9
1961	3,520	11,332	14,352	3,072[c]	10.7
1962	3,944	11,966	15,910	3,117	11.3
1963	4,393	12,482	16,875	3,162	11.8
1964	4,977	12,822	17,799	3,234	12.1
1965	5,390	13,130	18,520	3,344	12.2
1966	5,830	12,143	17,973	3,356	11.8
1967	6,192	12,018	18,210	3,421	11.7
1968	7,316	13,284	20,600	3,490	13.0
1969	7,962	12,917	20,879	3,561	12.9
1970	8,384	12,789	21,173	3,678	12.7
1971	9,064	14,609	23,673	3,706	14.1
1972	9,936	15,168	25,104	3,782	14.6
1973	11,301	15,189	26,490	3,818	15.3
1974	11,019	15,576	26,595	3,890	15.1
1975	10,305	13,360	23,665	4,033	12.9
1976	11,786	14,142	25,928	4,107	13.9
1977	12,302	15,577	27,879	4,182	14.7
1978	13,352	14,552	27,904	4,258	14.4
1979	13,979	15,898	29,877	4,336	15.2
1980	13,731	15,774	29,505	4,415	14.7
Growth rate[d]	567	212	779	70	0.216

[a] Consists of rayon, acetate and various non-cellulosic fibers representing the majority of man-made fiber tonnage.

[b] The total of cotton, wool and silk production.

[c] Interpolated.

[d] Growth rates are the slopes of lines fitted to the data by the least squares method. They are average annual rates expressed in the units in the column headings.

Sources: Production figures: *Textile Organon* (Roseland, NJ: Textile Economics Bureau Inc.), various issues 1960–1982. Population figures: United Nations, *Demographic Yearbook* and *Monthly Bulletin of Statistics*, New York, NY: United Nations, various issues 1960–1982.

presents data on the world population, per capita consumption and total production of textile mill products. The proxy measure chosen to represent textile mill production is the world production tonnage of selected fibers.[1] The changes taking place in the fiber production industry will mirror the changes taking place in the textile mill products industry, since the demand for fiber is derived from the demand for textiles.

Between 1960 and 1980 man-made fiber production increased more than 300 per cent while the natural-fiber increase was about 36 per cent and the combined increase of all fibers was about 100 per cent. At the same time, world population increased approximately 46 per cent. Since fiber production grew much more than the population, per capita consumption of textile fibers increased 35 per cent, from 10.9 pounds in 1960 to 14.7 pounds in 1980. Average annual growth rates in each item are shown at the bottom of the columns, adding a second dimension to the table.[2]

Comparison of Industrial Growth Rates
Indices of industrial production are published by several organizations. Table 4.2 presents the growth in the index for several categories of manufacturing in various regions of the world. The textile industry as a whole is seen to be growing more slowly than most other categories of industry, even in regions where textiles are experiencing comparatively rapid growth. This is presumably due to its already substantial base.

Comparison across regions shows that developing market economies and small economies (Caribbean, Central and South America) have grown faster than the older, more developed economies (Europe and North America) in textiles as well as other manufacturing. These findings are compatible with Figure 4.1 where the textile share of total output diminished as the economy grew. Essentially, the planned economies and the underdeveloped and small economies show the greater rates of growth. The degree of government control in planned economies allows concentrated efforts at expansion in any sector, and many of the planned economies are relatively small in absolute terms so that almost any amount of positive growth is translated into high percentage figures. Since the growth rate of any region reflects the region's particular characteristics, objectives and problems, probably the most meaningful figure for comparison purposes is the growth rate for world textile production (3.6 per cent). This figure represents a weighted average of the growth rates of all regions combined and, as such, tends to smooth the differences of interregional comparisons.

Table 4.2   *Annual Growth Rate of Indices of Industrial Production, 1967–1979 (1975 = 100)*

Region	Textiles	Light manufacturing	All manufacturing	All industry
World	3.6	4.1	5.1	4.9
Centrally planned	5.2	5.7	8.0	7.8
Market economies	3.1	3.5	4.3	4.3
Developed market economies	2.6	3.2	4.0	4.1
Developing market economies	4.4	4.8	6.6	5.8
North America	3.3	3.5	3.8	3.6
Caribbean, Central and South America	4.7	4.4	6.3	6.1
Asia	3.3	4.2	6.8	6.5
Asia – excl. Israel, Japan	4.1	5.5	6.9	5.8
Europe	2.2	3.2	3.9	4.0
EC[a]	1.8	2.9	3.7	4.0
EFTA[b]	2.2	2.6	3.5	3.9
Oceania	1.8	2.4	2.4	3.2

[a] European Community = France, West Germany, Italy, Belgium, Luxembourg, Netherlands, Ireland, Denmark and United Kingdom.
[b] European Free Trade Area = Austria, Norway, Switzerland, Finland, Portugal, Iceland and Sweden.

Source: United Nations, *Yearbook of Industrial Statistics*, Vol. I, New York, NY: United Nations, 1979.

World Trade

Interregional exchange, by the nature of its occurrence, is more conducive to data collection than is production. That is, traded commodities inevitably pass through customs stations, which are agencies of national governments. Thus records of such transactions are more meticulously kept. In addition there are several world-level organizations (United Nations, Organization for Economic Cooperation and Development) that gather and publish these data in consistent and comparable form. This relative abundance of information lends itself to better analysis of trade related matters.

The examination of international trade patterns begins with the description of the Standard International Trade Classification (SITC) of textile industry output. Table 4.3 lists the three-digit code numbers and their descriptions. Much of the data on world industry gathered by international organizations such as the United Nations and the

Table 4.3   *Standard International Trade Classification, Sub-sector Descriptions*

SITC No.	Description
651	Yarn and Thread
652	Cotton Fabrics, Woven (not including Narrow or Special Fabrics)
653	Non-Cotton Fabrics, Woven (not including Narrow or Special Fabrics)
654	Tulle, Lace, Ribbons, Embroidery, Trimmings, and Other Small Wares
655	Special Fabrics and Related Products
656	Made-Up Articles, Wholly or Chiefly of Textile Material, NES
657	Floor Coverings, Tapestries, etc.

Source: United Nations, *Yearbook of International Trade Statistics*, Vol. I, New York, NY: United Nations, 1979.

Organization for Economic Cooperation and Development are classified according to SITC categories.

Textile Trade by Commodity Groups
Table 4.4 shows the value of total imports of textile products by market economies. The series covers the entire decade of the 1970s and shows imports by three-digit SITC category. The figures indicate a nearly uninterrupted growth over all categories for the decade. Four categories (651, 652, 654, 655) had slight declines in 1975, a year of severe worldwide recession. The decade ended with import levels approximately four times as great as at the beginning of the period in all categories, and for two categories (656, 657) more than five times as great. During the same period, the US producer price index published by the American Textile Manufacturers Institute and applicable to textile mill products increased approximately 52 per cent.[3] This implies a rather strong increase in trade in real terms over the ten-year period. Using the totals at the bottom of the table and adjusting for inflation during the period it can be shown that worldwide textile imports grew by 160 per cent during the decade. On the same basis, worldwide imports of all goods grew more than 240 per cent from 1970 to 1979. This latter figure is, however, heavily weighted by the dollar value of crude oil imports after the quadrupling of oil prices by OPEC in 1973. A look at the percentage figures at the bottom of Table 4.4 shows that until 1973 trade in textiles was a consistent 4 per cent of trade in all goods. In 1974 textile's share of world trade dropped precipitously to around 3 per cent and remained at this level for the rest of the decade.

Table 4.4 Total Imports by Market Economies (US $ '000)[a]

SITC group	1970	1971	1972	1973	1974	1975	1976	1977	1978	1979
651 Yarn	3,089,427	3,619,116	4,049,941	5,759,111	6,717,405	5,984,013	7,273,897	7,737,808	8,859,951	10,870,002
652 Woven Cotton	1,700,619	1,894,835	2,363,240	3,279,813	3,954,224	3,627,153	4,583,697	5,069,672	6,016,775	7,223,578
653 Woven Non-Cotton	3,823,094	4,285,594	5,116,435	6,811,837	7,758,908	7,800,140	8,631,739	9,262,888	11,543,881	14,089,927[b]
654 Lace, Ribbon, etc.	284,837	298,597	339,246	454,173	515,820	498,145	582,315	668,585	894,518	1,176,068[b]
655 Special Products	1,041,127	1,171,660	1,338,808	1,826,701	2,471,317	2,319,998	2,455,211	2,854,038	3,343,600	4,155,303[b]
656 Misc. NES	671,667	739,798	950,322	1,297,572	1,662,749	1,717,590	1,998,714	2,388,571	2,875,334	3,429,502[b]
657 Floor Covering	864,613	1,042,283	1,292,791	1,833,385	2,107,334	2,109,883	2,524,899	2,947,066	3,713,516	4,370,815
Total trade (US $m.)										
Textiles	11,475	13,052	15,451	21,263	25,188	24,057	28,050	30,929	37,248	45,315
All goods	294,100	328,300	383,600	528,600	773,300	801,000	910,500	1,045,700	1,211,600	1,527,400
Textiles as % of all goods	3.9	4.0	4.0	4.0	3.3	3.0	3.1	3.0	3.1	3.0

[a] Includes imports from centrally planned economies reported by market economies; valuation is c.i.f. point of entry.
[b] Preliminary figures.

Source: United Nations, *Yearbook of International Trade Statistics*, Vol. II, New York, NY: United Nations, various issues 1970–1981.

Table 4.5 *Total Exports by Market Economies (US $ '000)[a]*

SITC group	1970	1971	1972	1973	1974	1975	1976	1977	1978	1979
651 Yarn	3,296,181	3,789,799	4,277,289	6,125,278	7,351,860	6,241,587	7,463,767	8,108,936	9,105,207	11,012,443
652 Woven Cotton	1,436,291	1,629,167	2,047,825	2,814,747	3,411,648	3,148,744	4,140,771	4,628,811	5,226,898	6,526,154
653 Woven Non-Cotton	3,967,451	4,612,712	5,390,634	7,006,307	8,136,383	8,037,605	8,625,352	9,377,100	11,618,803	13,909,744
654 Lace, Ribbon, etc.	270,282	284,722	326,635	425,884	492,101	547,430	652,969	724,365	948,136	1,107,848
655 Special Products	965,214	1,125,654	1,337,911	1,873,866	2,474,870	2,310,890	2,420,623	2,731,876	3,391,998	4,200,783
656 Misc. NES	664,683	754,671	895,828	1,162,120	1,552,877	1,598,362	1,799,832	2,152,720	2,515,277	2,986,643[b]
657 Floor Covering	770,410	926,080	1,169,791	1,614,859	1,891,829	1,913,644	2,251,966	2,618,988	3,591,633	4,226,756[b]
Total trade (US $m.)										
Textiles	11,371	13,123	15,446	21,023	25,312	23,798	27,355	30,343	36,398	43,970
All goods	280,000	314,100	372,300	517,900	767,900	788,000	896,400	1,018,200	1,175,100	1,488,900
Textiles as % of all goods	4.1	4.2	4.1	4.1	3.3	3.0	3.1	3.0	3.1	3.0

[a] Includes exports to centrally planned economies reported by market economies; valuation is f.o.b. point of departure.
[b] Preliminary figures

Source: United Nations, *Yearbook of International Trade Statistics*, Vol. II, New York, NY: United Nations, various issues 1970–1981.

Table 4.5 shows the data on world exports and reveals identical changes over the same period. Exports are not discussed here because they are essentially the mirror image of imports.

Growth in Textile Trade
The average nominal growth rates for each SITC category and total textiles are given in Table 4.6. Man-made fiber fabrics experienced the fastest worldwide growth during the 1970s, increasing by more than $1 billion per year on average. The growth in man-made fiber fabric constituted almost one-third of the growth in total textile trade of nearly $3½ billion per year. Although within the textile industry,

Table 4.6   *Average Annual Growth Rates of Textile Trade, 1970–9[a]*
(US $m. per year)

SITC group		*Imports[b]*	*Exports[c]*
651	Yarn	781.6	780.1
652	Woven Cotton	579.9	531.0
653	Woven Non-Cotton	1,026.9	989.2
654	Lace, Ribbon, etc.	86.1	90.3
655	Special Products	318.4	323.8
656	Miscellaneous NES	297.7	251.3
657	Floor Covering	367.3	357.2
Total		3,457.9	3,322.9

[a]These growth rates are the slopes of trend lines fitted by least squares method to the data in Tables 4.4 and 4.5.
[b] Valuation is c.i.f. point of entry.
[c] Valuation is f.o.b. point of departure.

Source: Slope of trend line fitted by least squares method to data in Tables 4.4 and 4.5.

cotton lost ground to synthetics, woven cotton fabric still added over $500 million per year (on average) to world textile trade. Yarn of all fibers added more than $750 million each year to the total of textile trade. Thus, increases in these three items made up more than two-thirds of textile trade growth in the 1970s. Again, exports are included but not specifically discussed because, on a world basis, they are simply the mirror image of imports excluding insurance and freight.

Regional Textile Activity

Thus far, aggregate world textile production and its growth, as well as total trade by commodity and its growth, have been examined. The next logical step to gaining insight into textile trade patterns is to examine the activities of the various regions of the world. In this section the production, trade and consumption of those areas of the world that can be quantitatively demonstrated as being most important to the world textile industry are described and compared.

Textile Production by Region

The usual method of interregional comparison that avoids the problems of incompatible data gathered from a wide variety of sources is the use of indices. Thus each region is compared with itself over time and a limited amount of information is derived.

Accordingly, Table 4.7 shows the textile production indices of the world's leading producing regions for the second half of the 1970s.

Table 4.7   *Indices of Textile Production by Selected Regions (1975 = 100)*

Region	1974	1975	1976	1977	1978	1979
EC*a*	109	100	110	107	105	109
USA	108	100	109	109	112	117
Japan	106	100	108	106	107	110
India	97	100	104	102	108	n.a.
Brazil	n.a.	100	106	107	113	123
Korea	79	100	131	142	163	182
World	101	100	107	107	109	113

a EC = the nine countries comprising the European Community during the period.

Source: US International Trade Commission, *Publication 1131*, Washington, DC: USITC, May 1981, Tables 127 and 128 converted to 1975 base year.

The regions are listed in descending order of production quantity. In general, the larger producers show relatively slow growth; in fact, the four largest producing regions ended the decade approximately at the same level of production that they had achieved prior to the mid-decade recession. Brazil, the fourth largest producer of textiles (mostly cotton products), increased output 23 per cent from 1975 to 1979 and gave the best showing of the large producers. Korea is important in this group not for the size of its output but for its phenomenal rate of growth. Korea began the 1970s with a small annual textile output ($715 million) but by the end of the decade its production had increased tenfold.

The production index for the world as a whole is a weighted average of all producing countries. As such it is more heavily influenced by the larger producers and can be expected to approximate their rates of growth more closely than those of the smaller producers. Such is the case in Table 4.7.

Textile Trade by Region

In most regions of the world, trade is effected by independent firms with specific objectives in mind. Among these objectives are:

(1)   to broaden markets for the firm's products,
(2)   to take advantage of economies of scale that may exist in an expanded output,
(3)   to take advantage of price differentials that may exist in different markets, and
(4)   to permit regional specialization in the production processes of multinational corporations.

These objectives are all oriented toward the firm's goal of increasing profits, but there are also consumer (thus governmental) incentives for trade, such as:

(1)   introduction of new and desirable products to a region,
(2)   foreign products that are more competitive in price and quality than domestic products, and
(3)   creation of additional jobs.

These reasons, among others, provide the incentive to trade that is no less evident in the textile industries of the various regions of the world than in any other industry.

Given the incentive and the fact of trade, an investigation should focus on which regions are trading which products and by how much. In Appendix 2, tables are provided that rank trading regions by commodity, share of world trade and year for the 1970s decade. Both imports and exports are presented.

Tables A2.1–A2.7 in Appendix 2 show the top ten textile importers by three-digit SITC commodity groups for each year from 1970 to 1979. Each trading country has been ranked according to its share of world imports of each commodity group. Shares are shown as percentages of total dollar value of textile imports by market economies (the first number under each country name). While rankings and percentages provide two modes of making comparisons among the import markets for the various textile commodities, they give no hint of scale. To provide this vital third dimension, total dollar values of imports are included (the second number under each country name). From these tables, both the relative and absolute positions of leading importers can be determined and advances and declines traced through the time period for each commodity group. For instance, West Germany was the leading yarn importer for the entire decade. The United States began the period in second place, but by mid-decade had dropped to near the bottom of the rankings and by 1979 had dropped completely out of the top ten importers of yarn. Canada appeared four times as a top ten yarn importer during the decade. Hong Kong represented the Far East every year and Japan joined Hong Kong in the top ten yarn importers intermittently for five of the ten years.

West Germany has been by far the largest importer of textile mill products. Germany consistently ranked first in six of the seven commodity groups and placed in the top three in the seventh group (SITC 652, woven cotton) throughout the 1970s, frequently absorbing 10–15 per cent of total world imports in the various commodities. No other country showed this great an affinity for imports or for a particular position in the rankings, although other countries would frequently hold a particular rank for several years before advancing or declining. The USA and Canada were also heavy importers of textile mill products, appearing in every commodity group nearly every year. The Far Eastern countries appearing in the top ten importers most often were Hong Kong, Japan and Singapore, in that order.

Totalling the percentages in each column shows that the top ten importers consumed more than half the world's total trade in textiles (55–65%). Particularly interesting, due to their size, were imports of floor covering (SITC 657) by the top ten, which remained between 73 per cent and 80 per cent for the entire decade, with Germany importing, on average, 29 per cent of the world's total trade each year, while the USA took 5–7 per cent annually. There was no participation by the Far East in the top ten importers of floor covering except for Japan, which took 2.8 per cent of world imports in 1979 only.

Reclassifying markets for imports of textiles in terms of continents, it is easily seen that Europe was by far the largest importer. North America was second, and Asia was a close third. Australia occasionally appeared in the top ten importers, while there was virtually no participation in the top ten by African countries and none from South American countries.

A similar set of tables, Tables A2.8–A2.14 in Appendix 2, shows exports of textile mill products by market economies. In these tables, the top ten countries supplying textile exports were ranked by percentage of total world exports of each of the seven SITC categories for each year during the 1970s. These figures present the supply side of trade and can serve to identify the countries that are the primary competitors in the world markets. The first number under each country name is that country's percentage share of the world's market for textile exports and the second figure gives the absolute size of the country's external market for each of the commodity groups. The tables identify West Germany as the greatest exporter of yarn (SITC 651) and special fabrics (SITC 655) for the entire decade. Germany also exported the most woven cotton fabric (SITC 652) during the last four years of the 1970s, with the first place for the first six years being divided among the USA (two years), Hong Kong (one year) and Japan (three years). Belgium–Luxembourg assumed first rank in exports of floor covering (SITC 657) for the whole period, while Japan did likewise with woven fabrics other than cotton (SITC 653). First place in exports of tulle, lace, etc. (SITC 654) was divided an equal number of years between France and Austria, while India and the USA did the same with exports of made-up articles (SITC 656).

As was the case with imports, the European countries as a group were the greatest exporters. It was in exports, however, that Asian countries made significant inroads into world trade, especially Japan and South Korea. Japan appeared in the top ten exporters in every category of textiles during the period, but was especially prominent in woven non-cotton (SITC 653) where it held first position for all ten years observed. During those ten years, Japan consistently exported 20–24 per cent of the world's trade in this category. These results were in keeping with Japan's strategy of moving into relatively high-value-added, high-technology goods.[4] As an exporter, North America was placed third overall, but only a few African nations put in occasional appearances in this upper group. Australia and South American countries never appeared among the top ten exporters during the period. These four areas (Europe, Asia, North America and Africa) accounted for nearly 80 per cent of total world textile exports by market economies.

Comparing the import and export ranks of a country for a particular commodity group resulted in a curious phenomenon. Often the same country ranked high in both imports and exports of a particular commodity group. For instance, West Germany led the world in both yarn imports and exports for the entire decade. While such an outcome is contrary to expectations on first examination, this apparent anomaly may be explained in several ways.

One reason is random market activity. In market-oriented economies, the trading entity is usually an independent firm, pursuing its own set of objectives, subject to its own set of constraints. This type of structure could create a situation in which a firm in one country is importing the identical item that another firm in the same country is exporting. Lack of marketing coordination at the industry level may be causing an unnecessary expansion in foreign trade.

A second explanation could be due to contracts. Two firms in different countries may have a supply agreement that prevents one of the firms (due to its capacity) from supplying firms in its own country. Of course this situation could have been an outgrowth of marketing inefficiencies explained above.

A third feasible explanation could be re-exports. Firms may import an item, perform some work on the item without changing its essential character, and re-export the item under the same commodity code. An example of this would be importing grey goods, bleaching, printing and then exporting finished fabric still under the same three-digit SITC code.

A final explanation, related to the third, is the level of aggregation of commodities under the three-digit codes displayed in Tables A2.1–A2.14. The fact that much detail is lost in the grouping process gives the false impression of redundancy in trade. For example, a country may import large amounts of wool yarn and at the same time export large amounts of synthetic yarn, both according to comparative advantage. The three-digit level of aggregation used in the tables does not distinguish among types of fiber.

Of the four explanations offered for importing and exporting the same item, the fourth is probably the most prevalent. Of course, a combination of all four explanations along with some others is entirely possible.[5]

Textile Consumption by Region
The sum of a region's production and its net trade (imports minus exports) is the amount of a commodity that a region consumes, ignoring stocks held in inventory. Consumption on a per capita basis is both a measure of welfare of the consumers of a region and a measure of potential market from the firm's point of view. With regard to textile products, the European Community, the United States and Japan are the world's largest consumers. In fact, the United States consumes approximately 20 per cent of the world's annual output of fiber. US per capita consumption of textiles and apparel is approximately 55 pounds per year.[6]

Table 4.8 shows fiber consumption by selected regions for several years during the 1970s. Consumption by each of the market-oriented economies tapered off in mid-decade showing the effects of the recession of 1974–5. Some rebound in consumption is noted by the end of the period shown, but none of the market economies had regained the pre-recession level of 1973.

The EC, USA and Japan as a group contain approximately 16 per cent of the world's population; however this group consumed about 42 per cent of the world's fiber output in 1973. This figure declined to around 34 per cent by 1979.

Table 4.8 Regional Consumption of Fiber[a] ('000 Metric Tons)

Year	United States	Western Europe EC[b]	Western Europe Other	Total	Japan	Socialist countries	Canada and Australia	Other countries	World
1973	5,219.8	3,265.2	1,517.7	4,782.9	2,305.8	7,120	412.0	6,183.5	26,024
1974	5,072.8	3,011.1	1,486.9	4,498.0	1,941.4	7,423	374.4	6,187.4	25,497
1975	4,522.1	2,640.7	1,354.0	3,994.7	1,737.6	7,471	324.5	6,410.1	24,460
1976	4,588.9	3,038.8	1,649.2	4,688.0	1,889.8	7,560	351.8	7,600.5	26,679
1977	4,775.7	2,737.6	1,537.0	4,274.6	1,840.1	7,866	332.3	7,888.3	26,977
1978	4,793.3	2,758.2	1,652.4	4,410.6	2,010.0	8,206	358.5	8,440.6	28,219
1979	4,872.9	2,930.6	1,779.3	4,709.9	2,184.7	8,466	394.1	8,874.4	29,502

[a] Cotton, wool and man-made fibers.
[b] France, West Germany, Italy and United Kingdom.

Source: International Cotton Advisory Committee, Quarterly Bulletin (Washington, DC), October 1980.

Table 4.9   *Consumption and Trade in the European Community,*
USA^a and Japan for Selected Years

		1968	1970–1	1974–5	1976–7
Textile mill products:					
Apparent consumption	EC	19,854	24,245	47,444	53,733
($m.)	USA	28,825	31,271	42,041	51,236
	JAP	8,911	11,836	21,554	25,389
External imports as	EC	3.68	5.83	7.29	8.36
% of consumption	USA	4.00	4.93	4.39	4.19
	JAP	1.54	2.04	4.11	3.51
Textiles and apparel:					
Apparent consumption	EC	33,471	41,716	75,043	86,157
($m.)	USA	56,351	60,449	80,313	98,890
	JAP	10,623	14,635	29,682	35,982
External imports as	EC	3.86	6.86	11.14	13.66
% of consumption	USA	4.90	6.70	7.92	9.31
	JAP	1.62	2.69	6.01	5.60

^a Figures for USA include Canada.

Source: United Nations Commission on Trade and Development, *Handbook of International Trade and Development Statistics*, Geneva: UNCTAD, 1980.

Table 4.9 shows apparent consumption of textiles and import penetration ratios (value based) for the European Community (EC), North America and Japan for selected years. The EC is roughly equal to the USA in consumption, but the ratio for the USA is significantly lower.[7] While the difference between these ratios is open to debate, it does seem to indicate that either the US consumer is more strongly disposed toward consumption of domestic textile products than is his European counterpart, or that barriers to trade are more successfully applied in the US market than in the European market.[8]

Exchange Rate Effects

Regional trade results such as those discussed earlier can be largely attributed to the price effects of movements in the exchange rates between currencies. Using the United States as an example, when the US dollar weakens against other currencies the prices of foreign goods are higher and US consumers will be more disposed to buy domestic products.[9] At the same time, the foreign consumers are induced to buy the lower-priced US products. Conversely, a strengthening of the US currency would act to reverse these tendencies. Thus changes in the exchange rates between the US dollar and the

Table 4.10 Average Annual Exchange Rates (Foreign Currency Units per US Dollar)

Country	1970	1971	1972	1973	1974	1975	1976	1977	1978	1979	1980	1981	Currency
West Germany	3.6600	3.4908	3.1886	2.6726	2.5878	2.4603	2.5180	2.322	2.0086	1.8329	1.8177	2.2600	Mark
Belgium	50.000	48.870	44.015	38.977	38.952	36.774	38.605	35.843	31.492	29.319	29.243	37.131	Franc
Denmark	7.5000	7.4169	6.9493	6.0495	6.9049	5.7462	6.0450	6.0032	5.5146	5.2610	5.6359	7.1234	Kroner
France	5.5542	5.5426	5.0443	4.4540	4.8099	4.2864	4.7796	4.9134	4.5128	4.2545	4.2260	5.4346	Franc
Ireland	0.4167	0.4108	0.3997	0.4078	0.4275	0.4501	0.5536	0.5729	0.5210	0.4884	0.4859	0.6185	Pound
Italy	625.00	619.93	583.22	583.00	650.34	652.85	832.28	882.39	848.66	830.86	856.45	1136.77	Lire
Netherlands	3.6200	3.5024	3.2095	2.7956	2.6884	2.5290	2.6439	2.4543	2.1636	2.0060	1.9881	2.4952	Guilders
United Kingdom	0.4167	0.4108	0.3997	0.4078	0.4275	0.4501	0.5536	0.5729	0.5210	0.4713	0.4299	0.4931	Pound
Luxembourg	50.00	48.870	44.015	38.977	38.952	36.779	38.605	35.843	31.492	29.319	29.243	37.131	Franc
Austria	26.000	24.960	23.115	19.580	18.693	17.417	17.940	16.527	14.522	13.368	12.938	15.927	Schilling
Finland	4.2000	4.1843	4.1463	3.8212	3.7738	3.6787	3.8644	4.0294	4.1173	3.8953	3.7301	4.3153	Markkaa
Norway	7.1429	7.0418	6.5883	5.7658	5.5397	5.2269	5.4565	5.3235	5.2423	5.0641	4.9392	5.7395	Kroner
Portugal	28.750	28.323	27.011	24.673	25.408	25.553	30.223	38.277	43.940	48.924	50.062	61.546	Escudo
Switzerland	4.3730	4.1342	3.8193	3.1665	2.9793	2.5813	2.4996	2.4035	1.7880	1.6627	1.6749	1.9637	Franc
Iceland	0.880	0.880	0.8826	0.9013	0.9995	1.5370	1.8217	1.9887	2.7111	3.5260	4.7976	7.2242	Kronur
Sweden	5.1732	5.1168	4.7624	4.3673	4.4394	4.1522	4.3559	4.4816	4.5185	4.2871	4.2296	5.0634	Kronor
Canada	1.0477	1.0098	0.9899	1.001	0.978	1.0170	0.9860	1.0635	1.1407	1.1714	1.1693	1.1989	Dollar
Japan	360.00	349.33	303.17	271.70	292.08	296.79	296.55	268.51	210.44	219.14	226.75	220.53	Yen
Australia	1.1200	1.1342	1.1923	1.4227	1.4408	1.3102	1.2252	1.1090	1.1447	1.1179	1.1395	1.1493	Dollar
South Korea	310.57	348.20	392.90	398.32	400.43	484.00	484.00	484.00	484.00	484.00	607.43	681.03	Won
India	7.500	7.501	7.594	7.742	8.102	8.376	8.960	8.739	8.193	8.126	7.863	8.659	Rupee
Pakistan	4.762	4.762	8.941	9.994	9.900	9.900	9.900	9.900	9.900	9.900	9.900	9.900	Rupee

Source: International Monetary Fund, International Financial Statistics Yearbook, Washington, DC: IMF, 1981.

currencies of other countries would affect the demand for US textile exports to those countries.

Without examining the reasons for exchange rate changes, a look at the actual changes in the dollar rate is informative. As shown in Table 4.10, with few exceptions, the US dollar weakened with respect to European currencies and the Japanese yen through the 1970s. In relation to Canada and Australia, the US currency remained constant to slightly stronger during the period, while the US dollar consistently strengthened against the currencies of South Korea, India and Pakistan.

Considering the price effects on the foreign demand for US exports, as the US dollar weakens against another currency, one expects exports toward that currency to increase. On the other hand, a strengthening US dollar would imply increased imports, other things being equal. Table 4.11 shows US textile trade by region of the world in millions of dollars and percentages of the total. In general, the price effects described above are reflected in the trade figures. The regions whose currencies were notably strong against the US dollar had strong affinities for US textile exports during the decade (EC, EFTA, Japan), while those regions with currencies weaker than the US dollar were sources of large quantities of imports into the USA (Asia). For Canada and Australia, whose exchange rates with the US dollar did not vary greatly over the period, the increases in exports from the USA must be attributed to factors other than price changes related to exchange rates, such as product price changes, long-term supply contracts or increases in their own domestic demand, to name a few.

From 1979 to 1982, the US dollar strengthened significantly against most world currencies. This change, according to the discussion above, should have brought about reduced exports and increased imports during 1981 and 1982 assuming other factors did not change. Indeed, in 1981 US textile imports increased 22 per cent over 1980, while exports fell slightly (0.4 per cent) (US Department of Commerce, 1982). To the date of this writing, the US dollar has remained strong against other currencies due to high interest rates in the USA. This fact should cause even greater decreases in exports and continued strong imports for 1982, provided import quotas are not tightened further.

Summary and Conclusion

In the first part of this chapter, the size and importance of the textile industry to the world economy was illustrated. It was seen that the

Table 4.11 United States Trade in Textile Mill Products by Region

Region	1966 Imports US $m.	% of total	Exports US $m.	% of total	1971 Imports US $m.	% of total	Exports US $m.	% of total	1977 Imports US $m.	% of total	Exports US $m.	% of total	1978 Imports US $m.	% of total	Exports US $m.	% of total	1979 Imports US $m.	% of total	Exports US $m.	% of total
EC[c]	217.6	24.0	112.5	20.3	495.0	33.4	144.0	23.0	496.3	27.7	547.2	27.7	611.9	26.6	616.7	27.4	584.2	25.5	1,046.6	32.4
EFTA[d]	49.3	5.4	24.7	4.5	62.0	4.2	35.0	5.6	53.0	3.0	51.1	2.6	61.9	2.7	49.5	2.2	63.2	2.8	81.9	2.5
Canada	20.7	2.3	159.8	28.8	29.6[a]	2.0[a]	170.0	27.1	30.2	1.7	546.3	27.6	34.5	1.5	567.8	25.2	34.7	1.5	765.1	23.7
Asia[e]	260.4	28.7	10.0	1.8	302.2	20.4	32.3	5.2	370.5	20.7	33.1	1.7	412.9	18.0	47.5	2.1	461.8	20.2	64.2	2.0
Japan	246.1	27.1	6.8	1.2	396.0	26.8	26.0	4.1	387.7	21.7	56.6	2.9	489.6	21.3	80.9	3.6	392.7	17.2	130.3	4.0
Australia	Neg.[b]		24.7	4.5	1.6	0.1	22.7	3.6	Neg.[b]		73.6	3.7	Neg.[b]		89.1	4.0	Neg.[b]		129.2	4.0
Rest of world (market economies only)	114.4	12.6	215.7	38.9	193.6	13.1	197.1	31.4	452.0	25.3	670.0	33.9	688.0	29.9	798.0	35.5	750.8	32.8	1,008.1	31.3
Total	908.5		554.2		1,480.0		627.1		1,789.7		1,977.9		2,298.8		2,249.5		2,287.4		3,225.4	

[a] Estimated.
[b] Negligible.
[c] EC = France, West Germany, Italy, Belgium, Luxembourg, Netherlands, Ireland, Denmark, United Kingdom.
[d] EFTA = Austria, Norway, Switzerland, Finland, Portugal, Iceland, Sweden.
[e] Asia = South Korea, Hong Kong, India, Pakistan.

Sources: United Nations, *Yearbook of International Trade Statistics*, Vol. II, New York, NY: United Nations, various issues 1966–1982; United Nations, *Foreign Trade Statistics of Asia and the Pacific*, New York, NY: United Nations, Series A, 1971; Organization for Economic Cooperation and Development, *Textile Industry in OECD Countries*, Paris: OECD, various issues 1966–1982.

world currently consumes more than 65 billion pounds of textile products per year or approximately 15 pounds per capita. World consumption is also growing at more than three-quarters of a million metric tons (1.7 billion pounds) annually. However, despite impressively large growth figures, a comparison of textile growth indices with those of other industrial sectors showed textiles to be among the slower performers. Comparison of textile growth rates across regions of the world showed that textile growth in developing economies and planned economies was faster than in the older, more developed market economies.

The second section of this chapter described world trade in textiles by market economies. Trade was broken down by three-digit SITC commodity groupings, total imports and exports in each group were noted, and the growth rate of each group was computed. In absolute terms, textile trade growth is large and impressive, but when compared to the growth in trade of all goods it falls behind. However, in some textile commodities (SITC 653, 656, 657) trade growth approaches the trade growth of all goods. Among the three-digit commodity groups, non-cotton woven fabric was seen to be the fastest growing trade item with more than a billion dollar annual increase in imports worldwide. This implies that the current major growth area in textiles is in synthetic fiber woven fabric, an area in which the USA is reported to have a competitive advantage.

In the third part of the chapter, textile activity by region was described. Indices of production for the world's leading producers of textiles were examined and large producers were seen to be experiencing relatively slow improvement while smaller regions showed the significant growth. Next, interregional trade tables were produced that illustrated both the absolute and relative positions of the ten leading traders for each year of the 1970s, by commodity, for exports and imports. Finally, a discussion of consumption by region showed that the leading producers of textiles are also the leading consumers of textiles. The shares of world textile output absorbed by these areas are disproportionately larger than their percentage of world population. Additionally, regional consumption has been lower since 1973 in many areas.

The final topic of this chapter was a discussion of the effects of exchange rate changes on textile trade. Using the United States as an example, tables on foreign currency exchange rates and US trade suggest a fairly strong correlation between the foreign exchange value of a currency and the direction of its commodity trade.

This chapter presented the pattern of international trade in textile mill products and in so doing raised a number of economic issues such as: industry growth, trade, specialization, regulation, and foreign exchange effects on prices. In subsequent chapters these points and others will be broadened and further analyzed with the aim of enhancing the international competitiveness of the world textile mill products industry.

Notes

1   The weight of fiber shown in Table 4.1 will overestimate the weight of textile mill products by the weight of fiber that goes into non-textile products. However, fiber weight will underestimate textile products by the weight of dyes and other treatments of the final output. An additional underestimate results from the exclusion of some fibers from the table. Under man-made fibers, the weights of textile glass fiber and olefin fibers are omitted. Natural-fiber weight includes cotton, wool and silk only. Materials such as jute, hemp, sisal, kapok and others left out are expected to comprise only a small percentage of the total, hence are not serious omissions. A rough estimate of all other vegetable fibers combined for 1975 is less than 1 million metric tons.

Given these considerations, it is most likely that the fiber weight shown in Table 4.1 is a conservative estimate of textile production. Nevertheless, the weight is still a considerable amount – over 65 billion pounds in 1980 (metric tons are converted to pounds by multiplying times 2204.6226).

2   In Table 4.1 and its discussion, fiber production is viewed in three manners: absolute weight, average growth in absolute weight and overall percentage change from 1960 to 1980. Point to point percentage changes can be misleading, however, depending on the particular years chosen to effect the calculation. Average growth rates smooth the distortion inherent in percentage growth calculations.

One caution concerning the information in Table 4.1 and its discussion is necessary. The growth rates shown are calculations based on historical data, and as such must be viewed with care in terms of predicting future levels of textile activity. However, in most forecasting it is fair to assume that the near future will be similar to the recent past so that some reasonable projections may be made.

3   The US producer price index is used because the imports are measured in US dollars in each year. The differences in inflation between the US and other countries are assumed to be removed via the exchange rates used to convert foreign currencies to US dollars.

4   For a greater exposition on this topic see Arpan, Barry and Tho (1981), particularly p. 43.

5   These four explanations are not meant to be an exhaustive list nor is the topic of extreme importance. However, the evidence could indicate a need for a greater emphasis on the coordinating function and information flow in an industry that is, by nature, fractionalized.

6   See Toyne, et al. (1983). Center for Industry Policy and Strategy. Exhibit 4–8.

7   Figures for USA include Canada, but the ratios are very near to those for the USA alone. Using data from different sources, penetration ratios (value basis) have been computed on the order of .049 for 1970, .040 for 1975, and .052 for 1980 for US textile mill products only.

8   For pertinent comments on US protectionism see Puchala and Zupnick (1982).

9   When the US dollar weakens with respect to other currencies, the exchange rate, expressed as the number of foreign currency units purchased by one US dollar, falls. As the dollar buys fewer foreign units the effect is an increase in the price of foreign goods.

5

The Economics of the Global Textile Industry

Introduction

The range of options available to a firm in formulating business policy and strategy is dictated by the firm's environment. Environment obviously encompasses many dimensions – political, cultural and economic – but the single most important dimension is the structure of the industry in which the firm competes. The profit potential of product differentiation, advertising, research and development, price competition, merger, etc., is substantially determined by industry structure. The purpose of this chapter is to describe the structure of the global textile industry and to discuss the conduct and performance of firms in major textile producing countries.

As we noted in Chapter 4, virtually every country has at least a rudimentary textile industry. Nonetheless, world textile production is largely concentrated in three regions – the USA, Western Europe and Japan. The discussion in the next two sections is therefore restricted to these three regions. The third section is devoted to some important trends in the textile labor force.

The US Textile Industry

The US textile mill products industry is composed of approximately 5,000 intermediate and small-sized firms that produce a variety of fabrics and related products.[1] In general, these firms pursue mass-market strategies – concentrating on long production runs for highly standardized products. Hence, within product categories, the outputs of US firms are relatively homogeneous.

This relatively modest product differentiation and the large number of small firms comprising the industry have kept market concentration among US textile manufacturers low. Table 5.1 gives the number of firms, total value of shipments and share of shipments (industry concentration ratios) attributable to the largest firms in each of thirty textile product categories. Generally, US industries are categorized as concentrated when the top four firms in the industry control 50 per cent or more of the domestic market or the top eight firms control 70 per cent or more. Based on this criterion, nine of thirty sub-sectors of the industry could be classified as concentrated. However, in 1977 these nine sub-sectors accounted for only 13 per cent of total industry shipments and only two of the nine, tire cord and finishing man-made and silk fabrics, had shipments valued at more than $1 billion. This general lack of concentration suggests a high degree of competitiveness in the textile industry.[2]

While the US textile industry has been, and continues to be, characterized by a lack of concentration, some sub-sectors of the industry have become more concentrated in recent years. For example, the top four, eight, twenty and fifty concentration ratios for weaving cotton and man-made fibers, hosiery, knit outerwear, knit underwear and finishing man-made fibers all increased from 1963 to 1977. At the same time, concentration in weaving and finishing wool, cotton finishing, throwing and winding mills, thread and floor covering declined. Table 5.2 gives a more complete list of sub-sectors with changing concentration ratios.

The relative ease with which firms can enter the industry is another characteristic that reflects the absence of monopoly power in US textile manufacturing. Monopoly power in an industry can persist only when barriers prevent new firms from entering and eroding the monopoly position of established firms. Such barriers could include large economies of scale, a high degree of product differentiation, high absolute costs, large capital requirements, control of input supplies, ownership of important patents and institutional or legal factors. None of these impediments appears present in the US textile industry.

Economies of scale can, at best, be only roughly estimated and there are no recent estimates for the textile industry. However, estimates by Leonard Weiss (1961, pp. 4 and 133) for 1952 suggest that cotton weaving plants with spindle and loom capacity equal to 0.3 per cent of total domestic capacity are sufficiently large to take advantage of all potential economies of scale. More recent estimates by the Council on Wage and Price Stability (1978, p. 15) suggest that economies of scale for an integrated weaving plant might exist up to 1.5 per cent of national production capacity. A survey of a sample of Italian cotton spinning and weaving mills (reported in Comitextil, 1979) reflects (1) little evidence of increasing returns to scale in ring spinning mills,[3] (2) significant increasing returns for open-end spinning

Table 5.1 *US Textile Industry Concentration, 1977*

Product code	Product class	No. of firms	Value of shipments US $m.	% of value of shipments accounted for by		
				4 largest firms	8 largest firms	20 largest firms
2211	Weaving mills, cotton	211	4,431.2	39	58	79
2221	Weaving mills, man-made fiber and silk	267	6,325.9	42	58	76
2231	Weaving and finishing mills, wool	153	583.3	31	47	74
2241	Narrow fabric mills	291	682.9	17	28	48
2251	Women's hosiery, except socks	176	871.2	50	62	78
2252	Hosiery, n.e.c.	382	921.3	20	30	46
2253	Knit outerwear mills	903	2,335.9	17	27	46
2254	Knit underwear mills	80	648.9	42	59	85
2257	Circular knit fabric mills	462	3,169.4	20	31	51
2258	Warp knit fabric mills	213	1,427.2	26	40	64
2259	Knitting mills, n.e.c.	191	95.7	30	42	59
2261	Finishing plants, cotton	194	759.5	29	47	75
2262	Finishing plants, man-made fiber and silk	248	2,404.3	60	70	80

2269	Finishing plants, n.e.c.	176	830.6	30	43	66
2271	Woven carpets and rugs	71	47.1	67	81	94
2272	Tufted carpets and rugs	397	4,520.7	21	35	59
2279	Carpets and rugs, n.e.c.	72	115.2	69	82	93
2281	Yarn mills, except wool	274	3,864.9	19	31	51
2282	Throwing and winding mills	170	1,510.1	44	54	71
2283	Wool yarn mills	71	194.9	51	66	87
2284	Thread mills	58	544.4	57	77	93
2291	Felt goods, except woven felts and hats	37	197.7	58	81	98
2292	Lace goods	68	45.9	51	68	87
2293	Paddings and upholstery filling	113	251.8	30	47	70
2294	Processed textile waste	95	178.4	43	60	82
2295	Coated fabrics, not rubberized	175	1,059.0	39	56	74
2296	Tire cord and fabric	8	1,013.2	80	100	—
2297	Non-woven fabrics	81	864.4	36	55	81
2298	Cordage and twine	151	332.2	34	50	73
2299	Textile goods, n.e.c.	432	231.1	21	35	48

Source: US Department of Commerce, *1977 Census of Manufacturers: Concentration Ratios in Manufacturing*, Washington, DC: US Government Printing Office, September 1981.

Table 5.2   *Changes in Concentration Ratios, 1963–77*

1977 Industry code	Industry
	Increasing concentration ratios
2211	Weaving mills, cotton
2221	Weaving mills, man-made fiber and silk
2251	Women's hosiery, except socks
2252	Hosiery, n.e.c.
2253	Knit outerwear mills
2254	Knit underwear mills
2262	Finishing plants, man-made fiber and silk
2279	Carpets and rugs, n.e.c.
2281	Yarn mills, except wool
2283	Wool yarn mills
2292	Lace goods
2293	Paddings and upholstery filling
2284	Processed textile waste
	Decreasing concentration ratios
2231	Weaving and finishing mills, wool
2259	Knitting mills, n.e.c.
2261	Finishing plants, cotton
2269	Finishing plants, n.e.c.
2271	Woven carpets and rugs
2272	Tufted carpets and rugs
2282	Throwing and winding mills
2284	Thread mills
	No substantial change in concentration ratios
2241	Narrow fabric mills
2291	Felt goods, except woven felts and hats
2295	Coated fabrics, not rubberized
2296	Tire cord and fabric
2298	Cordage and twine

mills only up to 5,000–6,000 rotors and (3) an apparent optimal size of 300 looms in weaving. More casual empiricism also points to a lack of substantial economies of scale in US textile manufacturing. That is, the economic survival of large numbers of small firms suggests a lack of large-scale economies. The general impression of textile experts appears to be that plant-level economies of scale are less important than length-of-run and plant-specialization economies.

High absolute cost and large capital requirements appear not to be important barriers to entry for textiles. Capital requirements for a weaving mill have been estimated at $19.5–25 million (1978 $) (see

Table 5.3 US Corporate Profits[a]

	1974	1975	1976	1977	1978	1979	1980	1981 01	1981 02
Profit[b] per dollar of sales:[c,d]									
All manufacturing industries	5.5	4.6	5.4	5.3	5.4	5.7	5.0	4.7	5.5
Textile mill products	2.5	1.5	2.4	2.4	3.1	3.2	2.2	2.3	3.3
Profit on total assets:[e]									
All manufacturing industries	8.0	6.2	7.5	7.6	7.8	8.3	7.1	6.6	7.9
Textile mill products	3.8	2.2	4.2	4.4	5.9	5.9	4.4	4.4	7.0
Profit on stockholders' equity:[e]									
All manufacturing industries	14.9	11.6	14.0	14.2	15.0	16.6	13.9	13.4	16.1
Textile mill products	8.0	4.4	8.0	8.7	11.5	11.9	8.5	8.8	13.8

[a] Profit data include certain foreign income.
[b] After federal and other income taxes.
[c] Sales are of net returns, allowances, excise and sales taxes.
[d] Percent or cents.
[e] Annual data are quarterly averages. Quarterly data are annual rates.

Source: reported in *Textile Hi-Lights* (Atlanta, Ga: McGraw Hill), December 1981.

Table 5.4 *Rate of Return on Assets*

Company	1972	1973	1974	1975	1976	1977	1978	1979
First Hartford Corp.	0.02158	0.023604	-0.09532	-0.04959	-0.02232	-0.02956	0.03705	0.0283
Intl. Stretch Prods.	0.00677	0.013032	0.03887	-0.21190	-0.02192	-0.09780	-0.06700	0.1751
Vertipile Inc.	0.03715	0.001091	-0.08587	0.00650	0.01545	0.04583	0.10387	0.1751
Barwick (E.T.) Industries	0.04049	-0.017467	-0.19225	-0.09041	-0.13920	-0.08172	-0.40366	-1.4443
Crown Crafts Inc.	0.09831	0.106488	0.02244	0.06055	0.05590	0.04937	0.03340	0.0069
Edmos Corp.	0.05986	0.023080	-0.00934	-0.01041	-0.07105	-0.02660	-0.05694	-0.3918
Alba-Waldensian Inc.	-0.07686	-0.016943	0.00075	0.03969	0.00225	0.02473	0.04405	0.0303
Liberty Fabrics of NY Inc.	-0.07639	0.009525	0.05836	0.05211	0.07974	0.07227	0.05767	0.0606
Gaynor-Stafford Inds.	0.04164	0.000063	0.01241	-0.09406	-0.06647	-0.39731	-0.07247	-0.0061
Fair-Tex Mills	0.10705	0.029116	-0.01223	-0.04459	-0.04441	0.00801	0.07638	0.0796
Berven Carpets Corp.	0.11349	0.078992	0.03929	-0.01230	-0.00150	-0.05392	-0.04421	-0.1367
Stevcoknit Inc.	0.06954	0.063159	0.03446	0.01718	0.04639	0.01296	0.00479	-0.0985
Adams-Millis Corp.	0.01014	0.026858	0.02232	0.01597	0.03520	0.06319	0.04722	0.0669
Concord Fabrics Inc.	-0.03853	0.007560	0.01566	0.09464	0.08225	-0.00466	0.00989	-0.0671
Galaxy Carpet Mills	0.08523	0.071480	0.02010	0.02391	0.03557	0.05827	0.07393	0.0394
Lehigh Valley Inds.	-0.17300	0.022504	0.20087	-0.01730	0.02353	0.06151	0.04251	0.0205
Martin Processing Inc.		0.157668	0.13943	0.15051	0.12514	0.12918	0.09824	0.0209
Compo Inds.	0.04700	0.042785	-0.03985	-0.03799	0.02174	0.00760	0.05068	0.0504
Opelika Mfg. Corp.	0.02393	0.050950	0.05769	0.03780	0.04791	0.02460	0.02736	0.0394
Fab Industries Inc.	0.05144	0.064221	0.02912	0.06089	0.09364	0.11084	0.13973	0.1409
Belding Heminway	0.04472	0.059121	0.04733	0.05166	0.04965	0.04081	0.05839	0.0609
Mount Vernon Mills Inc.	0.03644	0.047650	0.05466	0.01886	0.00887	0.00464	0.06482	0.0752
Standard Coosa-Thatcher	0.03572	0.051981	0.04578	0.00103	0.04486	0.05015	0.05426	0.0295

Masland (C.H.) & Sons	0.02356	0.027398	0.00572	0.02552	0.04615	0.04762	0.03059	-0.0384
Munsingwear Inc.	0.07950	0.048645	0.00485	0.04139	0.02946	0.06123	0.03951	0.0180
Tultex Corp.			0.04894	0.01750	0.07381	0.07671	0.07843	0.0681
Guilford Mills Inc.	0.09653	0.062664	0.05396	0.00578	0.06869	0.06041	0.13263	0.1639
Crompton Co. Inc.	0.03956	0.053405	-0.00250	-0.02889	0.04353	0.02026	0.07510	0.0991
Shaw Industries Inc.	0.10764	0.119379	0.10539	0.06005	0.06961	0.06716	0.04386	0.0421
Texfi Industries	0.04799	0.056844	-0.00238	-0.05023	-0.03671	-0.10182	0.02653	-0.0277
Ti-Caro Inc.	0.08247	0.059433	0.07192	0.05601	0.12269	0.12290	0.13202	0.1129
Avondale Mills	0.05437	0.076639	0.05341	0.03627	0.04520	0.04803	0.04028	0.0188
Russell Corp.	0.04629	0.053751	0.08389	0.07897	0.07312	0.09728	0.11248	0.1104
Graniteville Co.	0.05495	0.066384	0.12780	0.07898	0.09464	0.08006	0.00084	0.0343
Reeves Brothers Inc.	0.04667	0.071048	0.07891	0.02855	0.07746	0.06677	0.07225	0.1047
Riegel Textile Corp.	0.03422	0.058966	0.05789	0.05530	0.09304	0.08024	0.06830	0.0645
Albany Intl. Corp.	0.06970	0.076184	0.07624	0.02652	0.06314	0.06823	0.07444	0.0803
Fieldcrest Mills	0.04436	0.047202	0.00744	0.04977	0.05901	0.07567	0.08897	0.0821
Collins & Aikman Corp.	0.07561	0.058326	0.03413	0.07851	0.07437	0.08177	0.07794	0.0482
Lowenstein (M) Corp.	0.02298	0.028889	0.02857	-0.01677	0.02471	-0.02193	0.03290	-0.0097
Dan River Inc.	0.01441	0.033466	0.02237	-0.00956	0.04281	0.03551	0.04084	0.0631
Cone Mills Corp.	0.03916	0.039063	0.06092	0.08866	0.11378	0.12662	0.10475	0.1187
Cannon Mills Co.	0.05976	0.037750	0.05301	0.06044	0.05322	0.05810	0.06910	0.0938
United Merchants & Mfrs. Inc.			0.02897	-0.01749	-0.01789	-0.07609	0.00241	0.0200
Springs Mills Inc.	0.03977	0.043574	0.04663	0.02601	0.03508	0.03598	0.06167	0.0643
West Point-Pepperell	0.03741	0.058134	0.06930	0.05487	0.06110	0.05517	0.05929	0.0463
Stevens (J.P.) & Co.	0.02413	0.044060	0.05248	0.02633	0.04986	003938	0.03814	0.0458
Burlington Industries Inc.	0.03441	0.052085	0.06053	0.02539	0.06051	0.05081	0.03724	0.0390

Source: Raw data for these computations taken from COMPUSTAT® Data Base Services. New York, NY: Standard & Poors Inc.

Table 5.5 Rate of Return on Stockholders' Equity

Company	1972	1973	1974	1975	1976	1977	1978	1979
First Hartford Corp.	0.13991	0.200119	-3.1023	-3.7086	n.a.	n.a.	n.a.	0.0974
Intl. Stretch Prods.	0.01950	0.038660	0.1205	-0.6593	-0.0649	-0.3379	-0.27483	0.3282
Vertipile Inc.	0.10212	0.003095	-0.2838	0.0188	0.0408	0.1125	0.24346	n.a.
Barwick (E.T.) Industries	0.13672	-0.063619	-1.7932	-3.7893	n.a.	n.a.	n.a.	n.a.
Crown Crafts Inc.	0.18107	0.204622	0.0420	0.1186	0.1324	0.1062	0.07384	0.0152
Edmos Corp.	0.10124	0.040057	-0.0156	-0.0169	-0.1438	-0.0590	-0.12739	-1.3037
Alba-Waldensian Inc.	-0.15798	-0.031988	0.0014	0.0659	0.0039	0.0429	0.07329	0.0516
Liberty Fabrics of NY Inc.	-0.17998	0.019424	0.0948	0.0836	0.1261	0.1164	0.10132	0.1072
Gaynor-Stafford Inds.	0.14894	0.000330	0.0647	-0.9392	-1.2682	n.a.	n.a.	n.a.
Fair-Tex Mills	0.16948	0.051785	-0.0261	-0.1009	-0.1013	0.0187	0.16962	0.1635
Berven Carpets Corp.	0.17216	0.129622	0.0567	-0.0227	-0.0030	-0.1248	-0.08159	-0.3170
Stevcoknit Inc.	0.15631	0.137365	0.0738	0.0385	0.1189	0.0324	0.01189	-0.3038
Adams-Millis Corp.	0.02249	0.057392	0.0536	0.0300	0.0561	0.0919	0.06928	0.1132
Concord Fabrics Inc.	-0.10628	0.017204	0.0382	0.2132	0.1790	-0.0087	0.02154	-0.1610
Galaxy Carpet Mills	0.24844	0.229881	0.0676	0.0832	0.1100	0.1780	0.21621	0.1140
Lehigh Valley Inds.	n.a.	n.a.	n.a.	n.a.	n.a.	n.a.	2.37429	n.a.
Martin Processing Inc.		0.304456	0.2485	0.2661	0.1963	0.2179	0.15130	0.0333
Compo Inds.	0.10887	0.109705	-0.1023	-0.0895	0.0473	0.0172	0.12073	0.1319
Opelika Mfg. Corp.	0.04390	0.092262	0.1079	0.0673	0.0957	0.0513	0.05837	0.1054
Fab Industries Inc.	0.08827	0.108560	0.0482	0.1031	0.1345	0.1754	0.25710	0.2513
Belding Heminway	0.10446	0.122777	0.0955	0.0997	0.0915	0.0687	0.10007	0.1030
Mount Vernon Mills Inc.	0.04848	0.063346	0.0729	0.0247	0.0130	0.0069	0.09083	0.1065
Standard Coosa-Thatcher	0.04610	0.068450	0.0654	0.0018	0.0774	0.0860	0.08963	0.0501

Masland (C.H.) & Sons	0.05046	0.065346	0.0138	0.0556	0.1003	0.1053	0.07121	−0.0921
Munsingwear Inc.	0.12621	0.092291	0.0096	0.0688	0.0519	0.1060	0.07437	0.0379
Tultex Corp.	0.20396	0.136156	0.1608	0.0548	0.2220	0.2180	0.20315	0.1655
Guildford Mills Inc.	0.09494	0.080229	0.1329	0.0144	0.1608	0.1460	0.30798	0.3219
Crompton Co. Inc.	0.22096	0.277164	−0.0050	−0.0674	0.0876	0.0427	0.15184	0.1724
Shaw Industries Inc.	0.13396	0.157329	0.2582	0.1344	0.1578	0.1759	0.13667	0.1379
Texfi Industries	0.14024	0.096264	−0.0073	−0.1509	−0.1115	−0.3499	0.08271	−0.0908
Ti-Caro Inc.	0.08360	0.118639	0.1162	0.0874	0.1939	0.1900	0.20218	0.1614
Avondale Mills	0.09030	0.105411	0.0867	0.0546	0.0690	0.0752	0.06207	0.0290
Russell Corp.	0.08735	0.100508	0.1511	0.1409	0.1256	0.1693	0.19368	0.1859
Graniteville Co.	0.08606	0.116901	0.1843	0.1147	0.1422	0.1214	0.00134	0.0583
Reeves Brothers Inc.	0.07032	0.118749	0.1246	0.0424	0.1207	0.1157	0.12048	0.1766
Riegel Textile Corp.	0.12849	0.146459	0.1146	0.0992	0.1678	0.1369	0.12091	0.1147
Albany Intl. Corp.	0.08667	0.102864	0.1623	0.0528	0.1241	0.1273	0.13342	0.1443
Fieldcrest Mills	0.13157	0.111282	0.0159	0.1041	0.1211	0.1516	0.17562	0.1680
Collins & Aikman Corp.	0.05582	0.068634	0.0593	0.1346	0.1266	0.1367	0.13090	0.0858
Lowenstein (M) Corp.	0.03042	0.075290	0.0684	−0.0430	0.0578	−0.0527	0.07537	−0.0237
Dan River Inc.	0.05916	0.066845	0.0497	−0.0214	0.0883	0.0729	0.08322	0.1250
Cone Mills Corp.	0.06628	0.042445	0.0981	0.1374	0.1621	0.1837	0.14221	0.1531
Cannon Mills Co.			0.0601	0.0700	0.0606	0.0662	0.08542	0.1204
United Merchants & Mfrs. Inc.			0.1035	−0.0682	−0.0848	−1.6985	0.02333	0.1394
Springs Mills Inc.	0.05560	0.071339	0.0734	0.0387	0.0531	0.0538	0.09191	0.1044
West Point-Pepperell	0.05187	0.086572	0.1106	0.0843	0.1068	0.1005	0.11229	0.0942
Stevens (J.P.) & Co.	0.04336	0.081794	0.0976	0.0482	0.0931	0.0759	0.07489	0.0919
Burlington Industries Inc.	0.06438	0.099903	0.1123	0.0444	0.1079	0.0895	0.06810	0.0713

Source: Raw data for these computations taken from COMPUSTAT® Data Base Services, New York, NY: Standard & Poors Inc.

Council on Wage and Price Stability, 1978, p. 17). This is a very small sum compared to comparable estimates for other industries.[4]

Because of the large number of textile firms and their high degree of product homogeneity, individual US firms appear to have little price discretion. Textile prices respond quickly to changes in supply and demand (see Council on Wage and Price Stability, 1978, for more detail). This suggests that US textile firms are price competitive and that market conditions, rather than managerial decisions, are the primary determinants of textile prices.

The large number of firms in the industry, high degree of product homogeneity, relative ease of entry and pressure from foreign competitors have acted to hold down profits in US textiles. As Table 5.3 shows, rates of return on sales, assets and stockholders' equity are all substantially lower for textile manufacturers than for manufacturing industries taken as a group.

Of course, this does not mean that profits for all textile firms are low relative to firms in other industries. Indeed, some textile firms have been, and continue to be, very profitable. Tables 5.4 and 5.5 give rates of return on assets and stockholders' equity for forty-eight publicly held textile firms.[5] As these tables show, several textile firms have consistently earned profits in excess of average profits in manufacturing. It is also interesting to note that those firms consistently reporting above-average profits are all of intermediate size, with 1979 assets ranging from $60 to $370 million.

Employment in the US textile industry has declined continuously since World War II. In 1945 the industry employed approximately 1.3 million workers. By 1955 employment had fallen to 1.05 million and by 1965 it had fallen to 925,000. The late 1960s and early 1970s were growth years for US textiles, with employment reaching a peak of 1 million in 1973. However, textile employment has declined continuously since 1973. At present, the industry employs just over 800,000 workers.

Employment of these workers is highly concentrated in six Southeastern states. North Carolina, South Carolina and Georgia account for almost 58 per cent of total US textile employment, and Virginia, Tennessee and Alabama contribute another 12 per cent. Further, this geographic concentration is increasing. Textile employment in the Southeast is declining, but it is declining at a slower rate than total textile employment. Hence, textiles provide a declining share of economic activity in Southeastern states at the same time that the textile industry is becoming more concentrated in these states.

While employment has fallen, output for US textile manufacturers has increased. From 1967 to October 1981, textile output grew by 34 per cent.

Table 5.6 US Manufacturing Industry, Production Capacity (Percent of 1967 Output, Seasonally Adjusted)

Industry	1977 Q1	Q2	Q3	Q4	1978 Q1	Q2	Q3	Q4	1979 Q1	Q2	Q3	Q4	1980 Q1	Q2	Q3	Q4	1981 Q1	Q2	Q3
Manufacturing	133.1	136.9	138.7	139.9	139.8	144.4	146.7	151.7	153.4	153.1	153.3	152.8	155.0	141.0	143.9	148.6	151.3	152.4	152.5
Durable goods	129.2	135.1	136.1	137.7	137.9	144.0	144.0	150.3	157.3	157.7	158.7	158.4	158.3	131.3	140.6	144.3	150.9	152.3	152.7
Non-durable goods	149.5	154.6	154.7	155.0	158.0	163.2	163.0	170.3	172.2	173.4	175.7	175.7	179.3	168.0	161.9	176.3	179.2	178.4	175.8
Textile	111.3	110.9	113.2	115.3	115.3	117.1	116.8	119.5	118.2	119.6	122.3	123.8	120.6	116.4	113.4	113.7	114.8	114.5	115.5

Source: Federal Reserve Bulletin (Washington, DC: Publication Services, Board of Governors of the Federal Reserve System). November 1981. Table 2.11. pp. A46–47.

Table 5.7 US Manufacturing Industry, Capacity Utilization Index (Seasonally Adjusted Quarterly)

Industry	1977 Q1	Q2	Q3	Q4	1978 Q1	Q2	Q3	Q4	1979 Q1	Q2	Q3	Q4	1980 Q1	Q2	Q3	Q4	1981 Q1	Q2	Q3	Q4	Previous cycle[a] High	Low	Latest cycle[b] High	Low
Manufacturing	81.2	82.7	83.0	82.9	82.1	84.0	85.0	86.4	86.7	85.9	85.4	84.4	83.4	77.9	75.7	79.1	79.9	79.8	79.3	n.a.	88.0	69.0	87.2	74.9
Durable goods	76.5	79.4	79.3	79.6	79.3	82.2	85.3	87.4	87.3	86.2	86.0	84.1	82.8	74.6	69.1	75.7	78.7	79.0	78.7	n.a.	91.5	63.6	88.4	68.0
Non-durable goods	85.1	87.2	86.5	85.9	86.7	88.5	87.4	89.6	89.7	89.5	89.8	90.6	89.7	82.2	79.2	85.9	86.5	85.3	83.3	n.a.	94.5	67.2	90.9	76.8
Textiles	78.7	78.1	79.0	82.4	80.3	81.2	80.4	87.5	86.3	87.1	88.8	89.4	86.9	83.7	81.2	81.4	81.9	81.4	81.8	n.a.	92.6	57.9	90.1	79.5

[a] Monthly high 1973, monthly low 1975.
[b] Preliminary; monthly highs December 1978 – January 1980; monthly lows July 1980 – October 1980.

Source: Federal Reserve Bulletin (Washington, DC: Publication Services, Board of Governors of the Federal Reserve System). November 1981. Table 2.11. pp. A46–47.

Within textiles, the output of knitted goods increased by 87 per cent from 1967 to September of 1981. From 1967 to 1979 the output of carpets increased by 122 per cent, and, while the sharp decline in construction beginning in 1980 substantially reduced carpet output in 1980 and 1981, carpet production in September of 1981 was still 84 per cent greater than in 1967. In contrast, the September 1981 rate of production of woven fabrics was only 10 per cent higher than in 1967, and production of cotton fabrics fell by 33 per cent over this period.

US fiber consumption data confirm the modest growth in textile manufacturing and show a strong trend toward use of synthetics instead of natural fibers. Total consumption of fibers (measured in pounds) grew by approximately 40 per cent from 1965 to the third quarter of 1981. This change in total fiber consumption represents a decline in cotton and wool use of 33 and 68 per cent, respectively, and growth in the use of man-made fibers of over 140 per cent. In 1965, cotton represented 53 per cent of total fiber consumption, wool slightly less than 5 per cent and man-made fibers constituted almost 43 per cent. By the third quarter of 1981 the shares of cotton and wool in total fiber consumption had fallen to 23 and 1 per cent, respectively, and the share of man-made fibers had risen to 76 per cent.

Production capacity is inherently difficult to quantify. Hence, few data are available on capacity and capacity utilization. Further, because measurement problems are formidable, those data that do exist must be viewed with some skepticism. Nevertheless, it appears that several conclusions can be drawn from capacity data compiled by

Table 5.8 *Annual Average Capacity Utilization Index in Textiles, USA*

Year	Fabrics	Man-made fabrics
1967	98.1	86.3
1968	92.2	99.1
1969	92.7	98.3
1970	93.4	86.7
1971	96.3	80.8
1972	94.0	91.6
1973	91.4	100.2
1974	86.0	89.8
1975	79.3	74.9
1976	89.4	86.4

Source: Federal Reserve Board. Published by the Council on Wage and Price Stability, *A Study of the Textile and Apparel Industry*, Washington, DC: US Government Printing Office, 1978, p. 44.

Table 5.9 US Investment in New Plant and Equipment (US $m.)

Period	Total non-farm business	Manufacturing industries	Durable goods	Non-durable goods	Textile mill products	Paper & allied products	Chemical & allied products
1963	53,250	17,270	8,640	8,630	430	700	1,720
1964	61,660	21,230	10,980	10,250	590	910	2,100
1965	70,430	25,410	13,490	11,920	790	1,070	2,820
1966	82,220	31,370	17,230	14,150	960	1,320	3,350
1967	83,430	32,250	17,830	14,420	770	1,490	3,080
1968	88,450	32,340	17,930	14,400	650	1,270	2,800
1969	99,520	36,270	19,970	16,310	860	1,620	3,010
1970	105,530	36,990	19,800	17,190	800	1,740	3,380
1971	108,530	33,600	16,780	16,820	900	1,290	3,270
1972	120,250	35,420	18,220	17,200	1,060	1,460	3,380
1973	137,100	42,370	22,750	19,620	1,030	1,990	4,240
1974	156,980	53,210	27,440	25,760	1,090	2,890	6,470
1975	157,710	54,920	26,330	28,590	900	2,980	7,630
1976	171,450	59,950	28,470	31,470	1,050	3,110	8,120
1977	198,080	69,220	34,040	35,180	1,260	3,600	8,140
1978	231,240	79,270	40,430	39,290	1,380	3,990	8,460
1979	270,460	98,680	51,070	47,610	1,500	5,550	10,780
1980	295,630	115,810	58,910	56,900	1,620	6,800	12,600
1981[a]							
Q1	312,240	124,500	61,240	63,270	1,530	6,930	12,810
Q2	316,730	125,490	63,100	62,400	1,620	6,420	12,010

[a] Seasonally adjusted annual rates.

Source: Textile Hi-Lights (Atlanta, Ga: McGraw Hill), June 1981, p. 21.

the Federal Reserve Board. (These data are shown in Tables 5.6, 5.7 and 5.8.)

First, the textile industry has been faced with excess capacity since 1974 (see Tables 5.7 and 5.8). However, the magnitude of unused capacity is not substantially different from that in other manufacturing industries, i.e. stagflation has not differentially affected textile capacity utilization.

Second, despite existing excess capacity, production capacity in most manufacturing industries has increased, and the textile industry is no exception. However, capacity in textiles has grown at a substantially slower rate than for other manufacturing industries. This modest growth in textile capacity appears to be attributable to the modest growth in demand for US textile products and perhaps management uncertainty about the future foreign competition, government regulations and the rate of technological innovation.

Generally, increasing capacity is associated with increasing expenditures on new plants and equipment. As Table 5.9 shows, investment in textile plants and equipment is increasing, further evidence that US capacity in textile manufacturing is increasing.

From 1963 to 1980 annual expenditures on new plant and equipment by US textile manufacturers increased from $430 million to $1,620 million, an increase of 277 per cent. However, much of this increase is attributable to inflation. When adjustments are made for inflation, growth in textile investment from 1963 to 1980 was only 27 per cent. By contrast, over the 1963–80 period, annual inflation-adjusted investment expenditures in the US paper and chemicals industries increased by more than 400 and 300 per cent, respectively, and in all US manufacturing industries taken together by over 300 per cent. In short, while textile manufacturers have invested increasing amounts in new capital goods, the rate of increase in investment has been substantially lower for textiles than for most other manufacturing industries.

The Western European and Japanese Textile Industries

Western Europe encompasses a broad range of countries from the 'rich', such as West Germany and the Scandinavian countries with 1978 per capita incomes exceeding $10,000, to the 'poor', such as Turkey and Portugal with less than $2,000 per capita. In politico-economic terms, Western Europe can be broken into three groups: (1) the 'industrialized' EC, (2) other 'industrialized' Europe (predominantly Northern), and (3) semi-industrialized Europe (predominantly Southern). The relative size of these groups is shown in Table

Table 5.10   *Population and National Product, 1978*

Region	Population (millions)	GNP at market prices (US $m.)	GNP per capita (US $'000)	Growth of real GNP per capita 1960–70	1970–8
Total Europe	389	2,589	6.7	4.0	2.4
EC (9 members)[a]	259	2,039	7.9	3.8	2.4
Other industrialized North[b]	31	298	9.7	4.0	2.0
Semi-industrialized South[c]	99	252	2.5	5.6	3.3
North America	240	2,091	8.7		
Japan	113	737	6.5		

[a] West Germany, France, Italy, Belgium, Luxembourg, Netherlands, Ireland, Denmark, UK.

[b] Austria, Norway, Sweden, Finland, Switzerland.

[c] Portugal, Greece (EC member as of 1981), Spain, Turkey.

Source: Calculated from The World Bank, *World Bank Atlas*, Washington, DC: World Bank, 1980.

Table 5.11   *Indicators of Size of the Textile Industry*

Region	Woven cloth production[a] 1962 '000MT	%	1979 '000MT	%	Employment 1963 '000	%	1976 '000	%
Total Europe	2,237	100	2,250	100	3,147	100	2,415	100
EC (9 members)	1,857	83	1,564	70	2,430	77	1,699	70
Other industrialized North	153	7	127	6	230	7	167	7
Semi-industrialized South	227	10	559	25	487	15	549	23
USA	2,003		2,388		863		1,042	
Japan					1,312		877	

[a] The percentage breakdown by the three regions is virtually the same for yarn. Southern European countries tend to have a smaller share of other textile branches.

Sources: Calculations from data in Organization for Economic Cooperation and Development, *Textile Industry in OECD Countries 1969–1970*, Paris: OECD, 1971; OECD, *Textile Industry in OECD Countries 1978–1979*, Paris: OECD, 1981; Wolfgang Kurth, *Textiles and Clothing: A National and International Issue*, International Symposium on Industrial Policies for the Eighties, Madrid, May 1980.

Table 5.12 The Concentration of Large Firms in the EC, US and Japanese Textile Industries, 1965–80

	West Germany	Belgium	France	Italy	Netherlands	UK	Total EC	USA	Japan
Cumulative ratio of employment in largest firms (by size of sales) to total textile employment:									
1966									
3	4	7	10	6	23	16	8	16	6
5	6	9	12	9	30	21	9	20	8
10	11	11	14	n.a.	n.a.	28	11	29	12
1970									
3	6	n.a.	13	8	23	45	13	15	6
5	10	n.a.	17	10	25	52	15	18	8
10	15	n.a.	23	14	n.a.	57	19	25	11
1975									
3	5	n.a.	17	8	22	40	12	15	6

8	18	16	53	26	12	19	n.a.	7
10	26	17	70	n.a.	16	21	n.a.	16
1980								1980
3	13	12	43	22	(5)	22	(14)	4
5	17	15	56	25	(7)	26	(18)	7
8	24	21	67	n.a.	(10)^c	30	n.a.	14

Total number of firms with sales exceeding 100m. DM:

1965	13	42		13	4	3	7	1	21
1970	20	46		32	5	7	13	1	46
1975	22	50^a		30	4	10	14	2	44
1980	32	40^b		27	4	15	24	9	52

[a] Firms with sales exceeding 140 m. DM.
[b] Firms with sales exceeding 160 m. DM.
[c] 9 firms only.

Source: Textilwirtschaft (Frankfurt), 13 April 1967; 11 January 1973; 31 December 1981.

5.10. A similar representative breakdown of Western European textile production and employment is provided in Table 5.11.

As these tables show, the EC countries are the major European textile producers. Not shown but implied by relative population and GNP is the fact that the EC also dominates in textile consumption. Hence, our discussion of the European industry will focus on the EC.

As in the USA, textile industries in Europe and Japan are composed of many firms, each with a small share of their respective domestic markets. Table 5.12 gives ratios of employment by the largest three, five and ten textile firms to total in-country textile employment for the US, Japanese and major European textile producers. As these ratios show, the US textile industry is substantially more concentrated than the Japanese and approximately equal in concentration to that of the European Community (EC). Further, the concentration figures given in Table 5.12 may overstate the market power of EC firms relative to US firms for three reasons. First, the relative openness of European economies and the consequent high levels of import penetration dilute the market power of European firms. Second, the employment figures on which these ratios are based include foreign subsidiaries. Many larger European firms (particularly in West Germany, France and the UK) have important overseas investments. To cite an extreme example, Coats, the second largest UK company, had approximately 18 per cent of its 1980 labor force in continental Europe and 48 per cent outside Europe. Third, some textile firms have important non-textile activities. The most important example is Courtaulds (UK). Approximately 30 per cent of Courtaulds' 1980 employment was in non-textile activities, 40 per cent was in primary textiles and 30 per cent was in consumer products. If primary textiles only were considered, Courtaulds would probably be the world's second largest textile firm (behind Burlington) and the UK's 1980 concentration ratios would fall by approximately 13 per cent.

While textile industry concentration in the EC taken as a whole is roughly equal to that in the USA, degrees of concentration differ substantially between European countries. Specifically, the West German textile industry is dominated by medium-sized firms and the British by a few very large firms. On the other hand, the Italian and French industries have large shares of textile employment in both small and very large firms but only a few medium-sized firms (more detail is provided below).

As Table 5.13 shows, output trends in textiles for most developed countries have been similar to those experienced in the USA. For most developed countries, output increased up to 1973 and has remained approximately constant since 1973. There are some notable

Table 5.13 Textile Production Index (1973 = 100)

Country	1963	1970	1973	1974	1975	1976	1977	1978	1979	1980
West Germany	76	93	100	94	92	99	98	96	96	94
Belgium	87	94	100	96	82	92	81	77	83	86
Denmark	55	85	100	90	94	107	97	97	101	99
France	85	87	100	99	89	94	91	90	93	89
Ireland	43	79	100	94	88	99	108	125	130	
Italy	87	87	100	98	90	106	102	97	110	115
Netherlands	94	104	100	99	90	90	83	78	82	77
United Kingdom	90	94	100	92	87	90	89	87	83	70
Austria	58	83	100	196	83	89	90	87	91	95
Spain	74	99	100	101	90	86	90	95	100	96
Finland	62	88	100	109	112	112	107	101	113	113
Greece	41	68	100	100	118	136	133	141	152	149
Norway	103	105	100	98	92	93	95	98	99	103
Portugal[a]	44	70	100	104	86	87	84	86	101	109
Sweden	86	95	100	101	91	92	84	81	82	79
Switzerland	87	89	100	97	81	93	94	94	97	98
Canada	54	77	100	97	94	94	97	106	116	111
USA	56	78	100	93	85	94	94	96	101	97
Japan	50	90	100	89	85	91	90	92	94	93
Australia	78	89	100	75	94	86	79	83	82	81
New Zealand	37	77	100							

[a] Including clothing.

Sources: 1963–78 Wolfgang Kurth, 'Textiles and Clothing: A National and International Issue', International Symposium on Industrial Policies for the Eighties, Madrid, mimeo, May 1980; 1979 and 1980; Organization for Economic Cooperation and Development, *Indicators of Industrial Activity*, Paris: OECD, 1980–1 and 1981–2.

exceptions however. Greece, Italy, Finland and Canada have experienced above-average growth, while the Netherlands, the UK, Sweden, Australia, Belgium and France have experienced greater than average decline in output.

Within the EC, West Germany experienced growth of textile output in the 1960s, led by texturizing, knitting and carpets, but experienced stagnation in the 1970s with finishing and carpets showing some growth. In France, on the other hand, both decades witnessed a stagnant performance, with carpets and knitting offsetting large declines in spinning and weaving. In Italy, the data indicate substantial growth in the 1970s after stagnation in the 1960s. Every major area enjoyed growth in the 1970s, with knitting in the lead. Italy's textile recovery since 1973 is unique among major OECD producers. At the other extreme, UK textiles experienced moderate expansion up to 1973, as a result of a very strong performance in knitting, and a steady decline in output until 1979, followed by a veritable collapse in 1979 when the textile industry shrank by one-quarter. After moderate expansion in the 1960s, both Belgium and the Netherlands experienced declining output in the 1970s, with a poor performance in weaving being somewhat offset by expansion in carpets.

In contrast to developed countries in Europe and Asia, textile industries in the developing countries of Asia have grown substantially over the last decade. Unfortunately, comprehensive, cross-country comparable data are not available to document this growth. However, to the extent that spinning capacity is a reasonable proxy for textile production, Table 5.14 gives a rough indication of textile output for developing Asia Pacific countries. As this table shows, since 1971 spinning capacity has grown at very high rates in South Korea, Taiwan, Thailand and Indonesia. Growth in spinning capacity in China and the Philippines has been modest, while Hong Kong has experienced a small decline. Despite high rates of growth, textile industries in these developing countries remain small relative to those in Europe, North America and Japan.

Employment in textiles has roughly followed output trends. With the exception of Greece, textile employment in OECD countries has declined since 1973. From 1970 to 1978 textile employment in Japan fell by 34 per cent and in the EC by 28 per cent. By comparison, employment in non EC European countries remained approximately constant and Canadian and US textile employment fell by comparatively modest rates of 3 and 8 per cent, respectively (see Table 5.15).

The rapid increase in the rate of job losses in textiles, which occurred in virtually all OECD areas after 1973, took place under conditions of increasing unemployment. These developments have had a crucial influence on the outcome of the debate on protection in

Table 5.14 Spinning Capacity in Asia Pacific Countries

	Japan	Korea	Taiwan	Hong Kong	China	Thailand	Malaysia	Indonesia	Philippines
Spinning ('000 spindles):									
1961	15,951	544[b]	350	502	9,600	93	—	120[e]	501
1966	13,394	727[c]	700	749	12,300	246	—	230[f]	683
1971	14,710	962	1,080[d]	876	16,480	539	—	482	860
1976	14,105	2,091	3,159	900	18,000	1,112	—	1,239	993
1979	13,635	2,912	3,233	809	20,000[a]	1,240	391	1,741	1,129
Change in no. of spindles:									
1971/1961	0.92	1.77	3.09	1.75	1.72	5.80	—	4.02	1.72
1979/1971	0.93	3.03	2.99	0.92	1.21	2.30	—	3.61	1.31
No. of spindles per 10,000 people	1,204[a]	780	1,870	1,612	206[a]	269	295	123	244

[a] 1977.
[b] 1962.
[c] 1967.
[d] 1970.
[e] 1957.
[f] 1965.

Source: Compiled from data in Alcina Suehiro, *Comparative Advantage of Textile Industries in Asia* (a progress report). Tokyo: Institute of Developing Economies, 1980.

Table 5.15 *Employment in Textile Industries of OECD Countries, 1963–81 ('000)*

Country	1963	1965	1970	1973	1974	1975	1976	1977	1978	1979	1980	1981
West Germany	568	(547)	498	431	391	354	339	332	320	309	306	281
Belgium	148	(143)	126	108	104	95	90	82	73			
Denmark	24	23	23	21	19	16	17	16	16	17	16	14
France	(459)	(431)	(393)	406	387	371	365	345	329	318	307	285
Ireland	22	(22)	26	23	22	19	20	20	20			
Italy		(398)	419	377	359	352	335	331	315			
Netherlands	101	93	79	61	58	53	48	45	41	38	40	
United Kingdom	720	(706)	621	557	548	507	485	481	457	447	393	354
EC	(2,430)		2,185				1,699		1,571			
Austria	73	(70)	70	68	62	56	54	54	50	48	48	46
Spain	236	(222)	212	187	180	196	193	207	193			
Finland	31	(28)	30	30	30	28	26	24	22			
Greece	48	52[a]	44	54	64	68	61	63				
Norway	19	(18)	16	13	13	12	12	12				
Portugal	108	(106)	135	139	137	134	132		13	13	12	
Sweden	39	(39)	34	29	28	26	26	24	23	22	21	20
Switzerland	68	(73)	70	60	57	48	49	48	45	44	44	42
Turkey	95	107[a]	120		147	151	163	127	183	166	161	
Other OECD Europe	717		731				716		(730)			
Total OECD Europe	(3,147)		2,916				2,415		2,301			
Canada	81	(85)	97	107	105	99	95	91	94	97	94	94
USA	863	(891)	1,113	1,178	1,107	996	1,042	1,031	1,019	999	970	950
Japan	1,312	(1,086)	1,144	1,057	930	907	877	801	753	770	762	744
Australia	72		78	72	73	59	60	52	51	49		
New Zealand	12		17		18	18	16	17	15			
Total OECD	(5,487)		5,365				4,505		(4,233)			

[a] 1966.

Source: Wolfgang Kurth, 'Textiles and Clothing: A National and International Issue'. International Symposium on Industrial Policies for the Eighties. Madrid, mimeo, May 1980; Organization for Economic Cooperation and Development, *Indicators of Industrial Activity*. Paris: OECD. 1980–1 and 1964–82; Organization for Economic Cooperation and Development. *Textile Industry in OECD Countries, 1969–1970*. Paris: OECD. 1971.

textiles. If the amount of textile job losses in the 1970s is compared to the total size of the labor force or to the total increase in unemployment in major OECD textile producers, West Germany, the UK and Japan appear to have had the severest textile job losses, and Italy and the USA the least severe (see Table 5.16).

Among major EC countries, West Germany and the UK experienced the most rapid rate of textile job losses in the 1970s, although Belgium and the Netherlands lost jobs at a faster rate. Yet the 'structure' of job losses in these two countries differs in an interesting way. West Germany's losses were primarily due to labor productivity increase, and only secondarily to a deteriorating trade balance for textiles. For the UK, a significantly larger proportion of jobs was lost from the deteriorating textile trade balance, though labor productivity was still important. Thus, what West Germany lost on the swing of

Table 5.16   *Textile Job Losses, Major OECD Producers*

Country	All civilian employment			Textile job losses 1970–80	
	1980 total ('000)	Unemployment rate (%)		Number ('000)	As % of 1980 employment
		1970	1980		
West Germany	25,800	0.7	3.8	192	0.7
France	22,600	2.4	6.7	86	0.4
Italy	20,400	3.1	5.8	n.a.[a]	
UK	24,700	2.6	6.8	228	0.9
USA	97,300	4.9	7.1	143	0.1
Japan	55.400	1.3	2.0	382	0.7

[a] But small.

Source: As for Table 5.15 and US Department of Commerce, *International Economic Indicators*, Washington, DC: US Government Printing Office, June 1982.

improved labor productivity it partly compensated for on the roundabout of a less rapid deterioration in competitiveness

As with production data, employment data for developing countries are fragmented and of dubious accuracy. However, it appears that since 1970 textile employment has increased in Korea and declined in Singapore, Hong Kong, the Philippines and Taiwan (see US Department of Commerce, *Country Market Surveys* for the textile industry).

As noted above, US textile investment has increased in recent years. The US industry is somewhat unusual in this regard. Within the EC, gross fixed investment in 1964 exceeded that in 1978 for all countries except Italy, and among other European countries only Greece and Norway invested more in 1978 than in 1964. Also, for both Japan and Canada 1964 investment exceeded that in 1978. (See Table 5.17 for more deail.)

However, despite having lower rates of investment, European and Japanese textile manufacturers appear to be modernizing at a more rapid rate than their US counterparts. Evidence of this is provided in Table 5.18. The apparent contradiction of lower rates of investment coupled with higher rates of modernization for Europe and Japan appears to be attributable to a relatively higher rate of US investment for capacity expansion.

Important points to be made concerning establishment size are: (1) that size distributions of establishments vary greatly among OECD countries; (2) that these distributions have diverged over time; and (3) consequently that economies of scale appear weak. For example, Italy experienced a strong trend to smaller-scale plants (including a process of deverticalization) in the 1960s, a position that was at least maintained in the 1970s. This occurred across the board, although it was most strongly felt where scale was largest, i.e. spinning and weaving (cotton, silk and wool).[6] The UK, on the other hand, has experienced a substantial shift from medium-scale (50–500 workers) to larger-scale establishments in the last two decades. West Germany has seen precisely the opposite development, though less dramatically. By comparison, the US industry was dominated by small establishments during both decades. Thus Italy and the US now have a strong concentration of production in small, the UK in large, and West Germany in medium-sized establishments (see Table 5.19).

Table 5.20 provides comparisons in value terms for 1976 of output per worker in EC member countries and the USA. Caution needs to be exercised in making inferences about physical labor productivity comparisons because different countries may have different price levels, in large part due to exchange rate fluctuations. However, the direct comparisons of physical labor productivity in primary textiles for 1979 in Table 5.21 tend to support the rankings observed in Table 5.20. Not unexpectedly, countries tend to achieve similar labor productivity levels in terms of ranking with other countries across sectors. Thus the USA has consistently higher labor productivity levels than the top EC countries (West Germany, Belgium and the Netherlands). Italy and France tend to achieve productivity levels slightly lower than this first group, and the UK and Ireland achieve considerably lower levels of productivity.

It is difficult to judge how much of the level and trend in labor productivity reflect technical change that is embodied in new equipment or disembodied (i.e. depending on the efficiency with which labor is deployed). The impression is that the US textile industry was historically early to acquire new equipment and that much of the Western

Table 5.17 Gross Fixed Investment in the Textile Industries of OECD Countries, 1964–78 (US $m., at 1975 prices and exchange rates)

Country	1964	1970	1971	1972	1973	1974	1975	1976	1977	1978
West Germany	526.5	747.2	684.1	625.6	583.1	438.5	391.5	449.9	446.5	424.1
Belgium	136.7	177.2	136.2	153.6	185.5	197.6	151.2	112.7	110.1	94.8
Denmark	33.8	49.1	30.9	33.5	38.9	37.0	17.1	34.4	22.5	11.6
France	225.7	611.6	552.3	(581.4)	576.2	406.1	335.9	365.7	289.9	282.6
Ireland	(20.0)	26.4	30.7	32.0	15.6	18.7	17.8	26.2	48.9	36.0
Italy	275.8	353.0	392.5	452.4	501.1	504.9	348.4	447.8	449.2	402.6
Netherlands	105.9	115.7	96.7	78.3	97.2	76.5	65.3	63.7	57.7	51.0
United Kingdom	510.2	526.9	344.7	325.1	486.9	503.6	391.8	264.2	261.3	327.1
EC	1,834.7	2,607.1	2,268.1	2,281.9	2,484.5	2,182.9	1,719.0	1,764.6	1,686.1	1,629.8
Austria	63.7	87.4	67.7	71.4	93.8	77.7	57.6	69.5	60.1	51.5
Spain	113.9	127.9	125.2	177.4	188.3	128.6	160.8	74.1	132.7	(110.9)
Finland	45.8	37.4	34.3	41.0	53.5	60.7	36.0	24.8	17.9	32.1
Greece	55.2	80.7	107.2	129.8	133.0	163.9	173.2	193.9	(122.8)	(150.9)
Norway	9.8	26.8	20.8	(24.5)	16.3	22.2	17.2	15.6	17.5	25.0
Portugal	(165.7)	(146.2)	149.0	163.7	158.0	161.0	71.5	58.0	76.3	(58.6)
Sweden	65.9	55.5	38.0	42.2	57.8	57.7	55.7	42.2	46.5	43.1
Total Europe	2,354.7	3,169.0	2,810.3	2,931.9	3,185.2	2,854.7	2,291.0	2,242.7	2,159.9	2,101.9
Canada	112.2	134.0	122.3	135.5	170.2	175.1	164.2	109.3	73.6	82.7
USA	795.0	1,095.9	1,131.1	1,425.8	1,394.0	1,347.8	996.7	1,029.0	1,091.6	(1,155.3)
Japan	817.6	1,375.4	1,418.8	1,301.8	1,343.2	1,049.9	659.0	665.0	597.7	(590.0)
Australia	—	86.8	—	53.9	44.7	73.7	47.4	31.6	26.3	25.0

Source: Private communication from the Organization for Economic Cooperation and Development.

Table 5.18 Spindles and Looms in the Cotton Industries of Selected Countries

Country	Number of installed ring spindles 1978 (1)	Machines installed 1974–79 (million) Ring spindles[a] (2)	Machines installed 1974–79 (million) Open-end rotors (3)	Total equivalent ring[b] (4)	Degree of modernization [cols (4) + (2) × 100] (5)
EC	12.027	1.614	0.213	2.253	19%
of which Italy	3.338	0.911	0.73	1.129	34%
West Germany	2.971	0.374	0.48	0.517	17%
France	2.495	0.095	0.49	0.243	10%
UK	2.250	0.171	0.20	0.230	10%
Greece	1.349	0.416	0.9	0.443	
USA	12.5	0.449	0.139	0.862	7%
USSR	16.0	?	1.161	at least 3.48	
Asia	68.0	8.327	0.278	9.161	13%
World	151.4	15.448	2.230	22.638	15%

[a] No details are available for supplies from Western Europe, USA, Asia and Czechoslovakia. Ring equipment manufactured by state-trading countries for their own account is hence not included. In reality the number of ring spindles is higher.
[b] rotor = 3 rings.

| Country | Shuttle loom 1978 '000 | Looms installed 1974-79 | | Degree of modernization [cols (2) ÷ (1) × 100] | Technological level (Ratio of shuttle-less to total % of looms) |
		Shuttle '000	Shuttleless '000		
	(1)	(2)	(3)	(4)	(5)
EC	156.7	13.0	32.2	8%	19
of which Belgium	15.9	0.5	1.6	3%	±9
France	36.5	2.2	6.1	6%	±14
West Germany	36.1	3.3	6.8	9%	±16
Italy	42.7	3.9	12.3	9%	±22
UK	20.6	2.5	3.8	12%	±14
USSR[a]	270				
USA	246	9.4	21.7	4%	8
China	290				
Japan	180	28.0	8.6	15%	5
World	2,000				

[a] Only the number of advanced technology machines supplied by Western Europe or Czechoslovakia to Comecon is known (open-end spinning; loom/shuttleless weaving loom).

Source: Commission of the European Communities, Commission Communication to the Council on the Situation and Prospects of the Textile and Clothing Industries in the Community, COM(81)388 final, Annex IX, Brussels: the Commission, 1981.

Table 5.19   *Employment Distribution by Size of Establishment in Textiles (%)*

Size of establishment	West Germany 1979	UK 1978	Italy 1971	USA 1979
Small (1–49 workers)	8[a]	10	37	56
Medium (50–499 workers)	59	45	40	37
Large (500+ workers)	33	45	23	6

[a] *Excludes firms with 1–19 workers.*

Sources: M. Breitenacher, *Textilindustrie: Structurwandlungen und Entwicklungsperspektiven für die achtziger Jahre*, Ifo-Institut für Wirtschaftsforschung, Berlin: Duncker & Humblot, 1981, Table 30, p. 178; Business Statistics Office, *1978 Report on the Census of Production*, PA 1002, Business Monitor, London: HMSO; Ministero dell'Industria, del Commercio e del'Artigianato, *Programma finalizzato: Sistema della Moda*, Rome, 1979, Table 25; US Bureau of the Census, *County Business Patterns*, Washington, DC: US Government Printing Office, 1981.

European productivity increase in the late 1950s and 1960s represented 'catching up' (e.g. replacing non-automatic with automatic looms). For the 1970s, the impression is that Western Europe has been quicker to move into the more advanced technologies (e.g. shuttleless weaving and open-ended spinning). This is borne out by Table 5.18, which shows the higher share of more recent vintages of equipment in the cotton spinning and weaving capacity of the EC than the USA.

A comparison of Tables 5.18 and 5.21 brings out the paradox that the USA achieves higher levels of labor productivity with older equipment (on this see also American Textile Manufacturers Institute 1978). This appears to reflect the high degree of rationalization that US mills can achieve from long runs.

In 1955, wages paid to US textile workers were higher than those paid in any other textile-producing country. That situation has now changed. As Table 5.22 shows, the USA now ranks sixth in textile wages. Further, supplementary labor costs are now lower in the USA than in many other countries (see Table 5.23). More importantly, since 1970 the rate of increase in hourly labor costs for US textile manufacturers has been one of the world's lowest (see Table 5.24). In other words, hourly labor costs in the USA are declining relative to other OECD countries.

The relatively modest (and declining) US hourly labor cost and the relatively high labor productivity in the US textile industry yield labor costs per unit of output that are considerably lower than those for most major textile-producing countries in Europe and roughly equal to those for Japan. As Table 5.21 shows, unit labor cost for West

Table 5.20 Value-Added per Employee in Textiles in the EC and USA 1976 (US $'000)

	West Germany	France	Italy	Netherlands	Belgium	UK	Ireland[a]	Denmark	Average	USA
					EC[f]					
Cotton industry	12.1	10.1	9.1	13.2	11.3	7.0	6.0	13.8	10.1	15.3[b]
Silk industry	15.2	11.1	10.2	—	14.2	7.4	5.0	11.4	11.2	16.1[c]
Wool industry	12.6	12.1	10.3	16.0	11.7	7.3	7.2	12.6	10.2	16.6[d]
Knitting industry	11.6	9.5	7.2	10.1	9.2	5.6	5.1	11.4	8.4	14.9
Textile finishing	14.5	11.5	10.7	14.4	12.6	7.3	—	17.3	11.0	18.3
Carpets & floor coverings	15.5	13.6	9.4	—	15.0	8.9	8.0	21.7	11.7	24.7
Textiles	13.0	10.7	9.2	14.3	12.1	6.9	6.5	13.6	10.1	16.5[e]

[a] Figures for 1975, not included in EC average.
[b] Cotton weaving mills.
[c] Man-made fiber weaving mills.
[d] Wool weaving, finishing mills.
[e] Including yarn and thread mills, with a value added per employee of $14,600.
[f] Gross value added at factor cost ($1 = EVA. 8944).

Sources: Eurostat, Structure and Activity of Industry, 1976, Luxembourg: Statistical Office of the European Communities, 1981; US Bureau of the Census, Statistical Abstract of the United States 1978, Washington, DC: US Government Printing Office, 1978.

Table 5.21 *Comparison of Hourly Labor Costs, Labor Productivity and Unit Labor Costs in Primary Textiles in Selected Countries, 1979 (USA = 100)*

Country	Hourly labor costs	Labor productivity	Unit labor cost
West Germany	168	87	193
Belgium	171	87	196
Denmark	145		
France	116	74	157
Ireland	72		
Italy	115	76	151
Netherlands	185	86	215
United Kingdom	79	56	141
Austria	98		
Spain	70		
Finland	79		
Greece	47		
Norway	145		
Portugal	27	42	64
Sweden	163		
Switzerland	149		
Turkey	28	41	68
Canada	91		
USA	100	100	100
Japan	75	74	101
Egypt	6	14	43
Pakistan	6	13	46
Hong Kong	28		
Korea	12		

Sources: Werner Associates Inc., *Commentary on Hourly Labour Costs in the Primary Textile Industry Winter 78–79*, and *Spinning and Weaving Labour Cost Comparisons Summer 1981*, Brussels: Werner Associates Inc., n.d.

Germany are twice those in the USA and textile manufacturers in France, Italy and the UK have unit labor costs roughly 50 per cent higher than their US and Japanese counterparts.

On the other hand, growth in labor productivity for the US textile industry lags that of Europe and Japan. Hence, the USA appears to be losing its relative productivity lead. For example, between 1970 and 1980 textile labor productivity in the EC and Japan increased by 52 and 54 per cent, respectively, while the US figure was 42 per cent (see Table 5.25 for more detail). In 1967, EC countries achieved 30–60 per cent of US labor productivity in cotton spinning. By 1977, the range was roughly 60–95 per cent (see Table 5.26). The USA has

Table 5.22   Hourly Labor Costs in the Textile Industry in Selected Countries, 1955–81 (October rates)

Country	1955 DM	Rank	1960 DM	Rank	1965 DM	Rank	1970 DM	Rank	1975 DM	Rank	1978 DM	Rank	1979 DM	Rank	1980 DM	Rank	1981[a] DM	Rank
Sweden	3.17	2	4.08	2	6.22	2	9.28	2	16.27	1	16.56	3	18.02	2	21.03	1	24.31	1
Netherlands	1.72	11	2.55	10	4.35	6	6.63	6	14.38	3	17.04	2	18.73	1	19.97	2	21.04	2
Belgium	2.31	5	2.83	8	4.35	6	6.31	7	13.51	5	16.20	4	17.28	4	18.66	3	20.03	3
Switzerland	2.29	6	2.97	6	3.87	9	5.66	9	12.49	6	17.49	1	16.64	5	18.06	5	19.90	4
Denmark	2.29	6	3.08	5	4.78	5	7.05	5	13.54	4	15.85	6	17.65	3	18.19	4	18.30	5
USA	7.22	1	8.36	1	9.40	1	11.49	1	11.29	8	10.95	9	11.67	9	13.08	10	18.23	6
West Germany	1.87	10	3.13	4	4.79	4	7.40	3	12.30	7	15.00	7	15.91	6	17.06	6	18.01	7
Norway	2.42	4	3.23	3	4.80	3	7.36	4	14.43	2	15.90	5	15.38	7	16.63	7	17.86	8
Italy	1.97	9	2.52	11	3.94	8	6.17	8	9.91	9	11.56	8	13.36	8	14.93	8	16.58	9
France	2.54	3	2.81	9	3.69	11	4.96	10	9.58	10	10.59	10	11.55	10	13.40	9	14.17	10
Austria							4.69	11	8.36	11	10.09	11	10.36	11	11.40	11	12.34	11
Great Britain	2.20	8	2.86	7	3.84	10	4.61	12	6.83	12	6.87	13	8.56	12	11.17	12	12.20	12
Japan	0.80	12	1.06	12	1.94	12	3.04	13	6.47	13	9.64	12	7.95	13	9.59	13	12.07	13
Hong Kong			0.68	13	0.96	17	1.32	14	1.99	14	2.23	14	2.44	14	2.88	14	3.75	14

[a] July

Source: Arbeitgeberkreis Gesamttextil, Löhne und Arbeitskosten der Textilindustrie: Internationaler Vergleich, Frankfurt a/m. 1981.

Table 5.23 *Supplementary Labor Costs[a] as a Percentage of the Basic Hourly Wage Rate in Selected Countries, 1955–81*

Country	1965	1975	1978	1979	1980
Italy	78.6	102.2	105.9	104.2	100.2
France	54.4	61.1	64.2	65.8	67.0
Belgium	46.0	64.7	64.2	64.9	64.9
Netherlands	41.7	58.2	58.9	66.6	68.2
Japan	35.6	55.8	55.5	58.0	58.1
Sweden	21.6	39.6	54.7	56.7	57.7
West Germany	33.1	50.4	53.7	55.5	55.8
Norway	20.2	41.2	46.4	46.4	47.4
Hong Kong	23.9	22.8	36.9	37.0	35.6
USA	23.7	33.1	34.6	35.0	35.5
Switzerland	23.8	26.5	28.3	28.3	29.1
UK	13.6	20.1	23.3	27.7	27.7
Denmark	11.3	15.9	20.0	24.0	24.7

[a] Supplementary labor costs include bonuses, etc., paid leave, social security contributions, and other required payments.

Source: Michael Breitenacher, *Textilindustrie: Strukturwandlungen und Entwicklungsperspektiven für die achtziger Jahre*, Ifo-Institut für Wirtschaftsforschung, Berlin: Duncker & Humblot, 1981.

Table 5.24 *Index of Labor Costs per Unit of Output in Textiles, 1970–81 (1975 = 100)[a]*

Country	1970	1975	1978	1979	1980	1981	Annual Average Growth in Costs 1970–81 %
West Germany	83	100	104	107	116	121	9.9
Belgium	54	100	101	105			7.7
Denmark	78	100	110	123	122	107	2.7
France	56	100	96	99	115	125	7.6
Italy	77	100	98				3.1
Netherlands	59	100	105	100	113		6.7
United Kingdom	75	100	94	119	149	175	8.0
Austria	70	100	103	97	102	107	3.9
Norway	57	100	118	113	109		6.7
Sweden	71	100	100	106	123		5.6
Switzerland	60	100	114	94	101	108	6.1
USA	124	100	88	88	99	138	1.0
Japan	46	100	114	94	113	143	10.9

[a] Index based on labor costs in DM.

Source: See Tables 5.13, 5.15 and 5.23.

Table 5.25 Index of Labor Productivity in Textile Industries of OECD Countries, 1963, 1970 and 1973–81 (1973 = 100)

Country	1963	1970	1973	1974	1975	1976	1977	1978	1979	1980	1981
West Germany	58	81	100	104	112	127	130	131	135	134	135
Belgium	64	81	100	100	94	112	107	115			
Denmark	49	81	100	103	122	132	128	130	129	134	154
France	74	89	100	102	96	106	108	110	117	117	(114)
Ireland	45	70	100	97	104	114	121	143			
Italy		78	100	102	97	119	116	116			
Netherlands	56	80	100	104	102	113	112	115	133	125	
United Kingdom	69	85	100	97	95	98	99	102	100	104	97
Austria	55	82	100	105	103	113	115	120	130	136	(141)
Spain	59	87	100	104	86	83	81				
Finland	61	92	100	107	119	128	131	135			
Greece	46	83	100	84	93	119	114				
Norway	73	89	100	97	100	104	104	93	94	106	
Portugal					100						
Sweden	64	82	100	106	102	105	103	104	107	107	
Switzerland	77	77	100	104	102	115	118	125	145	146	150
Canada	70	85	100	99	102	105	114	120	127	126	(128)
USA	76	83	100	99	101	106	107	111	119	118	118
Japan	60	83	100	101	98	108	118	128	128	128	128
Australia	78	82	100	73	113	102	107	113	115	115	

Source: calculated from Tables 5.13 and 5.15.

Table 5.26   *Labor Productivity Indices for Cotton Mills, 1967, 1977 and 1979 (Based on Estimates by Werner), (USA = 100)*

Country	Cotton yarn 1967 $(205)^a$	Cotton yarn 1977 $(245)^a$	Woven polyester/ cotton shirting 1967^a	Woven polyester/ cotton shirting 1977^b	Primary textiles^c 1979^b
West Germany	59	95	43	68	87
Belgium					87
France	53	68	34	48	74
Italy		73		42	76
Netherlands	59		41		86
United Kingdom	31	63	47	39	56
Austria	56		36		
Spain		47		33	
Greece		44		29	
Portugal	14	52	16	32	42
Turkey		39		19	41
USA	100	100	100	100	100
Japan	33		32		74
Egypt					14
Pakistan	13		14		13
Hong Kong	25		22		
India	11		13		

Note: All the comparisons are based on data prepared by Werner Associates, Inc. and are therefore assumed to be comparably established.

^{a} 'Better' mills.
^{b} 'Average' mills.
^{c} 'Primary' textiles are understood to cover spinning and weaving in the cotton system.

Sources: 1967: Textile Council, *Cotton and Allied Textiles*, Vol. 2, Manchester, 1969, Tables 6 and 10 of Annex A; 1977: American Textile Manufacturers Institute, 'Older but Better', Economic Memo No. 18, Washington, DC, May/June 1978; 1979: Werner Associates Inc., *Commentary on Hourly Labour Costs in the Primary Textile Industry Winter 78–79*, New York: Werner Associates Inc., n.d.

maintained a greater productivity lead in cotton weaving but that too is deteriorating.

The extent to which textile firms generally specialize in a specific area of textiles or have moved to other textile areas (horizontal integration), to non-textile primary areas or abroad is a question of generalized impressions. Not unexpectedly, such moves seem the province of larger firms.

In West Germany textiles, still dominated by family-owned firms with a strong sense of textile vocation, horizontal diversification has not been a strong phenomenon. Vertical integration forward into making-up appears to have been minor and backward into fibers non-existent. There has also been little diversification. On the other hand, investment in textile production abroad has been significant (compared to other EC countries, not to other sectors, against which it loses significance). Much of this investment appears to have been in other industrialized, often Western European, countries and appears to play something of an 'export-substitution' role. While West Germany has invested in low-wage production bases, the industry gives no impression of beginning a 'flight off-shore', such as has happened in German apparel.[7] Overall, German textiles leave a strong impression of an intact, textile-dominated corporate structure.

In France, a small number of very large firms has taken a leading role in broadening their corporate base by: (1) forward integration into making-up (often with a considerable ownership of, or control over, apparel-retailing distribution); (2) some non-textile diversification;[8] and (3) considerable foreign investment, a significant proportion of it in former West African colonies. While Rhône-Poulenc, France's largest fiber producer, has in the past acquired textile capacity, it has not become a dominant actor in the industry. Indeed, it has reduced its textile capacity in recent years.

The UK is the only EC country to have seen significant new textile entrants. Courtaulds entered textiles massively in the 1960s, a strategy aimed at insuring its fiber outlets by assuring the survival of the rapidly contracting industry. ICI, the largest UK fiber producer, reacted to this by financing (but not managing) the growth of alternative large textile groups. Many of the large groups have integrated forward into apparel and have significant foreign investments, much of these in the Commonwealth. The recession-induced partial collapse of UK textile production since 1979 has perforce accelerated these trends. The larger groups have massively reduced their UK textile activities. Overseas activities are increasingly important. Indeed, at least one of the large firms, Tootal, may be in the process of systematically moving its center of gravity abroad, and Courtaulds is now stressing its non-textile activities.

The dominance of small firms in Italy generally means the continued dominance of highly specialized textile firms. There is, for instance, very little foreign investment in textiles and little backward or forward integration.

In summary, it might not be too fanciful to suggest three European 'models' of dynamic firms: (1) the 'German model', with dedication to medium-sized firms with specialization in textiles in modern, integrated plants; (2) the 'Italian model', with dedication to specialization in textiles in modern, but small plants and firms; and (3) the 'UK/

French model' of large, sophisticated, textile-based corporations with a strong philosophy of spatial and product diversification.

Trends in the Textile Labor Force

Following World War II, the US textile labor force was composed primarily of white, middle-aged males. That is now changing. US textile workers are increasingly likely to be young, or non-white or female. In 1960, approximately 50 per cent of the textile labor force in the Southeastern USA was composed of white males; almost 5 per cent were non-white males, approximately 45 per cent were white females, and non-white females contributed less than 1 per cent; 70 per cent of these workers were over 35 years of age. By 1980, that picture had changed dramatically. White males and females accounted for approximately 32 and 35 per cent, respectively, of the 1980 textile labor force. Non-white males and females constituted approximately 16 and 15 per cent, respectively. Perhaps most importantly, less than 50 per cent of these workers were over 35 years of age.

The changing demographic profile of the US textile labor force is attributable to two primary factors: (1) the changing demographic characteristics of the general civilian labor force and (2) increased competition for labor in Southeastern states and the failure of textile workers' compensation to keep pace with other manufacturing wages.

Since World War II, the civilian labor force has changed in two important ways. First, labor force participation rates for females have increased substantially. From 1959 to 1979 the proportion of manufacturing workers who are female increased from 26 to 31 per cent. Second, there has been an influx of young workers into labor markets as those who were part of the World War II baby boom reached working age. In 1960, 16 per cent of civilian workers were under 25 years of age, but, by 1973, 24 per cent of civilian workers were under 25. To some extent, changes in the age and sex composition of the textile labor force have reflected these changes in the general working population.

One non-demographic factor that has also influenced the US textile labor force is industrial growth in Southeastern states. This increasing industrialization increased competition for textile manufacturers in recruiting and retaining workers. The problems of recruitment and retention have increased for textile firms both because textile wages have traditionally been low and because the gap between wages in textiles and other manufacturing industries has been widening. Specifically, from 1960 to 1978 general manufacturing wages rose 173 per cent while textile wages rose 167 per cent. Textile wages now stand at approximately 70 per cent of the US average manufacturing wage (see Table 5.27 for more detail). Hence, as industrial growth increased employment options for Southeastern workers, more mobile workers (i.e. those who are most productive or who are less subject to labor market discrimination) have tended to leave the textile industry.

Evidence of the increased propensity of US workers to leave the textile industry is found in turnover and job quit data. Table 5.28 shows quit rates for manufacturing, non-durable manufacturing and textiles. As these data show, textile workers are considerably more

Table 5.27   *Average Hourly Earnings, (US$) in US Manufacturing Industry, 1960–80*

Year	Manufacturing	Durable goods	Non-durable goods	Textiles
1960	2.26	2.42	2.05	1.61
1965	2.61	2.79	2.36	1.87
1970	3.36	3.55	3.08	2.45
1975	4.81	5.15	4.37	3.42
1976	5.22	5.58	4.70	3.67
1977	5.68	6.06	5.11	3.98
1978	6.17	6.58	5.53	4.30
1979	6.69	7.13	6.00	4.66
1980	7.27	7.76	6.53	5.07
% change 1960–80	222	246	219	215

Source: J. S. Fryer, A. H. Barnett, A. S. DeNisi, B. M. Meglino, C. G. Williams and S. A. Youngblood, *The Textile Labor Force in the 1980s*, Columbia, SC: Division of Research, College of Business Administration, University of South Carolina, April 1981.

likely to quit their jobs than are workers in manufacturing generally. Moreover, when textile workers leave their jobs the departure is far more likely to be the result of a decision to quit on the part of the worker than an employer's decision to layoff. Table 5.29 shows the ratio of job quits to layoffs for manufacturing, non-durable manufacturing and textiles. As these data show, the ratio of quits to layoffs is high in textiles relative to manufacturing generally. This indicates that the composition of the textile labor force is more a matter of worker choice than employer choice.

One possible reason for this phenomenon is the role textiles has historically played as a transition industry for US workers. In the

1940s and 1950s the US textile industry provided a vehicle for white males to move from agricultural into manufacturing occupations. Over the 1960s these workers were siphoned off by other manufacturing industries, and employment opportunities in textiles were opened to blacks making the transition from agriculture and domestic service into manufacturing. This newer group can be expected to follow an exit pattern similar to their predecessors.

Table 5.28 *Quits per 100 Employees in Selected US Industries (Monthly Average) 1958–78*

Year	Manufacturing	Non-durable goods Manufacturing	Textiles
1958	1.1	1.2	1.3
1959	1.5	1.7	1.7
1960	1.3	1.6	1.6
1961	1.2	1.5	1.6
1962	1.4	1.7	1.9
1963	1.4	1.6	1.9
1964	1.5	1.7	2.1
1965	1.9	2.1	2.5
1966	2.6	2.8	3.5
1967	2.3	2.7	3.4
1968	2.5	2.8	3.6
1969	2.7	3.1	3.9
1970	2.1	2.6	3.5
1971	1.8	2.2	3.4
1972	2.3	2.7	4.3
1973	2.8	3.3	5.1
1974	2.4	2.8	4.1
1975	1.4	1.8	2.3
1976	1.7	2.2	2.9
1977	1.8	2.3	2.8
1978	2.1	2.5	3.1

Source: US Department of Labor, Bureau of Labor Statistics, *Employment and Earnings, United States, 1909–1978*, Washington, DC: US Government Printing Office, Bulletin No. 1313–11, 1979.

Postwar European textile firms have also experienced substantial difficulties in recruiting and retaining labor in the face of competition from growth sectors. As in the USA, this problem has not been solved via adjustments in wage levels. Instead, there has been an increase in the exploitation of segmented labor markets, i.e. an increasing use of labor that is not fully mobile or represented in the collective bargaining process. The high share of women in the textile labor force (typically above 50 per cent) is well known.

For the industrialized North of Europe, excluding Italy, there has been a substantial growth in the share of immigrants in the textile labor force. In West Germany, for instance, their share in the textile labor force grew from 2 per cent in 1960, peaking at 23 per cent in 1973 and since steadied around 20 per cent (Arbeitgeberkreis Gesamttextil, 1981). For the UK, the equivalent 1971 figure was 9 per cent; in the wool industry it appears that this figure grew from under 5

Table 5.29   *Ratio of Quits to Layoffs, 1958–78*

Year	Manufacturing	Non-durable goods Manufacturing	Textiles
1958	0.42	0.48	0.72
1959	0.75	0.85	1.31
1960	0.54	0.73	1.07
1961	0.55	0.68	1.23
1962	0.70	0.81	1.58
1963	0.78	0.80	1.58
1964	0.88	0.89	1.91
1965	1.36	1.31	3.13
1966	2.17	2.00	5.00
1967	1.64	1.80	4.25
1968	2.08	2.00	6.00
1969	2.25	2.21	5.57
1970	1.17	1.63	3.50
1971	1.13	1.38	3.78
1972	2.09	2.08	8.60
1973	3.11	2.75	10.20
1974	1.60	1.75	3.15
1975	0.67	0.90	1.53
1976	1.31	1.47	2.90
1977	1.64	1.64	3.50
1978	2.33	2.08	4.42

Source: US Department of Labor, Bureau of Labor Statistics, *Employment and Earnings, United States, 1909–1978*, Washington, DC: US Government Printing Office, Bulletin 1312–11, 1979.

per cent in the early 1950s to approaching 20 per cent in the 1970s. Cotton probably developed similarly. Immigrants come primarily from the Mediterranean basin (and from the Commonwealth in the UK case). The density of immigrant employment is generally higher in textiles than in other industries. The UK case suggests that the particular role of immigrants is to secure the night shift, which might be impossible to staff in their absence.

In Italy, market segmentation concerns not immigrants but

'decentralized production', which ultimately has a greater impact on competitiveness. It is largely connected with the structural shift from larger to smaller production units. First, firms employing less than fifty workers legally escape the payment of a considerable part of the heavy employers' contribution (social security, etc.). Second, the substantial development of outworking (primarily affecting knitting within textiles) permits illegal avoidance of this contribution (the so-called underground labor phenomenon). Third, small firms that employ primarily family labor do not necessarily, it appears, account for and remunerate the work of family members as would be done in an establishment employing wage-labor. Fourth, the gradual southward creep of textiles and apparel – probably affecting knitting and clothing more than the rest of textiles – reflects a move towards local labor markets with higher rates of open unemployment, hence greater possibilities for employing outworkers at low wages. Overall the phenomenon is complex and it would be wrong to ascribe Italian competitiveness solely to the wage advantage that decentralized production often brings (and this is increasingly true over time); the flexibility of this system is also important.

Summary and Conclusions

Textile industries throughout the world are highly competitive. In general, there are no significant economies of scale, only modest product differentiation, relatively small capital requirements and no significant technological or resource-based barriers to entry. Consequently, there appears to be little seller market power in world textile markets.

Further, despite recent labor-saving technological advances, textiles remains a labor-intensive enterprise. High labor versus capital requirements, coupled with apparent worker preferences for employment in other industries, contribute to making textiles a declining industry in most developed countries. Almost without exception, textile industries in OECD countries have negligible output growth, rising production costs and declining employment. On the other hand, several developing countries with a relative abundance of labor have small but rapidly growing textile industries.

Notes

1   The largest firms in the US textile industry are Burlington Industries and J. P. Stevens, with 1979 sales of $2.7 and $1.8 billion and industry shares of approximately 5 and 3 per cent, respectively.

2   Competitiveness, as the term is used here, refers to the structure of the textile industry. Competitive industries are characterized by a large number of relatively small firms producing a homogeneous product, by little price discretion on the part of sellers and by no substantial barriers to entry into the industry.

3   Mills in the sample with up to 10,000 spindles were not generally out-performed by larger mills.

4   For example, the Council on Wage and Price Stability has estimated capital requirements for an integrated steel plant are approximately $3 billion.

5   These forty-eight firms are those for which data are reported by the Compustat data service. The Compustat service provides a number of computer readable libraries of financial, statistical and market information through magnetic tape and time sharing. The companies covered are the largest and most significant companies traded on the New York, American and Regional Stock Exchanges. A full range of fundamental data is provided in Compustat. Specifically, a key balance sheet, income statement and market items are reported.

6   For branch details for 1961 and 1971 see Ministero dell'Industria (1979), Table 25. For more fragmentary information about the 1970s see Federtessile (1980).

7   Note that German tariff provision for offshore processing has been significant for the apparel industry. This has clearly increased German textile exports to Mediterranean processing locations, but the initiatives in this appear to have come more from apparel than textiles.

8   Agache-Willot's ill-fated takeover of Korvettes, the US retail chain, as well as its ownership of a French furnishing retail chain before its own collapse in 1981, is a premier example.

6

An Overview of Governmental Influence

Governments wield tremendous influence over the competitiveness of industries. Through adopted rules, regulations and policies, they can limit or even bar entry to industries and access to particular markets, and can restrict the size of domestic competitors. Unlike microeconomic and technological factors, which often tend to be similar between nations, the influence of governments may vary considerably and may focus on substantially different problems or on different solutions for similar problems. The rules, regulations and policies set by governments reflect their cultural, social and national differences.

The major regulations and policies affecting the textile industries of the United States, Asia and Europe are presented in the early part of this chapter. Governmental policies are then compared and, at the conclusion of the chapter, implications of relevance to the textile industry are drawn.

United States

Regulations
The United States has adopted many regulations that affect its textile industry. Listed in Appendix 3 are those most frequently cited. This list was developed by obtaining a 1977 US Department of Commerce publication, *Federal Regulation, Policy, Ruling, Etc.*, which was then circulated among members of the Advisory Board for their comments and updating. Several textile company lawyers also assisted in the updating of the 1977 list. Due to time and resource constraints, however, this list is undoubtedly incomplete. A more thorough investigation in the future would surely prove worthwhile.

Some of the regulations listed in Appendix 3 are of more importance than others. Through interviews and discussions with industry executives and with the help of the staff of the American Textile

Manufacturers Institute, the most important US regulatory issues as of mid-1981 were identified:

Care Labelling
Clean Air Act
Consolidated Permit Regulations
Davis-Bacon Act
Effluent Guidelines
Equal Employment Opportunity
Hazardous Waste Regulations
Industrial Revenue Bonds (proposed limitations)
National Energy Conservation Policy Act
Occupational Safety and Health Act
Powerplant and Industrial Fuel Use Act
Public Utility Regulatory Policies Act
Toxic Substances Control Act
Tris Reimbursement (proposed)
Vinson-Trammel Act
Walsh-Healey Act

A brief summary of each can be found in Appendix 4.

Government Support Programs
In the late 1970s the United States embarked upon a major long-term textile and apparel products export expansion program. This formal program was inaugurated in early 1979 and implemented by the Office of Textiles and Apparel in the Department of Commerce in cooperation with the Commerce's Bureau of Export Development. Among other things, the department coordinated a major study of the foreign sales potential for US textiles and apparel. Textile and apparel markets in forty-seven countries around the world were chosen for surveillance in order to gather information (e.g. where US products are competitive and in demand, the size of the market, the standards and trends, etc.).[1] In 1980, a series of seminars was planned and developed. These seminars, tailored to the needs of the manufacturers of textile apparel products, were held in major cities throughout the country.

In addition to these promotional campaigns, a number of other initiatives have been undertaken to improve the competitive environment for actual and potential exporters of textile products. For example, the Commerce Department has examined the viability of developing US export trading companies for textile and apparel products in order to facilitate the entry of firms that believe themselves to be too small or unfamiliar with foreign trade seriously to consider exporting (US Department of Commerce, 1981c).

An attack on foreign barriers to US exports of textile products has also been initiated and has already resulted in the removal of some barriers to trade. The Office of Textiles and Apparel of the Commerce Department has recently completed a publication that details the known non-tariff barriers to United States textile and apparel exports in 138 countries (US Department of Commerce, 1981a). These regulations will soon be examined in reference to the Multilateral Trade Negotiations with the hope of eliminating those rules in contravention of international commitments. In order to focus the efforts to eliminate textile export barriers, the Office of Textiles and Apparel recently established a special Trade Facilitation Staff, charged specifically with the investigation of non-tariff barriers and other trade problems that United States textile exporters are experiencing. This Staff supports the operations of the Committee to Eliminate Textile Export Barriers.

Export financing is another issue recently examined by the United States. Some exporters have complained that United States export financing for textile and apparel is not competitive. Therefore, the Commerce Department set up a task force to study the subject of export financing in response to suggestions and recommendations made by textile industry representatives. Included among the issues examined by the task force was the comparison of the financing for US exports of textile and apparel products and that available for firms in other countries. Freight rate disparities and other issues were also examined (US Department of Commerce, 1980)..

The US government also provides some trade adjustment assistance for both firms and employees. The program established by the Trade Act of 1974 provides adjustment assistance for firms whose businesses have suffered due to increased imports. It also helps workers who have become totally or partially unemployed as a result of increased imports. The objectives of the Act are to facilitate the orderly transfer of resources to alternative uses and to help with adjustments to new conditions of competition. A petition for certification of eligibility to apply for adjustment assistance may be filed by any firm, group of workers or their authorized representative. The specifics of this trade adjustment program are reported in Appendix 5.

Policy
The US governmental 'policy' concerning its textile industry has been in a state of continual change. The government has essentially moved

from supporting the concept of free trade to promoting a fairly protectionistic policy. This change occurred in three blending stages.

The immediate post World War II years were relatively problem-free for both the government and its industry: demand was high and foreign competition was low. A few tariffs were in effect, but most textiles were relatively free to enter the country. As overseas competition developed, however, the US textile industry, later joined by the US apparel industry, began to pressure the government for protection from imports. Finally, in 1961, the government agreed to negotiate a bilateral trade agreement with Japan in order to control cotton, textiles and apparel goods. Between 1961 and 1973, the government was convinced to negotiate additional bilateral trade agreements. These agreements were expanded from the one initiated in 1961 with Japan to include other fibers. The new agreements were more restrictive in other ways as well.

During the most recent period of government/textile industry interaction, numerous bilateral trade agreements and the Multi-fiber Arrangement (MFA) have been negotiated. These agreements are even more restrictive and also involve other Far Eastern suppliers. This trend of increased governmental protection has led a country that was identified as being fairly supportive of free trade in textiles to become a country that is now considered fairly protectionistic. No serious efforts, however, have been made to alter the current policy from one of protectionism to a more industrial policy in order to help restructure the industry in some manner. This point distinguishes the US policy from that of several major competitor countries.

Asian Policies

Each Asian country has its own set of regulations and policies that affect its textile industry. Some policies are similar to those of the USA, but many are different. This section identifies the governmental regulations and policies of some of the most important textile-producing countries in Asia.

Japan
The textile industry of Japan has experienced serious difficulties in recent years. The troubles have occurred as a result of a sluggish demand caused by a slackening in consumer spending on clothing, shrinking exports and ballooning imports, which were brought about by an intensification of competition from neighbouring developing countries and the sharp rises in the value of the yen.

During most of the prewar years, Japanese exports of textile goods accounted for 50 per cent of the nation's total exports. Today, they account for less than 5 per cent. During the intervening years, the import of textile goods increased dramatically. The ratio of imports (imports divided by domestic demand) climbed rapidly upward from 0.5 per cent in 1960 to 18.3 per cent in 1978. As a result, Japan's trade balance of textile goods deteriorated quickly, and the trade balance including textile raw materials dropped into the red in 1979.

In 1977, a total of 1,328 textile firms (manufacturers as well as marketing companies) went bankrupt. Outstanding debts amounted to an all time high of $1.3 billion. The number of business failures in ensuing years remained at a high level (reaching 1,388 in 1979). The continuing business slump took a heavy toll on textile jobs: in the eight-year period, 1970–9, the number of textile workers decreased by approximately 320,000 (18 per cent of the total employed in the textile industry). Consequently, the relative weight of the textile industry in relation to the nation's manufacturing industry eroded substantially. Its share of those employed in the manufacture of textiles fell from 23 per cent in 1955 to 13.2 per cent in 1979, with its share of industrial shipments dropping from 19.1 per cent to 6.3 per cent and exports from 37.3 per cent to 4.8 per cent (all in terms of dollar values).

To aid the Japanese textile industry in regaining its vigor and stability, the government decided that the industry must successfully meet the following challenges:

(1) it must work out a viable strategy to cope with the growing competition from neighboring developing countries in ways compatible with the ideal of international division of labor;
(2) it must find ways to meet the increasingly diversified preferences of domestic consumers; and
(3) it must restructure itself to create an industry capable of offering employment opportunities that appeal to the changing values of workers.

Since the first oil crisis of 1973, the textile industry of Japan has experienced a protracted slump. As late as the third quarter of 1980, industry production still lagged considerably below the level reached shortly before the oil crisis. The Japanese textile industry tried to retrench its operations by scrapping approximately 20 per cent of its production facilities and laying off excess workers. The nation also actively tried to restructure its product mix by emphasizing products embodying larger value-added components. The idea was to avoid direct competition with neighboring developing countries in the interest of a rational international division of labor.

In order to deal effectively with the problems facing the nation's textile industry, it was also considered necessary to diversify operations into areas where goods could be produced with larger value-added components. This was accomplished by tapping knowledge-intensive technologies and by vigorously switching over to non-textile businesses. However, due to the extremely limited operational scale of most of the firms and the consequent lack of funding capabilities (85 per cent of the looms are owned by small firms), supplementary measures were taken by the government to help these small firms.

To encourage the textile industry of Japan to diversify and enter higher value-added areas that could meet the increasingly diversified and sophisticated consumer market, the government took measures (pursuant to the Law on Extraordinary Measures for the Structural Improvement of Textile Industries enacted in July 1979) designed to encourage vertical cooperation between mills engaged in sectors such as weaving, apparel making and dyeing. The government's goal was to stimulate efforts for the development of new products or technologies. Specifically, tax and financial incentives were made available to firms that undertook projects within the guidelines laid out by the Minister of International Trade and Industry in the ministry's structural improvement program.

The textile industry also experienced excess capacity, which helped create an excess supply that undermined the health of the economy and created increasing pressures for an early disposal of the surplus capacities. When the cash strapped industry developed plans for scrapping excess capabilities on its own, the government released funds from government-run financial institutions. Such financial assistance was justified on the basis that it encouraged ailing textile mills to switch over to other areas with more promising business potential.

Table 6.1 describes the Japanese policies adopted in reference to its textile industry. It should be noted, however, that among the adjustment and assistance measures that are still in effect only A7 is concerned with the weaving sector. Trade policies affecting the weaving sector that may be in effect are B4, B6, B8 and B9. A brief summary of specific Japanese textile regulations is presented in Appendix 6.

Government-backed financial aid available to the Japanese textile industry comes from three major organizations: the Association for the Development of Small–Medium Sized Enterprises; the Small–Medium Enterprise Financing Bank; and the Japanese Development Bank. The contents and standards for the financial aid available through each of these three organizations is reported in Appendix 7. It should also be noted that, in addition to government-supported

Table 6.1 *Historical Developments in Japan's Policies Toward Textile Industry*

	1955	1960	1965	1970	1975	1980	1985	1990

Adjustment and assistance policies:

A1. Capacity adjustment based on old textile law ..... '56 ⟶ '64

A2. Capacity adjustment based on new textile law ..... '64 ⟶ '70

A3. Improvement of the textile structure based on special textile law .... '67 ⟶ '73

A4. Provisory and special measures for the textile industry, following the self-constraint exports to the US .... '71 ⟶ '73

A5. Measures on unregistered looms, based on special measures laws .... '73 ⟶ '78

A6. Improvement of the textile structure based on modernization and promotion law .... '63 ⟶ '73

A7. Improvement of the textile structure based on new textile law .... '74 ⟶ '79 ⟶ '84

A8. Joint scrapping of capacity based on business transformation law for small-and medium-sized firms .... '76 ⟶ '80

A9. Scrapping of excess capacity based on the law concerning extraordinary measures for specific depressed industries .... '78 ⟶ '83

Trade policies:

B1. Self-restriction of cotton products exports .... '57 ⟶ '60

B2. Short- and long-term agreement on cotton products .... '61 ⟶ '71 ⟶ '73

B3. Self-restriction of textile exports to the US .... '71 ⟶ '73

B4. Multi-Fiber Agreement (MFA) .... '74 ⟶ '78 ⟶ '81

B5. Kennedy Round (KR) .... '67 ⟶ '71

B6. General Special Preference (GSP) .... '71 ⟶ '81

B7. Provisional tariff reduction (non-reciprocal) .... '72 ⟶ '79

B8. Import quota on raw silk and silky products .... '74 ⟶ '80

B9. Tokyo Round (General Tariff Reduction) .... '80 ⟶ '87

Source: Ippei Yamazawa, 'Sen-i Sangyo no Kozo Chosei to Yunyu Seisaku', *The Hitotsubashi Review* (Tokyo), vol. 85, no. 5, May 1981, p. 24.

loans, the government guarantees the debt and provides preferential tax treatment.

In early 1981, the Textile Industry Council altered its position regarding the textile industry. Up to that time, Japan's policy-makers felt that the textile industry should produce high value-added textiles to meet domestic needs and should avoid competition from developing countries. But trends in Japan's textile exports in recent years have indicated that the Japanese textile industry is internationally competitive primarily in non-price areas for high-quality products. This has caused policy-makers to reconsider the future of the textile industry. For these reasons, various preparations have been made in order to revise the law (A7). These preparations have included: (1) the formation of a delegation sent to European countries and to the USA to study the situations in the advanced countries in order to learn from the experience of these countries; and (2) the formation of another delegation sent to the Asian developing countries to study the developments in their textile industries. These delegations returned to Japan in November 1981, and the preparation of their reports is under way.

Furthermore, in 1981 the Japanese government announced the initiation of a $70 million study that will examine the potential for the use of robots in the Japanese apparel industry – a major customer of the Japanese textile industry.

Other Asian Countries
Although other Asian countries set their own policies regarding the textile industries, many do support similar plans. In general, governments tend to protect, support and control the industry. Financial incentives are often available, and exporting (especially to non-Asian countries) is usually considered a primary goal. Listed in Table 6.2 are some of the specific government policies that have been adopted by some of the Asian countries.

In order to aid its textile industry, the Korean government enacted the Provisional Law for the Adjustment of Textile Facilities in 1967. This law emphasized the use of new equipment as a means of modernizing the industry. In 1979 the law was replaced by the Law for Promoting Modernization of the Textile Industry, which provided a special fund to be used to encourage specialization and integration, to obtain new technologies, and to train employees.

In 1980, Korea formed a semi-official organization, the Textile Industry Federation, financed by the government ($7 million) and by private firms (another $7 million). This group was created in order to help firms modernize plants and equipment as a means of becoming more competitive in the world market. Emphasis has been placed on

Table 6.2 Government Policies for Industrialization and the Textile Complex in Selected Asia Pacific Countries

	Korea	Taiwan	Philippines	Thailand	Malaysia	Indonesia
Textile policy	1967 Special measures for Textile Industry 1979 Textile Industry Modernization Act	1953 First Four-Year Economic Development Plan (import-substitution textile industry) 1961 Third Four-Year Economic Development Plan (export expansion of clothing)	1964–71 Textile Industry Subsidiary Act (exemption of import duties and sales tax)	1960–5 The first expansion and promotion of textile industries by Board of Investment 1968–9 The second promotion 1973– The third promotion (export-oriented)		1961 Eight-Year Over-All Development Plan 1969 First Five-Year Economic Development Plan
Incentives for investment		1961 Statute for Encouragement of Investment 1971 Statute for Encouragement of Investment (1971)	1946 New and Necessary Industries Act (import-substitution of textile industry) 1961 Basic Industries Act 1976 Investment Incentives Act (preferred area synthetic textiles)	1960 Industrial Investment Promotion Act B.E. 2503 1962 Promotion of Industrial Investment Act B.E. 2505 (import-substitution)	1958 Pioneer Industries Promotion Act B.E. 2503 1965 Pioneer Industries Act 1968 Investment Incentives Act	1968 Domestic Investment Act

Incentives for foreign capital	*1960* Promotion for Foreign Capital Inducement *1966* Foreign Capital Inducement Act	*1954* Statute for Investment by Foreign Nationals *1962* Statute for Technical Cooperation	*1962* Guaranty of Foreign Investments (remittance of earnings) *1967* Investment Incentives Act *1972* Positive introduction of foreign capital by President Marcos	*1958–9* Permission of remittance of earnings by foreigners Abolition of regulation on land holdings by foreigners *1962* Promotion of Industrial Investment Act	*1959* Guaranty of Private Investments (USA) *1960* Investment Incentives Act	*1967* Foreign Capital Investment Act
Incentives for Export	*1964–5* Reform of tax and financing system in order to promote export *1970* Law for Establishment of Free Trade Zone	*1965* Statute for Establishment and Management of Export Processing Zones	*1970* Export Incentives Act *1970* Starting of establishment of Export Processing Zones	*1972* Announcement of the Revolution Party No. 227 (promotion for export) *1977* Promotion of Investment Act B.E. 2520	*1967* Income Tax (Export Promotion) Act *1968* Investment Incentives Act	*1975* Draw Back System (export refund system) *1976* Package System for Export Promotion *1970* Devaluation of rupic

Source: J. Arpan, M. Barry and T. Van Tho, 'The Textile Complex in the Pacific Basin', in R. Moxon, T. Roehl and J. F. Truitt (eds), *International Business Strategies in the Asia Pacific Area*, Greenwich, Conn.: JAI Press, forthcoming.

low value-added textiles. The government has also encouraged the consolidation of firms.

Because textile exports account for about one-third of Korea's foreign exchange, the government has supported this key industry. Vertically integrated, the industry has been organized to be self-sufficient and export-oriented. In general, the domestic market is effectively shielded from imports by non-tariff barriers. Textile imports are not permitted except in the following instances:

(1) the imports are intended for re-export;
(2) domestic production capabilities are temporarily fully utilized; the imports are special items that meet temporary needs in the export market;
(3) domestic consumption is not large enough to justify local production; or
(4) the prices are so low that the material (primarily yarn) must be purchased in order to remain internationally competitive in other textile markets.

One reported result of this protection has been the lack of Korean fiber-producing plants large enough to enjoy major economies of scale. Consequently, the Korean textile industry has been burdened with relatively high-priced fibers. Korea frequently revises its regulations though, and trade restrictions have eased in recent years. However, the Korean regulations are still considered some of the most complex and restrictive in Asia.

Taiwan is another country that has adopted highly restrictive policies. In fact, Taiwan resembles Korea in many ways. Its textile industry, established primarily for exporting purposes, also helps to satisfy domestic needs and is highly protected – almost no textiles can be imported unless they aid the local textile industry. The fiber producers in Taiwan, however, are less protected and are therefore forced to sell fiber to the rest of the local industry at lower costs. This helps hold down the costs of woven goods and allows that segment of the industry to be more competitive in the world market.

Just as in Korea, the textile industry of Taiwan plays a key role in the local economy. In fact, the production of textiles is the largest industrial activity in Taiwan. It accounts for 19 per cent of all manufactured goods and employs 16 per cent of all manufacturing labor. About 90 per cent of the textiles produced are exported (about 25 per cent of Taiwan's exports).

Low value-added products from Thailand, Indonesia and the Philippines serve as Taiwan's major competition. Therefore, the Industrial Development Bureau of Taiwan encourages its industry to consolidate and modernize operations in order to strive towards producing higher value-added textiles. The development of a high-technology, higher-integrated industry is considered of primary importance. Exporting to a larger number of countries (especially those in Eastern Europe) as a means of achieving market diversification is also emphasized. A $600 million fund backs this emphasis on technology. This money, funneled through the Industrial Development Bureau, allows the textile firms to repay loans (often at subsidized rates) beginning a full year after production starts.

European Policies

The declining numbers of textile workers proved to be one of the major European social problems of the 1970s. Employment levels within the industry declined rapidly, beginning in the Netherlands and West Germany and spreading to France and the United Kingdom and then to Belgium and Italy. After enjoying years of prosperity through growth or stability, Europe was faced with a crisis, and by 1974 most European governments realized that they must act.

In general, the European governments pressed for time to allow their countries to adjust to the new economic conditions. Their arguments were quite similar: they needed time to transfer individuals from an increasingly uncompetitive textile industry into specialized components of the industry or into other industries. To obtain this necessary transitional time, they sought temporary protection. Rather than attempting the negotiation of many bilateral trade treaties, the European Community accepted the Multi-fiber Arrangement (MFA).

The European trade policy in textiles is distinctive in its approach to trade with the Mediterranean countries with whom the EC has concluded association agreements. Imports into the Community countries from these associated states are not covered by the MFA and have caused some problems for both European industry and governments. Controls on imports from the Far East or other low-cost sources threatened to be undermined by Mediterranean imports. Consequently, the agreement reached within the EC in 1977 on the Commission's mandate in the MFA II round of talks included a provision for the Mediterranean imports. Safeguard clauses in the association agreements were less restrictive than under the 1978 MFA, so the EC Commission was forced to seek voluntary agreements with these countries. Since Greece, Spain and Portugal had applied to join the Community, these negotiations were particularly difficult. The

Commission finally reached agreement with Portugal in January 1979 on a three-year voluntary restraint agreement, which limited import growth to 1–2 per cent. Agreements were also reached with Greece (now a member of the Community), Spain and other Mediterranean exporters, usually for a one- or two-year duration. In order to reach agreement, however, the Commission has to make concessions on quotas, which in some cases breached the global ceilings agreed by the Nine. These concessions should be viewed in the context of the general need to promote trade with these countries in order to support the new democracies only recently established in all three.

The primary plan of the European Community, however, was to accept the MFA as a temporary measure to help countries prepare for free trade. In the meantime, each country was free to make any preparations deemed necessary. Nevertheless, most European countries instituted a similar approach: they sought to identify the strengths and weaknesses within their own textile industries and then tried to concentrate on strengthening those sectors holding the greatest comparative advantages. This long-term strategy implied the country's willingness to sacrifice weak firms. However, the political realities varied from country to country as did the resultant actions taken by governments.

West Germany and the Netherlands were the most prepared to allow the free market to operate. They were able to do this because they were both experiencing strong economies and strong currencies. Both governments encouraged their textile firms to invest in lower-cost countries (a suggestion readily accepted – especially by the German firms). Some of the investment went to the USA, but much of it went to Eastern Europe and the Mediterranean. As a result, employment levels in both countries continued to decline. The West German government appeared more prepared to accept this decline than the other European governments. However, over one-half of all textile jobs in the Netherlands disappeared between 1970 and 1976. This sharp drop proved too great for the Dutch, and governmental policy switched from support of the free market to support of job preservation.

The preservation of jobs was also a major concern of Belgium, Italy and the UK. As a result, substantial subsidies were offered. When this strategy failed, some firms were nationalized (especially in Italy). 'Temporary' measures were usually renewed each year and eventually they essentially became 'permanent'. Unfortunately, these job preservation attempts were not successful. Employment continued to drop – often even at faster rates than before. This phenomenon caused the UK and other European countries to begin re-evaluating their policies.

France approached the problem differently. In addition to providing transitional assistance to small and medium-sized firms, the French encouraged extensive technological research. Their goal was to become more competitive through increased productivity. Unfortunately, this strategy was not particularly effective. Productivity rose no faster than anywhere else, and employment levels continued to fall. In fact, some even claimed that the emphasis placed on productivity caused greater declines in labor levels.

These unsuccessful results led the Europeans to re-examine their governmental strategies and search for new approaches. The strategy presently pursued is one of restructuring the industry.[2] The Dutch were the first to attempt this approach when they established the Dutch Industrial Restructuring Corporation (NEHEM) to authorize governmental guidelines for streamlining the industry. According to their policy, the least efficient firms (25 per cent) are considered helpless and will not be granted aid. The other firms are encouraged to consolidate and to concentrate on areas that appear to hold a viable future. Grants of up to 20 per cent of investment costs are available for these purposes. Whether or not such restructuring efforts will work, however, remains to be seen. The risks and costs are high, as are the political repercussions of failure.

Currently, policies supporting aid and protectionism continue to be in effect in Europe. In fact, popular support for these approaches may even be growing. France, for example, recently announced a new aid program for its textile industry. Under this program, companies will receive relief from social security payments for employees. Greatest reductions are granted to companies that increase employment over the year and sustain investment at average levels for manufacturing. Slightly lower benefits accrue to companies that either maintain investment at 10 per cent above the average for the sector or that invest 20 per cent more than the average and make reductions in employment but avoid collective redundancies. There is also a provision for relief for companies experiencing difficulties. Each firm must conclude a contract with either the industry association representing the government (in the case of large companies) or the regional authorities (for firms employing less than 100 people). The objective of the scheme is to promote investment while slowing the decline in employment.

The EC Commission has recently approved a Belgian proposal to grant loans and provide other forms of financial support to textile mills involved in its restructuring program. To qualify, though, a firm must retain at least 90 per cent of its labor force and contribute a minimum of 30 per cent of all restructuring costs. Interest rate subsidies (of 7 per cent) are available on only 30 per cent of the investment and state participation in the investment is limited to 45 per cent.

It should be noted that most European governments typically provide two types of assistance: financial assistance used to compensate for plant closures, etc.; and investment incentives used to motivate firms to adopt the plan. Regional assistance schemes are usually also provided, but it should be pointed out that regional plans have not been very extensively used (except in the United Kingdom). While perhaps the most economically defendable of all economic intervention schemes, they are not politically the easiest to implement.

Several EC-oriented studies have also been funded by the EC Commission in order to determine the strengths and weaknesses of the textile industry. Although most of these studies have now been completed, the governments have not had sufficient time to react fully or to implement any new programs.

The EC Commission does not intend to force industrial changes, but has left this task to be undertaken primarily by the countries. The Commission has, however, developed guidelines to encourage restructuring. It has also launched two programs (one to encourage research and the other to facilitate the central collection of consumption and production data), and it is trying to serve as a forum for consensus.

In May 1978, the Commission sent a policy statement on industrial aid schemes to the Council. The statement listed three conditions (approved by the Council) that must be met prior to aid disbursement:

(1)   an emergency must exist;
(2)   the aid must not remove normal business risks; and
(3)   the aid will not preserve the status quo.

Basically the aid program assists a corporation only when its bankruptcy obstructs the adjustment program. A firm receives no assistance if its failure does not affect the general restructuring plans.

In summary, the political and legal environment for the textile industry in Europe is highly complex. It involves both national and EC dimensions. Concern for employment has resulted in a recent increase in tax and investment incentives. However, in an effort to maintain a competitive and viable textile industry, most emphasis has been placed on trade regulation.

Before comparing European policies with those in other parts of the world, a brief comment about outward processing is necessary. Outward processing refers to the practice of exporting cloth or semi-finished items of clothing to low-cost countries for completion. The finished products are then re-exported and distributed by the company that supplied the cloth. West German companies have taken a lead in this form of trade and have been able to improve their competitive position by doing so. Since costs can be reduced by this method, integrated textile and clothing manufacturers in West Germany have been able to balance high domestic costs, and thus compete with lower-cost sources within the Community (such as the UK and Italy where labor costs were considerably lower during the 1970s). Producers in the Netherlands and Belgium were first to emulate this policy during the 1970s but with less success. Today many companies in the EC are moving in this direction as a means of competing and to some extent strengthening the position of the textile industry. As parts of the clothing manufacturing process are being transferred to Mediterranean and East European countries, labor unions in the apparel industry have been particularly critical of outward processing. But some national governments, in particular the UK, have also opposed it and have sought to introduce means of controlling the growth in such trade.

Because of the pressure from these sources, the EC Commission has made various proposals to limit outward processing to a certain percentage of a given manufacturer's annual production. However, the regulations to date have not been very constraining, so unions and the clothing industry are still upset.[3]

A Comparison of Policies

In many respects it is quite difficult to compare the various countries' governmental policies. The United States, for example, has not actually adopted a comprehensive policy that encompasses the textile industry. Instead, the set of regulations is fragmented, often conflicting, and produces varying impacts upon the industry. Most of the other countries enjoy a more unified and integrated approach.

Nevertheless, an examination of governmental policies and regulations reveals an extremely important finding: almost all nations have become more protectionistic of their textile industries – even the Far Eastern countries. The US government, however, primarily limits its support to protectionistic policies while most of the other governments also provide financial support for restructuring of the industry.

The financial assistance programs offered by most governments are aimed towards preparing the industries for a time when free trade might again prevail. Most governments claim that their protectionistic policies are only temporary and that they are 'buying time' to allow the industry to make crucial structural adjustments. The temporariness of these policies remains uncertain, but it appears that most governments of the major textile-producing countries assist their textile industries with important amounts of financial aid.

There are exceptions, of course. Of all developed countries, West Germany seems most prepared to accept free trade and its effect on the West German textile industry. West Germany also seems less interested than most countries in subsidizing any necessary transitions. German policies, however, have been partially modified in order to be consistent with EC policy. As an example, West Germany is a member of the MFA agreement basically because the EC has accepted the MFA. Furthermore, Germany's 'Law for the Promotion of Employment' provides assistance to workers adversely affected by its essentially free trade policy. Enterprises are not aided, but the social costs of such a policy are reduced by this cushioning impact upon labor.

Nevertheless, the West German government basically seems the most prepared to allow its textile industry to die, to struggle on its own or to relocate in other countries. Most German policy-makers reportedly feel that the economy can absorb these changes without undue disruption. However, each of the other countries has taken major steps at least temporarily to protect its industry, and all of them except the USA also provide financial assistance in order to permit structural changes.

Implications

If we accept the assumption that the world may soon be faced with an over-capacity problem and that some governments will continue to subsidize their textile industries, then it can be concluded that protectionistic policies are needed to assure the survival of the other textile industries. Protectionism, however, may be necessary only for those sub-sets of the industry facing significant competition. Specialization, therefore, may be a means to avoid disaster without adopting permanent protection.

Governments not desirous of permanently subsidizing or protecting their industries will need to encourage restructuring. Countries following a policy of promoting protectionism without restructuring will have long-run problems if the other countries' industries are so greatly assisted that they become more competitive. Less world interest would exist for agreements resembling the MFA, and world pressures might force the reduction of all textile barriers. If such pressures are successful, it might then become too late for countries to initiate restructuring, and their textile industries could shrink considerably in the environment of these new economic realities.

Notes

1 These August 1980 reports are now available by country (with six regional summaries) under the general title *Country Market Survey* (US Department of Commerce, 1980).
2 It should be noted that, when compared to US anti-trust law, most national anti-trust legislation in Europe is permissive. National competition policy seldom stands in the way of industrial restructuring and nationalization efforts.
3 It should be noted that regulations and restrictive clauses differ from country to country. In the USA, for example, only cut fabric can come under Item 807, but both cut apparel parts and uncut fabric can be processed and then returned to Europe. For more information on Item 807, see American Apparel Manufacturers Association (1980). For specific details on foreign customs practices concerning the return of national merchandise, see US Tariff Commission (1980), pp. 27–32.

7

Corporate Strategies and Adjustments

Interviews were conducted with top management representatives from eight United States textile manufacturing companies, three Japanese firms and three European companies. A structured interview format (see Appendix 8) was adhered to throughout. Results from these interviews are presented in four sections. The first three order the interview findings by geographic areas, and the final section synthesizes the findings.

A conscientious effort was made to capture the views of all interviewed firms rather than giving undue consideration to, say, the largest companies only. Rarely do the data represent consensus opinion of all executives. The information, however, does reflect the major shared views rather than merely highlighting isolated examples.

It is important to emphasize that the contents of this chapter represent the opinions and views of industry representatives. The research team does not necessarily share each and every view.

A United States Perspective

Four of the eight US textile companies are privately owned and four are publicly held corporations. The companies range in size from one having fewer than ten production facilities to another with over 100 plants. The delineation of companies by 1981 performance includes two with sales less than $200 million, two with sales between $300 and $500 million, and four with sales in excess of $500 million. Included in the eight interviews are companies involved primarily in grey goods production as well as those that engage in a full range of production of finished goods marketed to the home furnishings, apparel and industrial markets.

Perceived Threats

A primary objective of the interviews was to ascertain textile executives' perceptions of the major threats confronting the industry and their firms over the next five–ten years. The major conclusions are organized into five categories: substitute products, technology, government, foreign competition and other sources of threat.

The substitution of non-woven fabrics is regarded as a definite source of competition, particularly in those narrow product applications and market segments (e.g. diapers) that have turned almost exclusively to non-woven fabrics.

Technological developments are regarded more as an opportunity than a threat, yet optimism is tempered by the recognition that major innovations in equipment may also represent a threat to certain companies, especially those that cannot afford to modernize. However, even for those firms that are able to incur anticipated heavy capital expenditures, the possibility remains that technological advancements may not be justified in return on investment (ROI) terms. One executive suggested that the industry take a hard look at modernization opportunities and assure that capital investments promise sufficient returns, especially in light of the fact that ROI in the textile industry has averaged around 10–11 per cent, when in fact it should be averaging closer to 17 per cent given current interest rates.

Industry representatives overwhelmingly perceive the US federal government as an obstacle to the efficient conduct, profitability and growth of the US textile industry. Attitudes toward government divide into two major categories – those concerning domestic regulations and policies and those dealing with international trade considerations. The interviewees alleged that regulations (e.g. cotton dust standards and noise abatement requirements) increase the cost of business, thereby placing US firms in a less competitive position. Regulations also are perceived as contributing to industry concentration, because smaller firms are less able to incur the costs of modifying existing processes and plants or building new ones to meet government standards. A fundamental fear is that the textile industry could find itself in the unpleasant position of the US shoe industry unless the government's position and policies regarding international trade are altered. For example, it was alleged that the government has not strictly enforced the previous MFA growth policy of 6 per cent, and that for some items the actual import penetration has amounted to 12–14 per cent, or even greater growth.

The consensus view is that foreign competition is the major threat faced by the US textile industry, with the People's Republic of China (Mainland China) regarded as *the* major threat, a 'sleeping giant'. The absence of a profit motive and the need to employ a massive work force were reasons given for the Chinese ability to achieve certain competitive advantages over US textile producers. This purportedly has created a state of unfair competition, particularly in view of the relatively low freight rates to the USA from Asia and given the assertion that man-made fiber prices charged to Chinese textile manufacturers are as much as 20 per cent lower than those available to US producers.

Other perceived sources of threat and grounds for complaint involve the government's treatment of Korea, Hong Kong and Taiwan as developing countries. Some respondents asserted that more stringent quotas should be required because the textile industries are highly developed in these specific countries.

Some of the interviewed executives acknowledged that all textile products are not equally affected by foreign competition. The shirt business and other similar end-use categories, characterized by relatively high concentration among apparel manufacturers, represent a more vulnerable market for US textile producers than, say, the women's blouse business. This is because the blouse business involves a greater number of smaller manufacturers who are less able to purchase from foreign suppliers. Moreover, frequent fashion changes require that these firms be able to alter sources quickly, thus reducing the impact of foreign competition.

Two additional perceived threats to the US textile industry are the leverage of man-made fiber suppliers and the trend toward increasing textile industry concentration in the USA. The leverage of domestic fiber suppliers over textile producers is manifest in the form of greater foreign competition, as US export fiber prices to these competitors were alleged to be lower than prices charged to American producers. The trend toward greater use of man-made fibers may exacerbate this threat.

Industry concentration poses a clear threat to smaller manufacturers, who find it more difficult to incur the capital investment created by the need to modernize and to meet government regulations. Also, the advantages associated with production integration (from spinning to finishing) place the larger, more sophisticated firms in a superior competitive position. Further acceleration in industry concentration is perceived as likely to result from financial pressures stemming from higher labor costs and greater capital-investment requirements. Penetration of the US market by foreign competition was an additional factor cited as underlying the likelihood of greater textile industry concentration, as this may lead to a continuing shakeout of less competitive domestic textile producers. The implication is 'modernize or go'; many smaller firms apparently will have to specialize in order to survive.

Opportunities and Industry Viability

In addition to examining perceived threats, the interviews also investigated the perceived opportunities available to the textile mill products industry within the next five–ten years and what the industry must do to remain competitive. There are four major categories: technology, markets, marketing sophistication and external relations.

Technology perhaps more than anything else is regarded as the major opportunity available to the US textile industry and the primary means to maintain or achieve a superior competitive position. A consensus view is that heavy investment in plant and equipment modernization (e.g. air-jet looms) is a competitive imperative that will serve the dual function of reducing costs by improving productivity and of increasing quality by permitting production of more defect-free textiles.

The opportunities associated with modernization are perceived to be most available to the better capitalized companies that can more quickly replace existing machinery with costly advanced machinery and can sustain temporary reductions in ROI. This requires a management attitude of willingness to invest in the future although the short-term impact may be negligible or even detrimental.

Man-made fibers is another area in which technology is thought to provide opportunities. Some industry representatives believe that sufficient advances in the treatment of man-made fibers will make them practically indistinguishable from natural fibers. This, however, is thought to represent a double-edged sword. On the one hand, US textile manufacturers possess production superiority (particularly over the Mainland Chinese) in working with man-made fibers, while on the other, greater use of man-made fibers would increase fiber suppliers' leverage by eliminating the neutralizing impact of natural fibers.

Markets that have not historically received much industry-wide attention are considered to offer opportunities for some companies. The greatest domestic growth potential is perceived to be in a variety of home furnishing and industrial textile products, which in comparison to apparel are regarded as relatively more insulated from foreign competition.

Perhaps the greatest growth potential is expected to be in international markets. Comparatively, average textile consumption per capita in the USA is approximately 60 pounds per year, whereas worldwide it averages around 14–15 pounds. Though recognizing this potential opportunity, optimism is tempered by the perception that demand in developing countries is erratic and varies inversely with the strength of the dollar.

US textile leadership resulted historically from superior production capabilities. While this competitive advantage has not vanished, it has eroded. Textile executives recognize the need to enhance marketing sophistication in order to maintain or improve their competitive positions. Greater customer orientation was identified as a step in the right direction. For example, because apparel manufacturers are beginning to demand 60-inch widths, production of 60-inch widths by the US textile industry would effectively nullify in certain markets the impact of the Mainland Chinese, who do not produce 60-inch fabric (and, in fact, are not even producing much 48-inch material).

Improving relations with various participants in the textile industry is seen as another way to increase the industry's competitiveness. For example, some of the interviewed executives believe that the industry must work more closely with the government to achieve reasonable controls over imports, perhaps leading ultimately to quotas pegged to actual increases or decreases in consumption of particular items.

Improving its image so that it can attract a more qualified pool of laborers and managers is viewed as another imperative for the industry. This will necessitate efforts to present the industry as progressive and viable. The interviewed executives consider the American Textile Manufacturers Institute to be an appropriate mechanism for facilitating improvements in the industry's image.

Corporate Objectives and Strategic Focus

This section summarizes the interviews with US textile executives in terms of six major categories of corporate objectives and strategies: financial, production, marketing, physical distribution, supplier relations and management/planning.

A complicating factor in attempting to synthesize the interview results arises from the inherent heterogeneity of the interviewed firms – evenly divided between privately and publicly owned enterprises, some very large and others quite small, etc. Against this backdrop, the results are integrated as best as possible and without giving undue consideration to any one type of firm. However, the discussion of financial objectives and strategies focuses primarily on the publicly owned firms, as their financing alternatives are less restricted than those available to privately owned companies.

The major financial-related results from the interviews were that several of the interviewed firms operate under a policy of no external debt, whereby all growth and modernization objectives are financed by internally generated funds, and that, for those that go into capital markets for funds, the targeted debt/equity ratio averages around 35 per cent and 65 per cent equity. The desire to achieve greater leverage is limited currently by high interest rates and fully extended credit lines.

A return on investment (ROI) of 15–16 per cent was the objective given by those executives who were willing to divulge this information. The desired ROI of course increases with increases in the cost of money. There is a willingness to accept a lower short-run ROI to achieve long-run benefits.

One thought characterizes textile executives' perspectives on what must be done to enhance the competitive posture of the American textile industry. In a word, that view is 'quality'. There is virtual consensus that high quality is imperative to maintain and improve the industry's competitive position. Various firms reflected great pride in recognizing themselves as the quality leaders in the industry. However, one executive made the point that the important objective should be to produce an acceptable level of quality, but not to go overboard. The reason, in his opinion, is that the premium on quality above a certain level is less than the return to be obtained from superior service and fashion. Another executive said that his firm attempted periodically to place a value on quality in order to demonstrate to customers the comparative value of his company's products.

Heavy investment in modernization to improve quality and enhance production efficiency is a core objective of the US textile companies. As one executive put it, the air-jet loom *is* the future. His company as well as others are converting their equipment as rapidly as feasible. New spinning systems to produce open-end yarns and computerized finishing at the other end of the production process are additional technologies that are receiving widespread acceptance. Greater attention to process controls and energy efficiency further reflects the rapid technological developments in the industry.

With few notable exceptions, it is a well-known fact that the textile industry in the USA has not historically invested heavily in R&D. While the US textile executives appreciate the importance of sophisticated R&D, most do not feel it feasible for their firms to invest heavily in basic research. Several executives indicated their objective as being rapid followers rather than innovators. Most of their research is directed at specific applications, with the industry turning to fiber suppliers, textile equipment manufacturers or the Institute of Textile Technology for major developments in textile technology.

All of the interviewed firms desire a more efficient mix of capital and labor. A move toward greater capital intensification is an explicitly stated objective in some firms while implicit in others. One rationale for greater capital intensification is improved productivity. Another factor is the purported disadvantage that the textile industry has in competing for labor with higher paying industries that have recently located in the Southeast. Several executives acknowledge that the industry must be willing to pay more in order to attract and retain skilled labor.

The interviewed firms have concentrated their production facilities in the Carolinas and Georgia in order to enhance political clout and provide access to a less unionized labor pool.

Two of the interviewed firms have offshore production facilities, but neither intends to enlarge these operations. There is absolutely no desire to locate offshore among the firms that have never tried it. The prevailing view is that such operations are more trouble than they are worth, owing to cultural barriers and other problems. One executive perhaps best summarized the industry view in saying that past industry success with offshore production has been dismal.

A major issue confronting textile executives is the choice of market sectors to which to devote their efforts: apparel, home furnishings, industrial applications, foreign markets, etc. Responses were highly varied to questions involving market share objectives, in terms of both specificity and content. Perhaps the most consistent revelation was that apparel remains the preferred market for all of the interviewed firms. Not a single firm indicated a conscious intent to reduce dependence on the apparel market. However, two companies indicated a desire to increase market share in home furnishings while maintaining their relative shares of apparel textiles. Their modest move toward home furnishings was explained by the fact that this market is growing rapidly and competition is less intense than in apparel.

Half of the companies had specific goals regarding foreign markets. For example, one spokesman stated that his company has a goal of generating 15 per cent of revenue from exporting. The goal is supported by a sales force budget, and while currently directing efforts from New York, the company plans eventually to set up offices in Europe. Another executive indicated that his company operates only in politically stable markets. This company enters foreign markets on a selective product basis in which its product possesses some unique competitive advantage. This product then provides a springboard for expansion into other markets.

Overall, the interview results reveal great variability in the degree of clarity and explicitness of market share objectives. Most firms, in fact, appear to be operating from rather vague and implicit objectives. Two exceptions are worth noting. One executive said that his company entered a new product/market only if it foresaw the opportunity to be a major competitor, i.e. be number one, two or three at worst. Another executive was even more explicit in stating that his company did not enter a particular market unless two conditions are met. First, the company's product offering has to equal or exceed competitive offerings and, second, the company has to believe it can secure a 30–40 per cent market share. This share objective is predicated on the notion that 'experience effects' cannot be enjoyed at lower levels of output.

Product lines and improvements are sought continually. Some recent product developments include the expansion of warp knit production and manufacture of wider width materials. Increasing the use of man-made fiber was identified by several firms as a specific objective. In fact, one interviewee claimed that cotton would decline considerably because man-made fibers will be able to do everything that natural fibers do today.

Finally, it is important to point out an additional product objective cited by a company that sells the bulk of its output to the apparel sector. The company has no objective to alter this focus to any significant degree, but it does intend to move away from commodity products and into areas where it can achieve greater autonomy and flexibility.

In the US textile firms' promotional arsenals, personal selling emerged as the dominant activity. Advertising remains a relatively minor tool. Trade advertising in the apparel sector is perceived by most of the interviewed companies as relatively ineffective and consumer advertising is regarded as infeasible if not wasteful. Home furnishing advertising is evaluated more favorably, probably because of the more direct nature of the home furnishing market. A company actively involved in home furnishings marketing indicated that it would not increase its advertising budget to any measurable degree, but it did intend to improve the budget allocation by seeking better media vehicles and better means of achieving retail advertising cooperation.

Conducting research on how businesses price their products is always difficult, and these interviews were no exception. Several noteworthy findings did emerge, however. One spokesman argued that there has been excessive price focus in the textile industry, with companies presuming falsely that they could compete successfully on the basis of price alone. In terms of specific pricing objectives, it is apparent that pricing objectives are conditioned by market share performance. One executive claimed that his company has very specific gross margin targets but that prices are largely a function of uncontrollable market forces. Several of the larger firms acknowledged their policy of charging above average prices. Their policy is to be the price leader when they dominate a market and to meet competitors' prices in other instances.

A distinction should be made between marketing research and market research. The former focuses on customer preferences, buying motives, changing behavior, etc., whereas the latter emphasizes the analysis of competitive activity, economic developments, and so forth. The interview results clearly showed a dominance of market research in the textile industry. Most companies do not believe it feasible or even necessary to perform studies of the end-users of their products. Only one of the interviewed companies conducts extensive surveys of end-users. The remaining firms perform varying degrees of market research. Research staffs typically are very small, often depending upon consultants for specific studies.

The interviews also sought to obtain opinions about the possibility of textile companies integrating their operations backward (into fibers) or forward (into, say, manufacturing and marketing apparel items). When companies were asked their intentions in these directions, the response was an overwhelming 'no'. Textile executives believe that their primary business mission is textiles and not apparel. Requirements to manufacture and market apparel successfully are perceived to exceed the abilities of most textile companies. There is also the fear of alienating apparel firms (their major customers) if textile companies engage them in head-on competition.

In recent years firms in the textile industry have undertaken vigorous efforts to enhance management quality and to increase the level of planning sophistication.

All of the interviewed firms have ongoing management development programs, though they vary considerably in sophistication and formality. At one extreme are informal programs tailored to individual manager needs. At the other extreme are formal programs that employ a combination of in-house training and external specialists. The more sophisticated development programs operate at all levels – plant, division and corporate. Some of the interviewed executives hold the opinion that good training programs are essential because the highest quality candidates out of colleges and graduate programs purportedly are not attracted to the textile industry.

Annual planning and longer-term strategic planning are standard practices with the interviewed firms. All reported the use of annual planning. These plans typically are updated either quarterly or semi-annually. Though relatively new among the interviewed firms, strategic planning is warmly embraced, particularly by the larger firms. Their strategic planning cycles are either three or five years, with annual updates typical. An argument provided by one executive in favor of the three-year cycle is that this period supposedly corresponds with the industry's equipment improvements and fabric changes.

Procedures for implementing the strategic planning process vary considerably. Some of the larger firms have corporate planning staffs, whereas smaller companies tend to designate a single individual as head of strategic planning. This person more likely than not occupies a financial position (e.g. treasurer, financial vice-president) as his primary job responsibility.

In most of the interviewed firms the strategic planning process involves a combination of top-down plans from corporate headquarters with bottom-up inputs from plants and divisions. All corporate units and functional areas are usually involved in the planning process. Several of the larger firms use state-of-the-art planning tools, whereas smaller firms rely more on executive judgement when formulating strategic plans.

A Japanese Perspective

Interviews were conducted in Japan with three large Japanese textile enterprises. While these firms do not represent a cross-section of the Japanese textile industry, the interview results nonetheless help to highlight the perspectives and strategies of major textile executives in Japan.

All three firms recorded total sales in recent years between $700 million and $1.3 billion. These companies are fully integrated textile producers, and the smallest has more than 6,000 employees and the largest over 10,000. All firms are diversified into non-textile areas (plastics, auto parts, etc.), with non-textiles representing as much as 25 per cent of total sales. Therefore, in comparison to the sample of US firms, the Japanese companies are generally larger, more integrated horizontally and vertically, and less dependent on textile business.

Perceived Threats
Two major sources of threat stood out in the minds of the interviewed Japanese textile executives: foreign competition and changes in the demographic and socio-economic composition of Japan. The former threat results primarily from producers of lower-value textiles in developing Asian countries, whereas demographic changes have a twofold impact on the Japanese textile industry. First, the reduced birth rate is perceived as contributing to reduced textile demand from end-use segments that are particularly sensitive to the birth rate, namely baby's wear and the fashion industry that is dependent on younger consumers. The second and perhaps more critical negative consequence results from the increasingly severe problem of recruiting young laborers to work in textile mills. The industry's traditional labor pool (young females with limited education – high school

diplomas or less) is increasingly favoring the pursuit of higher education or work in industries that have more attractive working conditions.

Opportunities and Industry Viability

The perceived opportunities and imperatives for maintaining Japanese textile viability correspond to the threats described above. The development of labor-saving technology (computers, sophisticated equipment, and even robots) is seen as one means of dealing with the labor shortage problem as well as increasing productivity. The other major opportunity, one shared by all three Japanese firms, is the move toward higher value-added textiles directed at both domestic and foreign markets. This perspective illustrates the widespread Japanese attitude toward competition, which advocates competing from a position of comparative strength in relatively insulated markets rather than engaging head-on in highly competitive, undifferentiated product markets.

Corporate Objectives and Strategic Focus

Financial matters do not appear to dominate the strategic thinking of Japanese textile executives. Indeed, one executive indicated that his company's financial position is the best among Japanese textile firms and that the company has no goal or strategy to alter its financial programs. The other firms are concerned primarily with improving the financial strength of their subsidiary operations.

The production-related objectives and strategies of the three Japanese firms can be summed up in four points. First, the declining textile labor pool in Japan makes it essential for these textile companies to invest heavily in labor-saving equipment. Second, the threat of intensified foreign competition has prompted the Japanese executives to increase investment in R&D as a means of identifying high value-added products that are less susceptible to competition. Related to the threat of increased competition, a third strategy is to increase production and sales of non-textile products. A final point is that none of the interviewed firms has any plans for additional offshore production. The largest of the three has about twenty offshore production projects located in Latin America, Southeast Asia and elsewhere, but it does not plan to invest further into offshore production because of political and economic risks.

The specific marketing objectives and strategies vary somewhat, but all three Japanese firms demonstrate a clear marketing orientation. An objective shared by all is the desire to increase cooperative efforts with apparel makers. This includes joint research and product development activities. For example, one company establishes 'area committees for textile use' as a means of strengthening connections with apparel makers and retailers. Subcommittees are formed to promote cooperative efforts in three product areas: men's wear, uniforms and apparel for exports. Another area of agreement is the perceived need for greater marketing research to understand changes in demand better and the need for heavy investment in R&D to identify opportunities for high value-added products.

In addition, each firm has its own special marketing emphasis. One firm is particularly concerned with establishing brand name identity for its new products. Another stresses the desire to increase its domestic market share, but not at the expense of profitability. This represents a reversal of past efforts where many Japanese firms focused on building share, whether profitable or not.

Considerable attention is devoted to planning. All three firms have formal planning units at the corporate level. Planning involves short- and mid-term planning at the division level and longer-term, strategic planning at the corporate level. One firm, for example, is already formulating its 1990 plan.

A European Perspective

The material in this section is based on interviews with a French company and two West German textile firms. All are large textile producers by European standards, with the smallest enjoying 1980 textile sales of approximately $200 million. The largest company is a fully vertically integrated agglomeration of textile companies (from production to retailing); the others practice integrated production (from spinning to finishing) but restrict their operations to production and some diversification in non-textile areas. In terms of size and diversification, the two West German companies are more similar to the previously described US firms, whereas the French company is more akin to the interviewed Japanese firms.

The following review differs in several fundamental respects from those presented for the Japanese and US firms. The major distinction is the elimination of a section concerning perceived threats and opportunities. Emphasis, instead, is devoted to strategic concerns. Discussion focuses on three areas: production strategies and practices; marketing philosophies and practices; and management organization, strategy and planning.

Corporate Objectives and Strategic Focus
An outstanding characteristic of the three European firms is their commitment to modernization. In recent years each has invested 3.5– 5 per cent of sales into new plant and equipment. The West German

firms are particularly progressive: most of their weaving capacity is shuttleless, a large percentage of spinning is open-end, and there is substantial computerization of finishing. Quality control receives considerable attention. In fact, in one firm the quality control manager reports to top management rather than to production management.

In terms of production location, domestic production prevails. Two of the firms have engaged in offshore production, but neither intends to increase this activity. One firm had a particularly unsuccessful experience. It attempted in the 1970s to relocate some production to low-wage countries. This proved unsuccessful, apparently because of insufficient control over the production process. The present philosophy is that close control, requiring physical proximity of management and plant, leads to greater flexibility and higher productivity, thereby offsetting the advantage of lower wage rates from offshore production.

Marketing orientation pervades the three European firms. Promotion of brand identification and image is perhaps the most notable indicator of marketing commitment. It is seen as a means of having products viewed as something more than mere commodities. Further indication of the desire to avoid commodity status is an intense fashion orientation. Two major collections of fabrics are designed for spring/summer and autumn/winter showings. This requires considerable investment in studying the fashion industry and translating this knowledge into creative new designs. The effort to discover the changing needs of the market and to maintain flexibility in the production process in order to answer these needs quickly illustrates dedication to marketing. A third indicator of the European firms' marketing orientation is the effort to pursue markets whenever the opportunity arises. International marketing and sales activities are significant. Both of the West German firms receive over one-half of their sales from exporting activity.

The desire of the interviewed firms to react quickly to market changes is reflected in organizational structures: decentralized organizations prevail. This is typified in one firm where each product group acts virtually as an independent firm in product development, financial control and selling.

The future-oriented strategies of the interviewed firms vary considerably in individual characteristics, although continued innovation and the ability to meet changing market needs are common to the strategic thinking of all. Several specific strategic themes are worth noting. One firm emphasizes high quality and advanced technical specification of fabrics. Another sees its future growth depending upon achieving better competitive position via modern technology and product specialization. The third firm intends to diversify into areas both within and outside of textiles that exploit the company's existing managerial and technical skills. Formal planning structures, short-term and strategic, are present in all three European firms. Considerable time is devoted to strategic planning.

Synthesis of Findings

The interviews with US, Japanese and European textile firms revealed some interesting and noteworthy similarities as well as differences in the practices, objectives, philosophies and strategies. This synthesis attempts to capture the major points of concurrence and disagreement among the geographically diverse textile executives. A point of qualification is needed. The interviews were conducted with small samples of textile executives in each area. To speak of a Japanese perspective, for example, is appropriate only to the extent that the three Japanese firms represent the overall thinking among textile executives throughout Japan. The same applies of course for the US and European cases. While it is doubtful that three Japanese, three European and eight US firms are perfectly representative of all textile companies in these areas, it also is improbable that these firms are unrepresentative. Therefore, the interview results are suggestive if not perfectly definitive.

Similarities in management philosophies, strategies and practices are fewer than differences. However, US, Japanese and European textile executives all agreed that improvements in technology are critical to the survival and growth of their companies. Associated with modernization was the consensus that product quality must improve. Increases in textile production by developing countries would seem to be at the heart of this concern. Another area of agreement was the similarity of attitudes toward offshore production. Difficulties arising from inability to achieve desirable levels of control have created disappointments with past efforts to produce offshore. Additional offshore production was eschewed by the vast majority of the interviewed firms.

The interviews revealed four major areas of differences among textile companies in the US, Japan and Europe. The greatest differences were in the areas of international focus and marketing orientation. With regard to the former, it is apparent that Japanese and European companies think in terms of international markets to a much greater extent than do US companies. There are obvious socio-economic factors to account for this, but the fact remains that US firms (although certainly not all) are more insular and domestic-oriented than are their competitors.

Japanese and European firms also reflect significantly greater marketing orientation. The desire to meet customer needs and to react quickly to changes in these needs is much more apparent than it is in US firms. Indeed, marketing is more of a driving force in Japanese and European textile companies than it is in the USA. Organization structures with an emphasis on decentralization, and production technology emphasizing flexibility, are natural extensions of the greater marketing orientation found in Japanese and European companies. The promotion of brand name identification/image further reflects Japanese and European thinking that marketing can be used effectively to differentiate a company's products and thereby lessen price competition.

Investment in R&D was another point of distinction between US and Japanese/European firms. US textile companies invest less in basic research and development and depend more on external agents to perform this function. The European firms and particularly the Japanese companies are more inclined to perform R&D in-house.

Diversification outside of textiles is a final area of distinction. US firms, with minor exceptions, have limited their operations and investments to textiles. The Japanese in particular, but also the Europeans, are more willing to make non-textile investments.

8

Strategic Adjustments in Textile
Mill Products Industries

Introduction

Chapters 3–6 cut across national industries by analyzing worldwide trends in several environmental factors that affected competitiveness within and among national textile mill products industries: technology, trade patterns, economic structure and political action. Chapter 7 presented and evaluated the opinions of Asian, European and United States textile mill executives concerning these trends and the strategies some of them were currently pursuing to remain competitive.

This chapter synthesizes these trends, opinions and strategies at the national and firm levels. The first section briefly summarizes the major changes that have affected the competitive environment of the global textile industry since the late 1950s, and identifies the major strategic options that have been used by national industries. The second section assesses the strategic adjustments and performance of five European industries, two Asian industries and the US industry over the last two decades. Within the European area, the industries of West Germany, Italy, France, United Kingdom and the Netherlands are analyzed. The two Asian industries analyzed are those of Taiwan and Japan. The third and final sections present the implications and conclusions that can be drawn from the first two sections and that are of value to specific industries and individual firms.

The Basis of Competition within and among National Textile Industries

The textile industries of industrialized and developing countries have undergone considerable adjustment since World War II as a result of changes in their competitive environments. Pressures for adjustment in the industrialized countries of Europe and the United States were the result of four major forces: first was the formation of the European Community (EC) in the late 1950s and the dismantling of trade barriers among member nations; second, the trade liberalization movement among OECD countries (e.g. Dillon, Kennedy, Tokyo rounds) was important, not only in stimulating textile trade among industrialized countries, but also in stimulating textile imports from low-wage countries; third was the increasingly more sophisticated competition from developing countries, particularly in high-volume, low-cost textiles and apparel; fourth was the slow-down in the growth of textile consumption in industrialized countries and the increase in the growth of textile consumption in other regions of the world. Table 8.1 summarizes the major changes in estimated fiber consumption for various regions of the world.

The industries of countries such as Japan and Taiwan also experienced pressures for adjustment as they matured. They first encountered stiffening market barriers imposed first by the United States and then by the European countries. Second, they were challenged by other even lower-cost developing countries such as the Philippines and Indonesia pursuing their own industrialization and economic development goals.

As a result of these increasingly severe competitive pressures, the textile industries experienced growing pressure for structural adjustment, technological change and political action. Adjustments appeared to be based on several major strategic options: tariff and non-tariff (mainly quotas) protection measures; minimization of production costs through modernization of equipment and plant and/or the exploitation of international wage differences (e.g. offshore manufacturing); product specialization; increased emphasis on marketing; unplanned and planned industry restructuring; and internationalization (e.g. foreign direct investments and contractural arrangements). National industries eventually pursued a combination of these strategies. However, national conditions such as domestic market size, international perspective and stage of industrialization imposed limitations on the single and combined effectiveness of these strategic options.

For example, unlike the US textile industry, which has a large, diverse and high-consumption domestic market, the economic success of most other textile industries is highly dependent on their abilities to compete for market share in world markets. Consequently, they are generally 'outward looking', aggressive and committed to enhancing their international competitiveness. They view all foreign markets as extensions of their domestic markets, and do not hesitate to take the necessary competitive steps to maintain and increase their

Table 8.1 *Estimated World Fiber Consumption, 1976, 1981 and 1991*

Nation description	1976			1981			1991			Analysis of 15-year increase (1976–91) (million lb)		
	Population (millions)	PCFC[a] (lb)	Consumption (million lb)	Population (millions)	PCFC (lb)	Consumption (million lb)	Population (millions)	PCFC (lb)	Consumption (million lb)	Due to population increase	Due to PCFC increase	Total
Developed nations	760	39.9	30,300	790	47.1	37,200	865	59.5	51,500	6,250 (13.0)	14,950 (31.1)	21,200 (44.1)[b]
Developing nations	2,015	6.4	12,950	2,280	7.3	16,700	2,870	9.4	26,850	8,000 (16.6)	5,900 (12.3)	13,900 (28.9)[b]
Latin America	330	10.5	3,450	375	12.1	4,550	490	16.6	8,150			4,700
Near East	190	11.6	2,200	215	13.7	2,950	270	18.5	5,000			2,800
Far East	1,185	5.1	6,000	1,320	5.6	7,450	1,630	6.8	11,000			5,000
Africa	310	4.2	1,300	370	4.7	1,750	480	5.6	2,700			1,400
Centrally planned nations	1,290	13.4	17,250	1,360	15.2	20,800	1,505	20.1	30,250	4,350 (9.0)	8,650 (18.0)	13,000 (27.0)[b]
Total	4,065	14.9	60,500	4,430	16.9	74,700	5,240	20.7	108,600	18,600 (38.6)	29,500 (61.4)	48,100 (100.0)[b]

[a] PCFC = per capita fiber consumption.
[b] Numbers in parentheses are percentage increases in 1991 based on 1976 consumption.

Source: 'The big textile picture for 1991', *Textile Industries* (Atlanta. Ga: Smith Publishing Co.), July 1980. p. 82.

market shares. On the other hand, the US textile industry is more concerned with its domestic market and the competition that prevails in this market. Most initiatives undertaken by US textile mill companies were designed to enhance domestic competitiveness, not international competitiveness.

Competitive Strategies of Textile Mill Products Industries

The five European industries were selected because of substantial differences in the adjustment strategies adopted and their success in enhancing the international viability of the various industries. The successful West German, Italian and Netherlands industries permitted market forces and domestic conditions to mold their strategic responses to changes in their competitive environments.[1] The relatively unsuccessful French and British industries relied on strategic responses that required substantial government intervention.

The two Asian industries were selected because of substantial differences both in their adjustment strategies and in comparison to those of the European and United States industries. They were also selected because, unlike the industries of other Asia Pacific nations, their industries can be classified as mature, technologically advanced and highly sophisticated in their international operations. They also pose considerable competitive threats for the US and European industries.

The US industry was selected because of its rather unique market characteristics (e.g. size, leader in accepting new fabrics). It was also a leader in the development of such agreements as the Multi-fiber Arrangement Regarding International Trade in Textiles (MFA).

The adjustment strategies adopted by the European, Asia Pacific and United States industries are classified according to the industry strategy[2] matrix shown in Figure 8.1: (1) undifferentiated, (2) proliferated, (3) concentrated, or (4) differentiated. The classification depends on the firms' perception of the market (actual or imagined), and the number of product offerings. A homogeneous perception implies that firms ignore, or do not recognise, that a market consists of sub-markets or segments that have different needs or requirements to be satisfied. Some firms that have this perception of the market will go after the market with one product offering (e.g. denim), trying to attract as many customers as possible. This is called an undifferentiated strategy. Other firms, recognizing the competitive value of product differentiation, will use several product offerings (e.g. denim, shirting, coat lining). This is called a proliferated strategy. It is impor-

Number of Products Offered by Company	Perspective of Market	
	Homogeneous	Heterogeneous
Single	Undifferentiated	Concentrated
Multiple	Proliferated	Differentiated

8.1 Strategy Matrix

Source: Adapted from Philip Kotler, *Marketing Management: Analysis, Planning, and Control*, 4th edn, Englewood Cliffs, NJ: Prentice-Hall, 1980.

tant to recognize that this strategy is not based on an analysis of market segment needs or requirements. Rather, it is an attempt to differentiate one firm's offerings from those of other competing firms. A heterogeneous perception, in contrast, recognizes that markets can be subdivided or segmented according to need or requirement differences. Firms with this perception of the market will go after one or more segments of the market, using one or more product offerings, respectively, that are specifically based on an analysis of the market segment's needs or requirements. The single product offering strategy is called concentrated, and the multiple product offering strategy is called differentiated.

European Industry Strategies[3]

West Germany With the formation of the European Community, the West German textile and apparel industries were faced with heightened intra-EC competition but protected from low-cost imports from developing countries. The West German textile industry reacted to this intra-EC competition in the early 1960s by consolidating vertically and horizontally to exploit economies of scale and to achieve market power in a rapidly growing market within the EC. It also made major investments in an effort to become capital intensive, and adopted an undifferentiated strategy by concentrating on the production of standardized fabric and clothing. However, there was some specialization among smaller firms in fashion-related fabrics and apparel, home furnishings and industrial goods.

By the mid-1970s, however, the undifferentiated strategy floundered. In 1975, for example, at least seven of the top forty-nine textile firms were receiving subsidies from provincial (or *Land*) governments,[4] and employment was contracting at about 7 per cent annually. The reason for this strategy failure was the growing liberalization of extra-EC low-cost imports by the federal government, an import policy it pursued until about 1978. (West Germany was a reluctant supporter of the EC, signing the MFA in December 1977. Relative to other EC countries, Germany tends to be more liberal in the interpretation and enforcement of MFA's restrictive clauses.)

From the early 1970s, the larger textile firms began to change to a differentiated strategy, and placed increased emphasis on smaller production units, more flexible production, substantial exports and modern technology. The industry also supported industrial research encouraged by the federal and *Land* governments. Offshore manufacturing, mainly in Eastern European countries, was used extensively, and several firms made foreign direct investments.

The two West German companies discussed in Chapter 7 are probably representative of other West German textile mill companies in that they emphasize export markets, a divisional approach to management,[5] a steady flow of innovations (e.g. semi-annual showings of new collections based on a two-year planning cycle) to meet the changing and heterogeneous demands of a worldwide market, and the creation of strong brand awareness for their fabrics. Both companies also spend a considerable amount of time and effort on long-term planning for the future, and are more concerned about market position than market-share targets.

The success of this more recent differentiated strategy is noteworthy. In spite of high wage levels and a substantial reduction in the textile labor force, West Germany has emerged as one of the world's largest exporters of textiles (see Chapter 4). This success is partially the result of the strategic initiative taken by German clothing firms to manufacture apparel offshore using uncut fabric exempt from duties upon re-entering into Germany.

The West German textile industry continues to be a strong supporter of free market principles, and does not believe that the federal government should be responsible for its survival. However, survival probably has been helped by trade unions that the industry regarded as enlightened and cooperative, an economy capable of absorbing a large number of redundant textile and apparel workers,[6] *Land* government assistance and banks (Shepherd, 1981, pp. 32–3).

Italy Throughout the 1960s, Italy's textile industry was the principal beneficiary of the rapid growth in demand for textiles within the EC.

Italy's competitive success was the result of a concentrated strategy and unique structural development in the private sector that fostered the development of a cooperative 'cottage industry' structure for production, and eventually marketing. Although government intervention directed at maintaining employment resulted in the nationalization of some ailing large textile firms, these public firms represent only about 5 per cent of official textile employment, and are inefficient and uncompetitive.

The development of cooperative small-scale production units was the result of (1) political conditions in Italy, (2) the presence of a strong trade union movement to preserve employment regardless of the cost involved, and (3) certain peculiarities in the Italian labor market that resulted in the extensive use of 'underground' labor.

The reorganization of vertically integrated operations into small-scale production units started in the 1950s, and was in response to over-capacity and trade unions. Lacking a strong, centralized and stable government, a strong trade union movement emerged to fill the vacuum. The union movement created substantial pressure on the government and large firms to preserve employment with two contradictory results. The public sector's response was the nationalization of large textile firms at great public expense. The private sector's response was the decentralization of operations and the employment of 'underground' workers (Shepherd, 1981, p. 34).

The existence of a pool of underground labor in Italy was the result of the government's approach to financing social welfare programs with heavy employment taxes. Social security and other indirect charges in the Italian textile industry were more than 110 per cent of direct labor costs (i.e. direct labor costs are 45 per cent of total compensation) (de la Torre and Bacchetta, 1979, p. 38). This situation resulted in the creation of a large pool of part-time, non-reported workers, which the industry was not slow to use.

Like other textile industries, the Italian industry was affected by the 1973–6 recession. Unlike other industries, however, the worldwide recession accelerated the restructuring process started in the 1950s. The Italian industry is now an aggressive international competitor in specialized quality synthetics and high-fashion design. It is supported by highly specialized small, yet vertically cooperative production units that benefit from an ability to remain flexible, to make product changes quickly, and to upgrade technology without having too great an impact on production.

France   The French textile industry's adjustment to the competitive changes of the 1960s and 1970s was not as successful as that of West Germany or Italy. The reasons for this relatively poor performance are varied and too complex to explore fully in this report. However, several of them can be highlighted.

The influence of governmental intervention on the adjustment made by the French industry is quite evident. The government was a persistent supporter of the industry's demands for heavy protection against extra-EC, low-cost imports of textiles. It pushed hard for the renewal of the MFA and the strengthening of its restrictive clauses among EC member countries. In order to justify this position on extra-EC competition, the government argued that its textile industry was scattered and antiquated, modernization was only starting, and the industry needed protection until this process was completed.

The industry also went through a process of mergers that had the backing and encouragement of the French government. It was thought that larger firms would be more capable of upgrading the industry's technology, and thereby increase its competitiveness in other countries. Although the process of consolidation resulted in a high degree of concentration, it was lopsided. While a small number of large and powerful groups emerged that were technologically advanced, much of the industry remained fragmented and technologically backward. In addition, the large French firms often lacked the flexibility to keep abreast of rapidly changing market conditions. This was in sharp contrast to the more uniform, technologically advanced and flexible West German industry, and the highly specialized, efficient and market-responsive Italian industry.

A notable exception is the French company discussed in Chapter 7. Although fully integrated from wool trading to finished wool apparel, the company has been steadily decentralizing its operations since 1974. Today, each division is largely autonomous, contains several profit centers (e.g. in clothing, each brand is a profit center), and can purchase inputs from outside the company. Also, there is an increasing tendency by the divisions to adopt a more differentiated strategy (similar to the German approach). However, because the company recently negotiated a loan with the French government, capacity expansion will be encouraged in the near future.[7]

The French industry has concentrated on technological superiority and on improving production at the expense of developing marketing-oriented strategies similar to those of the West German and Italian industries. It is also dependent on a distribution system that is increasingly prone to import textile products, yet that retained the initiative in design and marketing. (The same is somewhat true of the US textile industry, which is dependent upon an apparel sector that is increasingly dependent on large retailers who often use offshore sourcing – see Chapter 2.)

It needs to be noted, however, that while the French government presently is firm in its protectionistic policies, its structural policy is in a state of flux. This occurred because of the failure of Agache-Willot, France's largest textile firm, and the threatened bankruptcy of several other large firms (Shepherd, 1981, p. 34).

United Kingdom   The lackluster performance of the British textile industry relative to other EC countries during the 1960s and 1970s can be traced to the strategic option initially selected and the method used for its implementation: development of an undifferentiated strategy concentrating on standard cotton and man-made fiber fabrics while protected from low-cost imports.

The undifferentiated strategy pursued by Courtaulds and other large textile groups formed in the 1960s required vertical and horizontal integration and the infusion of advanced technology and techniques of production. The goal was to displace low-cost Commonwealth suppliers who had been gaining an increasing share of the cotton textiles markets since before 1960. It was believed that the economies of scale and market power achieved as a result of consolidation and modernization would reduce costs sufficiently to make domestically produced textiles competitive with imports in an open market.

However, by the early 1970s it became clear that the strategy was not a complete success. Although some mass-produced standardized textiles were competing with low-cost imports domestically and in other EC markets, a Commonwealth tariff was introduced in the early 1970s, and extended to include man-made fiber textiles in the mid-1970s.

Currently, the British industry is weak by industrialized country standards. However, it does contain a few well-developed, technically advanced, competitive sectors that cover all aspects of textile manufacturing. It is strongly influenced by vertically and horizontally integrated firms that operate in many sectors: one man-made fiber producer (Courtaulds) and two textile producers (Tootals and Carrington–Viyella) extend into retailing.

The Netherlands   Severe contraction of the Dutch textile and apparel industries was the main thrust of adjustment strategies followed by firms and the government in the 1960s and 1970s. Between 1973 and 1978, for example, employment in the textile industry declined by 40 per cent, or from 58,700 to 35,200 workers. Contraction of the apparel industry was even worse, declining from a labor force of 40,200 to 19,800 persons. Over the same period, the number of apparel firms decreased from 446 to 349. (GATT, 1980.)

The differentiated strategy pursued by the textile industry and supported by government programs designed to aid displaced workers was based on free market principles (comparative advantage within the EC) and a minimum of artificial supports. Inefficient firms were allowed to disappear or be taken over by stronger and more efficient firms.

However, the survivors were helped by the Dutch government to improve planning and efficiency of production, and to upgrade the range of production. Market research was also provided by the government together with certain facilities aimed at encouraging a common approach among firms towards exports.

Asia Pacific Industry Strategies

Taiwan The backward-linking development of the Taiwan textile complex is typical of the development process being pursued by other Asia Pacific and third world countries: first the development of an apparel industry initially designed to replace imports, then the development of a closely linked textile fabric industry, and finally the development of a man-made fiber industry. In the case of Taiwan, this development process was initiated by the Taiwan government in the early 1950s and eventually aided by Japanese foreign investments and transfers of technology.

An undifferentiated strategy was pursued during the period extending from the 1950s to the late 1970s in high-volume, low–medium-priced apparel and textiles for local and foreign markets, coupled with the rapid development of the other two segments of the textile complex. Exports expanded rapidly in the 1960s as Japanese textiles and apparel lost competitiveness. By 1980, exports of the textile complex were $100 million in fibers, $1.8 billion in yarns and fabrics, and $2.4 billion in apparel. The USA was the most important foreign market for apparel, and Hong Kong, Japan and Singapore for yarns and fibers. ('Taiwan plan. . . .', 1981.)

The strategy depended for its success on three critical factors: (1) the continued expansion of export markets; (2) the availability of low-cost labor, and (3) the willingness of small Chinese apparel and textile firms to merge into larger groups.

Starting in the early 1960s, Taiwan exports of apparel and textiles encountered increasingly restrictive barriers and mounting competition from new low-cost producers like Thailand, Indonesia and the Philippines. The USA imposed quotas on Taiwan cotton textile imports in 1963 and man-made fiber textile imports in 1971. European countries followed suit in 1970 and 1975, respectively. As a result, exports to the United States and the EC declined from 68 per cent of total exports in 1975 to 50 per cent by 1979 as Taiwan diversified into other higher growth markets. Shipments to the Near East,

Africa and Latin America rose from 10 per cent to 30 per cent during this period. (Tanzer, 1981.)

Similar to Japan and South Korea, Taiwan's success in developing other, relatively higher-technology industries (e.g. electronics) resulted in a severe labor shortage and spiraling labor costs. Monthly factory wages doubled between 1976 and 1980, thereby requiring an adjustment in its strategy.

Finally, the Taiwan textile complex remained relatively fragmented during the 1960s and 1970s as a result of a cultural resistance to mergers by Chinese owners of apparel and textile firms. As noted by Pai-hui Hsueh, president of Hualon Corp., a leading synthetic fiber producer, 'Chinese all like to be their own bosses, so I don't foresee many mergers'.

In reaction to these changes and to the reluctance of small apparel and textile firms to merge into larger vertically integrated groups, the Taiwan government's Council for Economic Planning and Development adopted a differentiated strategy and announced plans in 1980 to consolidate the industry into larger groups as a result of incentives, increase productivity, and upgrade the quality and value-added of apparel and textile exports. Large investments in labor-saving machinery are also planned to replace departing workers. (Tanzer, 1981.)

Japan[8]   Shortly after World War II, the Japanese textile industry adopted an undifferentiated strategy and emerged as the first major Asian source for high-volume, low–medium-priced apparel and textiles. Although the initial development of the Japanese textile complex was similar to the development process described for the Taiwan complex, several important differences emerged that influenced subsequent adjustment strategies. First the sequential development of first apparel, then textiles and finally fibers resulted in a dualistic complex dominated by a few tightly linked textile groups (e.g. Toray, Teijin). Second, Japan experienced labor shortages and currency revaluations and resulting wage increases long before other Asia Pacific countries such as Taiwan, Thailand and South Korea embarked on the sequential development of textile complexes that threatened to displace Japanese exports to those countries and erode its competitiveness in important European and US markets. Finally, the US–Japan textile agreement of 1971 severely restricted Japanese exports to the USA, and the system of preferential tariffs enacted by European countries about the same time gave developing countries other than Japan relatively easier access to the markets of industrialized countries.

Unlike the industrialized countries of Europe and the United

States, Japan could not react defensively by imposing additional quota restrictions (although non-tariff barriers increased substantially). Also, the markets upon which it depended were the same markets being penetrated by its Asia Pacific competitors. To solve this problem, several of the major Japanese textile groups embarked on a strategy of internationalization through foreign direct investments (FDI) in Asia Pacific countries that threatened its export markets. Investments in Asia Pacific area, shown in Table 8.2, started in the 1960s and accelerated in the early 1970s.[9] These investments, combined with Japan's extensive network of contractural arrangements, were an important force in the development and growth of textile complexes in the Asia Pacific region. For example, the manufacture of synthetic fabrics in many Asia Pacific countries was initiated as a result of Japanese investments and technological transfers. Also, Japan's joint ventures still control most of the synthetic fiber sector of the entire region.

Toray, the largest fiber company in Japan and a leader in foreign investments, provides a good example of the complexities of the internationalization strategy undertaken by the Japanese industry. In addition to the textile mill plants identified in Chapter 2, Toray partially owns fiber plants in Brazil, Taiwan, Indonesia (5), Malaysia (5), Thailand (6), Philippines and Singapore, in addition to those in Japan. Several of these plants are joint ventures with Japanese trading companies: Mitsubishi in Taiwan, Mitsui in Thailand and Korea, and Itoman and Toyo Menka in the Philippines. Intra-group trade in fibers, yarns, fabrics and apparel is extensive, in order to minimize manufacturing costs and/or gain access to markets that impose restrictions on Japanese exports. This international production rationalization process is not uncommon among other large Japanese fiber companies.

In addition to adopting an internationalization strategy to maintain markets in the Asia Pacific region and to gain better access to industrialized countries, the Japanese industry also undertook strategies designed to provide it with regional superiority in technology and the production of synthetic and blended fabrics and apparel. Both strategies have been successful.

Japan's leadership role in textile technology was achieved in a sequence of stages. They first learned the basic technology of apparel production developed by other more advanced countries, then fabric formation and finally man-made fiber production. They then modified and improved these technologies for domestic application. They later introduced innovations such as the water-jet loom (invented in Czechoslovakia) and robotics. At each stage, they transferred the more mature and tested technologies to less developed Asia Pacific

Table 8.2 Japan's Foreign Direct Investment by Period (as of September 1980)

Periods	Stages	Taiwan	Hong Kong	Korea	East Asia	Thailand	Indonesia	Philippines	Malaysia	Singapore	ASEAN	Southeast Asia
Until 1965	Fibers										1	1
	Fabrics	2	3		5	5			1	1	7	12
	End-products	2			2	5			1	1	7	9
1966 — 1970	Fibers	3		2	5	1		1			2	7
	Fabrics	16	1	2	19	9	6			1	16	35
	End-products	19		6	25	2	1			1	4	29
	Shareholding		1		1							1
1971 — 1973	Fibers			3	3		4	1	1		6	9
	Fabrics	3	6	4	13	4	9	2	3	3	21	34
	End-products	1	4	22	27	1	2	5		1	9	36
	Shareholding		1		1							1
1974[a]	Fibers							2			2	2
	Fabrics	1	2	3	6	3[b]	5	1	6		15	21
	End-products	1	2	5	8	1	1	1	2	1	6	14
Total		48	20	47	115	32	28	13	14	9	96	211

Note: Ten projects are double-accounted.

[a] Most projects in the period beginning from 1974 were undertaken during 1974–6. Since 1977, almost no new textile projects have been undertaken by Japan in Southeast Asia.

[b] Investment period is not known.

Source: Adapted from Jeffrey S. Arpan, Mary Barry and Tran Van Tho, 'The Fiber, Fabric and Apparel Complex in the Asia Pacific: The Patterns & Textures of Competition and the Shape of Things to Come', paper prepared for the University of Washington's Conference on 'International Transfer of Resources: Strategic Company Responses in the Dynamic Asia Pacific Environment', Montreal, 1982.

countries to upgrade their FDI and maintain their international competitiveness in other countries. In addition to this basic pattern of technological development, Japan also learned, adopted and adapted other forms of technology including the management of overseas production and international logistics and, more recently, the technology of marketing research and design.

Japan's current strategies appear to be two-fold: (1) improve the technologies of apparel and textile production in order to increase productivity and fabric quality, and decrease its dependency on labor, and (2) put increased emphasis on high value-added apparel and textiles by increasing marketing research and the development of the Asia Pacific area as a fashion center.

Thus there has been a marked shift by Japanese textile companies away from an undifferentiated strategy to a differentiated strategy, initially in Japan and increasingly in other Asia Pacific countries. To gain comparative strength in segmented markets, Japanese firms are emphasizing market and marketing research, the substitution of capital for labor and superior process technology. They are also aided by the forward integration of fiber companies into fabrics and their contractual arrangements with other fabric and apparel companies. Their recent emphasis on sophisticated fibers and fabrics, developed to meet the demands of domestic and foreign consumers, provides them competitive advantages over smaller and less marketing-oriented firms.

US Industry Strategy
Compared to the adjustment responses of textile industries in Europe and the Asia Pacific area between 1960 and 1980, the US industry's responses were less marked and more gradual. The only government involvement in the adjustment was to reduce tariffs on textile imports from industrialized countries and increase quotas to protect the industry from the low-cost imports of developing countries, including Japan. Unlike the European industries, the US industry was not forced to make the types of adjustments required by the redefinition of competition arising from the formation of the EC. Nor was it faced with the kinds of competitive threats that the newly emerging textile industries of developing countries posed for the maturing Taiwan and Japanese industries. It also had a very large and diverse domestic market that consumed about 20 per cent of the world's textile output, and was the leader in the introduction of man-made fiber textiles and apparel. Consequently, the US industry was comparatively insulated from international developments during most of the period, and its adjustments were primarily the result of internal changes in the domestic competitive environment.[10]

In contrast to most European and Asia Pacific textile firms, most US firms are not involved overseas as exporters, or as investors. Only about 4 per cent of US textile production is exported, and only a few firms have foreign subsidiaries.

Even before 1960, the US textile industry had undergone major technological and structural changes as a result of the US market's rapid acceptance of man-made fiber textiles. The market-dominated pressures that resulted in these changes were not to reach Europe until the early 1960s and the Asia Pacific area until the late 1960s.

Although the US market's tastes are sophisticated, a high degree of product standardization is possible because of its size. As a result, the US industry concentrated on an undifferentiated strategy in the 1950s and early 1960s that resulted in horizontal and vertical integration within the textile mill sector of the complex. Its mills became larger and highly rationalized, and emphasized the economies of long production runs of a relatively limited number of fabrics. Integration occurred as textile mill companies sought to increase cost control over the entire textile manufacturing process, to capitalize on the generally higher margins of finished textile products, and to improve market effectiveness by providing a full line of textile products.

The US industry is still the most productive in the world. The structural characteristics of the industry, its production requirements and the variety and size of its end-users combined to emphasize increased productivity, replacement of labor with capital and productive flexibility. An analysis of the major textile mill companies' annual reports to their shareholders and to the US Securities and Exchange Commission reveals that all of them have in fact placed considerable emphasis on these three areas. The evidence presented in Chapter 7 suggests that the smaller textile mills also place considerable emphasis on these areas.

However, as the analysis in Chapter 5 disclosed, capital expenditures in the industry have lagged those of other US industries. More important for the future, perhaps, capital expenditures have also lagged the expenditures of other textile industries. For example, historical data for the early 1970s, based on OECD and national statistics, indicate the following investment-to-sales ranges: West Germany 4–6 per cent; France and the United Kingdom, 3–5 per cent; and the United States, 2–3 per cent. Additionally, like the USA, European investments in recent years have been primarily for modernization, not capacity.

The claim that the USA is the lowest-cost producer of textiles, at least among industrialized countries, is also justified. Several reasons can be suggested for this performance. First, economies of scale in the textile industry are primarily dependent on the length of the production run, and the size and structure of the US market have provided US textile mill firms with a distinct advantage. Second, the slow growth in the economy and the substantial devaluations of the US dollar in the 1970s resulted in a slower rise in US wages relative to the increases that occurred in other major textile countries. Third, it is alleged, at least by the European industries, that the US industry until recently enjoyed a price advantage in the production of man-made fibers (derived from the US system of pricing oil and natural gas).

The undifferentiated strategy of the 1960s and early 1970s gradually gave way to a strategy that combined the cost-reducing undifferentiated approach with a proliferated strategy. However, some companies have adopted a differentiated strategy. For example, the industry led the world in promoting synthetic and blended fabrics in the 1960s and 1970s, and turned home furnishings into a fashion center in the 1970s. There are also signs that the industry is shifting from a strategy of large, fully integrated mills to smaller, more flexible and more specialized mills as a result of this new strategy.

As part of this combined strategy, US textile mill firms have become increasingly involved in styling, making changes in the fibers used, and changing their product mixes. Such strategies are cited by Burlington, J. P. Stevens, West Point-Pepperell and Dan River in their annual reports as major reasons for improved performance in many of their lines.

It is not clear, however, that these changes are the result of end-user marketing research. Rather, the changes appear to be the result of competitive forces identified as a result of market research (e.g. what are other textile mills doing, usually the larger ones, and so what must we do to remain competitive) and accentuated by the trend toward a proliferated strategy.

Implications for National Textile Mill Industries

There are many elements common to the adjustment strategies undertaken by the European, Asia Pacific and US industries. Some of the more significant and easily discernible ones include:

(1) all countries used protectionistic measures (tariff and non-tariff restrictions) against imports;
(2) all countries, industrialized and developing, sought to reduce the impact of wage increases with productivity increases and with strategies that minimized wage increases (e.g. use of

immigrant labor in the European Community, and offshore investments by Japan – and increasingly by South Korea);

(3)   all industrialized and maturing developing countries sought some degree of specialization at the company or national levels (proliferated or differentiated strategies);

(4)   all countries sought to integrate (or link) their textile complexes vertically and/or horizontally except the Netherlands and the United States; and

(5)   all countries sought to upgrade their technologies and their manufacturing processes.

However, the results have been quite mixed when measured in terms of performance and international competitiveness. Of the European countries, West Germany and Italy emerged as the most successful at the close of the 1970s, and France and the United Kingdom as the least successful. Taiwan and Japan emerged as highly successful international competitors,[11] but for different reasons. And finally, the United States industry emerged as a successful international competitor without specifically pursuing international strategies.

The reasons for this variation in industry performance and international competitiveness are many and too complex to be fully explored here. However, several of the more significant ones need to be discussed. They include (1) the international scope of each industry's competitive environment, (2) the speed at which change occurred in this environment, (3) the adjustment strategy or strategies selected to cope with this change, and (4) the emphasis placed on particular elements of the selected adjustment strategies.

The remainder of this section addresses these major differences in terms of the four adjustment strategies identified in Figure 8.1, in order to reveal underlying trends that may have significant implications for the relative international competitiveness of the studied industries in the 1980s. The roles that protection and government assistance played in the adjustment strategies of the various industries covered in this chapter were presented in Chapter 6.

The US textile industry, insulated from the relatively more dynamic international competitive environment, adjusted more slowly to competitive change than did the successful European and mature Asia Pacific industries. In contrast, the French and UK industries adjusted more slowly because of the adjustment strategies adopted. As a result, the US industry was able to enter the 1980s as a recognized world leader in productivity and the lowest-cost producer of textiles. The French and UK industries were not so fortunate.

The size and diversity of the US textile markets and the structure of the industry are sufficient to insure adjustment will continue. However, it is not clear from the evidence presented in this book that its international superiority as the lowest-cost producer of textiles and a leader in productivity will continue, or that this superiority is sufficient to make it a leading international competitor in the 1980s. There are several reasons for this prediction.

First, the domestic rates of growth of textile demand in Europe and the USA, particularly in apparel fabrics, have declined considerably in recent years, yet the rates of growth of apparel imports have increased. This trend will, of course, increase pressures for further adjustments, probably through even greater specialization (a competitive reaction) and a call for heightened protection (a passive reaction).

Second, the successful European and Asia Pacific industries have already adopted strategies that emphasize specialization in fibers and fabrics. This is not the case for the US, French and UK industries, whose movement towards a specialization strategy is still overshadowed by their long-entrenched undifferentiated strategies. This suggests that these industries will be faced with foreign competition in domestic and overseas markets that is increasingly more specialized and narrow, yet highly sophisticated in meeting the special demands of market segments.

Third, capital expenditures by the US textile industry continue to fall behind the capital expenditures of other textile industries (mea-

Table 8.3   *Wage, Productivity and Labor Costs Indices for Textiles: 1962, 1969, 1979 (1960 = 100)*

	US $ wages		Labor productivity[a]		US $ unit labor costs	
	1962	1979	1962	1979	1962	1979
European Community of the Six	55	500	70	200	75	250
United Kingdom	70	350	80	140	75	250
United States	70	200	90	140	80	140
Japan	35	700	70	190	50	350
South Korea	90	400	60	200	150	200

[a] ATMI and BLS data indicate that US productivity increased 49 per cent between 1969 and 1979. The discrepancy is probably due to the different data bases used. The indices shown in the table are based on OECD and ILO data, and were used to reduce problems normally encountered when comparing national statistics. It is just as conceivable that the productivity increases for the other countries are also understated.

Source: Geoffrey Shepherd, *Textile-Industry Adjustment in Developed Countries*, Thames Essay No. 30, London: Trade Policy Research Centre, 1981, Table 3.2.

sured in terms of output). A possible outcome of this trend if it were to continue is a relative decline in the productivity of the industry. As Table 8.3 indicates, labor productivity in the textile industries of other countries has increased considerably *vis-à-vis* the USA.

Fourth, the declining value of the US dollar, which aided the US textile industry during the 1970s, was a lengthy adjustment to the overvalued dollar of the 1950s and 1960s. Dollar exchange rates cannot be expected to favor the US industry to the same extent during the 1980s.

Finally, the textile industries of other countries are well along in the process of rationalization of the worldwide production of textiles,[12] a process in which the US industry has not participated. The formation of the European Community forced European textile industries to rationalize, and the emergence of new, low-cost industries in Latin America and the Asia Pacific area has done the same for Taiwan, Japan and South Korea.

Much can be learned from the adjustment strategies of the various industries studied that should be of value in meeting the challenges of the 1980s. These strategies are shown in Figure 8.2.

The undifferentiated strategy (production of standardized fabrics) followed by West Germany and Japan in the 1960s, the United Kingdom and Taiwan in both decades, and France in the 1970s failed to provide these industries international viability. The USA's undifferentiated strategy succeeded in both decades primarily because of the size of its domestic market. The reasons for failure of the undifferentiated strategy included: inadequate market base, inherent inflexibility, and continued emergence of low-cost industries.

The United Kingdom industry failed because of a wrongly focused (in retrospect) emphasis on domestically displacing low-cost imports from developing countries of the Commonwealth. The combination of low UK wages (about two-thirds of those of other EC countries) and an emphasis on the production-oriented use of technology (productivity) was not sufficient to offset the favorable wage differential enjoyed by developing countries and overcome the limitations imposed by a market that is relatively smaller and less standardized than the US market.

The undifferentiated strategy adopted by the textile industry of West Germany, and eventually France, failed because the strategy depends for its success on a large and stable market. The European situation in the 1960s and 1970s required flexibility in production, something that the undifferentiated strategy inherently lacks, in order to adjust simultaneously to the mounting pressures for the rationalization of the EC textile industry and to the rapid changes occurring in man-made fiber and blended fabrics.

Strategies of the 1960s

Homogeneous Market	Heterogeneous Market
UNDIFFERENTIATED	CONCENTRATED
Japan Taiwan United Kingdom (largest firms) United States West Germany (majority of larger firms)	Italy (many firms were shifting to this strategy and away from proliferated or differentiated strategies)
PROLIFERATED	DIFFERENTIATED
United Kingdom France*	Netherlands West Germany (minority of larger firms)

Strategies of the 1970s

Homogeneous Market	Heterogeneous Market
UNDIFFERENTIATED	CONCENTRATED
France (larger firms) Japan (through FDI) Taiwan (plans to shift to a differentiated strategy in the 1980s) United Kingdom (larger firms)	Italy (high-value segment)
PROLIFERATED	DIFFERENTIATED
United States (still over-shadowed to some extent by an undifferentiated strategy)	Japan (many segments) Netherlands (few segments) West Germany United Kingdom (recent shift to a low-value segment strategy)

*In the 1960s, France pursued a strategy that emphasized technological superiority.

8.2 Adjustment Strategies of Textile Industries in the 1960s and 1970s

The textile industry of Japan, and eventually Taiwan, had to abandon the undifferentiated strategy because of competitive pressures from new emerging low-cost industries, and increasing protection by the industrialized countries.

The concentrated and differentiated strategies – finding or creating market segments – had provided those industries that adopted them with international viability. The differentiated strategies adopted by West Germany in the 1970s, Italy in both decades and Taiwan for the 1980s emphasized productive flexibility, advanced technology, a marketing orientation and a strong export orientation. Italy and Taiwan also emphasized the development of linkages (cooperative or ownership) with their fiber and end-market sectors.

The Japanese textile industry was unique in its development of a strategy that combined the undifferentiated and differentiated strategies through an internationalization process (South Korea is in the process of adopting a similar strategy). This strategy emphasized the international rationalization of production to gain from lower costs in other emerging industries, productive flexibility, advanced technology, direct linking with other textile sectors (required if internationalization is to be maximized), a marketing orientation and a strong export orientation.

The US industry is the only industry of an industrial country to emerge from the 1970s with a successful undifferentiated strategy. Yet it increasingly adopted a new strategy in the late 1970s as a result of domestic competition. However, unlike other industries that increasingly viewed markets as heterogeneous and therefore catered to specific market segment needs or requirements, the US industry tended to adopt a proliferated strategy, which assumed market homogeneity. While this strategy inherently emphasizes productivity, productive flexibility and advanced technology, it lacks a marketing orientation, a reason for linkage with other textile complex sectors and an export orientation.

The four strategy alternatives used to identify the adjustment strategies of European, Asia Pacific and United States industries result in firms placing differing emphases on various strategy components. This difference in emphasis directly affects the international competitiveness of these industries. The components and the type of emphasis placed on them are shown in Table 8.4.

The four strategies all place considerable emphasis on technology, but for different reasons. The undifferentiated and proliferated strategies emphasize modern and advanced technology in order to increase productivity, fabric quality and the replacement of increasingly costly labor in the production of standardized or undifferentiated fabrics. Since economies of scale are important in the production of

Table 8.4 *Major Strategy Components of Textile Mill Firms and the Influence of Strategy Alternatives*

Strategy component	Homogeneous market-orientation		Heterogeneous market-orientation	
	Undifferentiated strategy	*Proliferated strategy*	*Concentrated strategy*	*Differentiated strategy*
Technology	Technological improvements that reduce costs and/or increase fabric and yarn quality are emphasized: productivity, fabric and yarn defects, and the replacement of labor with capital.		Although the same technological improvements are sought for these strategies, greater emphasis is placed on productive versatility and product diversity in order to be responsive to changes in the needs and/or requirements of market segments.	
Production	Tendency is for textile mills to be large and integrated to gain economies of scale from long production runs.	Tendency for textile mills to be smaller (shorter runs), and have productive versatility.	Tendency is for textile mills and companies to be smaller. The mills are basically emphasizing the production of highly specialized yarns and fabrics of shorter production runs. Diseconomies of scale are generally offset by charging premium prices for products designed to meet specific needs and/or wants. Productive versatility is stressed.	
Marketing & linkage	Major emphasis is placed on price and quality. Market research is used to identify short and intermediate demand changes, and trends in competitors' product offering(s). Little, or no, emphasis is placed on developing relationships with other sectors of the textile complex except as buyers and sellers.		Although price and quality are important, emphasis is on non-price factors. Both market and marketing research are used. Marketing research becomes increasingly more important as the market segment(s) becomes a higher value-added segment(s). Also, direct linkage with other sectors of the textile complex is important to insure an adequate knowledge of the market segment(s) is gained, and the firm's ability to satisfy specific needs and/or requirements is enhanced.	
Strategic planning	Long-term planning is not emphasized. Since demand tends to be stable over time and broad-based, major emphasis is on correcting production for short-term or intermediate-term variations resulting from economic changes or technological changes associated with production. Thus, the planning activity of firms pursuing undifferentiated or proliferated strategies involves short or intermediate time horizons.		Long-term planning is emphasized. Since product offerings cater to specific end-market needs and/or requirements of market segments, a major emphasis is placed on predicting long-term trends in factors that affect these needs and/or requirements and the firm's ability to satisfy them (e.g. demographic changes, end-user technologies, market segment size, competitors' offerings, distribution channels, suppliers). The narrower market-base(s) of concentrated and differentiated strategies necessitates a long-term planning horizon to offset the inherently higher risks associated with these strategies.	

undifferentiated products, mills tend to be large, relatively inflexible, dependent on large volume orders and relatively unresponsive to market changes. Also, textile mill companies pursuing such strategies need not have strong ties with textile machinery manufacturers since their products tend to be stable over time.

The concentrated and differentiated strategies, in contrast, while seeking the same technological advantages of the undifferentiated and proliferated strategies, place considerably more emphasis on productive flexibility and versatility and on the development of new fibers and fabrics. Because the fabrics are differentiated and, of necessity, are developed to meet specific demands, shorter and more varied production runs result, and smaller mills can be used (diseconomies of scale in producing these shorter runs are generally offset by premium prices). In addition, much closer ties are required between textile mill companies pursuing such strategies and textile machinery manufacturers, man-made fiber producers and end-markets.

For example, the increasing dependency of the US textile industry on foreign textile machinery manufacturers (discussed in Chapter 3) is probably due to its later and relatively weaker market-oriented proliferated strategy. Since the textile machinery industries of West Germany, Japan and Switzerland are the major US sources for advanced technology, it can be construed that these industries were responding directly to their indigenous textile industries' earlier adoption of concentrated and differentiated strategies. This is further supported in the Japanese case because of the close ties that exist as a result of the overriding influence of Japanese trading companies. These trading companies are directly involved in marketing textile machinery, textiles and apparel, and act as catalysts in the development of new fibers, fabrics, apparel and textile machinery.

The potential decline in the US textile industry's status as a low-cost producer *vis-à-vis* other major industries that are pursuing highly marketing-oriented strategies suggests that these strategies have greater international viability. The viability arises from the need to invest more heavily not only in modern and advanced technology, but also in manufacturing techniques related to productive flexibility and product diversity. The strategy also appears to stress small–medium-sized firms, which tend to be better industry performers.

The undifferentiated and proliferated strategies place little emphasis on market needs and changes in these needs. As a result, textile mill firms pursuing these strategies tend to be production-oriented and do not develop an in-depth capability for forecasting demand and changes in demand. More importantly, perhaps, they are not responding to fundamental changes that are occurring in the international market place.

The international market place is increasingly being divided into two distinct markets. The first market is for undifferentiated yarns and fabrics, which can only be satisfied with an undifferentiated or mass-market strategy. Yet the comparative advantage for this type of strategy is increasing with the new emerging industries. They have large pools of low-wage labor and have ready access to modern production technologies. The only way that this advantage can be exploited by the high-labor-cost industries of Europe, Asia Pacific and the United States is through an internationalization strategy similar to that adopted by Japan, or by increased protection of domestic markets.

The second market is for differentiated yarns and fabrics. It has grown substantially since World War II, and is partially the result of textile mill firms seeking to become dominant in particular market segments by satisfying the specific needs of these market segments (concentrated or differentiated strategies). However, unlike the homogeneous market approaches of the first market, the success requirements for the heterogeneous market approaches of the second market include: (1) a considerable in-house capability for forecasting future demand (market research); (2) a sophisticated marketing research activity capable of identifying the changing needs of end-users (apparel, home furnishings and industrial), and (3) a close cooperative (if not direct) relationship with man-made fiber producers attuned to end-user needs.

At the present time, the European and mature Asia Pacific industries have a clear and distinct advantage over the US industry in this second market in terms of developing these success requirements. First, their industries are committed to heterogeneous market strategies, whereas the US industry's reaction has been a continued persistence in viewing its markets as homogeneous. As noted in Chapter 7, although the US textile mill executives stressed the need for greater specialization, they were more concerned with improving productivity (i.e. a proliferated approach). Second, the European and Asia Pacific industries have been involved in developing their marketing-oriented strategies for much longer than the US industry, particularly West Germany, Italy and Japan. Third, they have developed close cooperative or direct links with their fiber producers and their apparel manufacturers. This has resulted in a greater sensitivity to the needs of their end-users. For example, the Japanese trading companies have not only played a significant role in expanding and diversifying the market bases of Japanese textile firms, they have also provided an impetus for a stronger marketing orientation. US textile mill companies, in contrast, devote little of their resources to developing such an orientation or capability.

With an increased emphasis on marketing-oriented strategies, the need for long-term, formal and systematic planning is increased. The inherently higher risks associated with such strategies increase the need to be aware of long-term domestic and international trends that will ultimately affect specific market segments, and how they may impact on short- and intermediate-term plans and objectives of the firm. This can only be accomplished by individual firms if a longer time horizon is used.

Conclusions

During the past two decades the textile industries of industrialized countries have undergone varying degrees of adjustment as a result of changes in the competitive environments of their local and international markets. The most profound adjustments occurred in European and Asian industries, and the least noticeable occurred in the US industry.

While the industries of the developed countries of Asia, Europe and the United States had to adjust to increased competition from low-priced, high-volume apparel from low-wage developing countries, the European industries also had to adjust to the redefinition of local markets and the Asian industries to increased market barriers. The US industry had to adjust gradually to changes in its large and diverse domestic market. Three types of strategic response evolved during the 1960s and 1970s.

The strategic responses of the Italian, Japanese, Dutch, Taiwanese and West German industries focused increasingly on a growing international market for differentiated yarns and fabrics. Additionally, the governments of these countries acknowledged that the comparative advantage of producing low-priced, high-volume apparel and textile fabrics was increasingly with low-wage developing countries, and that sectoral adjustment was necessary. Consequently, these governments supported their industries' shift from the production of undifferentiated to differentiated fabrics, encouraged the offshore manufacture of apparel and/or foreign direct investments in apparel production in developing countries, and facilitated the transfer of apparel and textile workers to other growth industries. The textile industries of these countries increased their international competitiveness.

The strategic responses of the French and United Kingdom industries were to retain superiority in the production of undifferentiated fabrics and apparel as a result of technologically induced increases in productivity. Additionally, the governments of these industries actively supported these industry responses by protecting their industries from international competitive trends and shifts in comparative advantage, encouraged consolidation and adopted 'employment maintenance' programs. The international competitiveness of these industries steadily declined during the past two decades.

Finally, the United States industry increasingly focused on a proliferated strategy in response to domestic market changes and competition. Its government, while providing protection from international competitive trends and shifts in comparative advantage, consistently refused to play an active part in the industry's adjustments. The relative, if not absolute, international status of this industry as a world leader in productivity and as a low-cost producer of fabrics and yarns declined during the 1970s and will be seriously challenged in the 1980s.

The challenge posed by low-wage developing countries will persist well into the 1980s, if not into the 1990s. The technological superiority sought by the French and UK industries indicates that technology and modernization are not sufficient to offset the medium-term comparative advantage enjoyed by the third world. The experiences of Japan and Taiwan suggest, however, that this comparative advantage will tend to weaken in the long term as third world countries become more industrialized.

Notwithstanding the advantages third world countries presently have in the production of textiles, particularly apparel, there are strategies available to the textile industries of developed countries that can insure their profitable continuance during the next decade. These 'industry' strategies and their implications for individual firms are discussed in Chapter 9. Also discussed are the implications that international trends and international competition may have for third world countries.

Notes

1 Successful in terms of an ability to compete in foreign markets, even if the ability was not exercised. All of them experienced contraction in terms of employment.
2 An 'industry strategy' is defined as the prevailing or dominant strategy adopted by an industry's larger and 'progressive' firms. It is not meant to imply that all firms within an industry have adopted identical strategies. In addition, some firms may pursue all four strategies at any one time.
3 The discussions of the strategic adjustments undertaken by the West German, French, Italian and UK textile mill products industries draw heavily from Shepherd (1981). Shepherd, however, used a two-way strategy classification system: mass-market strategy and specialization strategy.
4 German provincial governments are loosely equivalent to state governments in the US.

5   The West Germans quickly discovered that the differentiated strategy requires close management attention at the product group level. As a result of the need to be responsive to the changing needs of market segments, each product group acts virtually as an independent firm in marketing, product development and financial control. This has required the building-up of a larger and more sophisticated management team.

6   Between 1973 and 1977, only 10.5 per cent of the 172,000 workers lost to these industries were added to the industries' registered unemployed. In West Germany, workers are classified by the industries in which they work since the industries are required by law to help their unemployed.

7   Government assistance emphasizes investment and employment maintenance.

8   The discussion of the strategic adjustments undertaken by the Japanese industry draws heavily from Arpan, *et al.* (1981).

9   The individual Japanese firms often had little influence because of the number of firms involved in the internationalization process. Individual firms were generally only involved in a small number of projects, many of which were small in scale. Ownership in many joint ventures was minor, and a large number of FDI projects were undertaken by groups of Japanese firms (e.g. fiber firms, spinners and trading companies).

10 The US textile mill industry continues to be concerned about the penetration of the US apparel market, since imported apparel displaces domestically produced apparel fabrics (see Chapter 2).

11 Trade data on Japan's international competitiveness in the 1970s are somewhat misleading since they do not include data on its activities in other Asia Pacific and Latin American markets.

12 The European industries' adjustment in the 1960s and 1970s resulted in national industries becoming specialized in those sectors of the textile industry in which they had comparative advantages. The result generally has been an EC textile industry with efficient national sub-parts. The Taiwanese and Japanese industries are undergoing a similar process in the Asia Pacific area.

9

Future Challenges and Responses

Introduction

The 1980s cannot be expected to provide the same economic and political conditions for the global textile mill products industry that the 1960s and 1970s did. These two decades were decades of adjustment for the industry at the national and global levels as a result of many interrelated events including the formation of regional economic and political blocs (e.g. the European Community), the general acceptance of 'orderly market arrangements' (e.g. the Long Term Arrangement Regarding International Trade in Cotton Textiles and the Multi-fiber Arrangement) by the developed nations, and the emergence of new, export-oriented textile industries in many developing nations. Events such as these have resulted in a global industry in which the industries of developed and developing nations are inextricably interwoven. The actions of individual firms and governments affect and are affected by the actions of other firms and foreign governments. The 1980s therefore will be a decade during which individual firms will be required to become increasingly sensitive and responsive to what is occurring within the global industry and what both domestic *and* foreign firms and governments are planning and doing.

This chapter is divided into two major parts. The first part presents an assessment of the future challenges confronting national textile mill products industries and individual firms. The second part discusses various options available to firms in both developed and developing countries.

Future Challenges

Chapters 2–8 have described the major structure and dynamics of the global textile mill products industry, the major problems these dynamics have posed for firms, and how a number of firms have reacted.

Although generalization is difficult and dangerous, the evidence presented in this book suggests that the following trends and changes occurred in the past two decades.

(1) The nature, degree and complexity of competition within the textile mill products industry increased internationally and will intensify in the future, particularly as national industries and individual competitors increase their efforts to position themselves in world markets rather than in domestic markets.

(2) A major weakness of the textile mill products industries of developed countries was their dependence on fragmented, relatively high-cost, labor-intensive and low-profit domestic apparel industries for a major portion of their outputs. This dependency increasingly became a strategic weakness as the apparel industries of developing countries became more sophisticated internationally. The comparative advantages enjoyed by developing countries because of lower labor costs, augmented by the rapid and relatively easy transfer of apparel manufacturing technology, proved to be superior to the productivity gains of the textile mill products industries of developed countries (see Chapter 8 – France and the United Kingdom).

(3) Changes in technology accelerated rapidly, primarily in the form of textile manufacturing equipment (for yarns and fabric forming, dyeing, printing and finishing) and fiber combinations. The international diffusion of technology also accelerated, and increasingly emanated from firms based in Europe and Asia. There was also increasing emphasis on technologies related to global market-positioning strategies (e.g. production flexibility and short production runs).

(4) Most governments became more actively involved in their textile complexes. The essential focus in the developed countries was on policies of higher non-tariff protection and industry restructuring, and in the developing countries on rapid textile-complex development, often accompanied by import substitution and export-development policies. Also, the industry restructuring/rationalization policies of many European governments (notably West Germany and the Netherlands) appeared to be based on the assumption of increased future trade liberalization, and on their need to transfer resources into higher-growth, higher-profit, more internationally competitive industries.[1]

(5) The international competitive effects of these changes on the textile industries of various countries were highly mixed. There was explosive growth in the Asia Pacific area (although Japan's domestic employment and number of firms contracted), in contrast to significant contraction in employment and firms in Europe with a general decline in international competitiveness (with the exception of West

Germany and Italy). In the United States, the textile industry generally increased its international competitiveness, although it too experienced reductions in total employment and the number of firms in the industry.

(6) Individual corporate strategies were equally varied. The larger Asia Pacific firms aggressively moved internationally, particularly within the Asia Pacific area by investing (e.g. Taiwan, Indonesia, Thailand), and all over the world via exporting. While most smaller European firms tried unsuccessfully to retrench in protected domestic markets, the larger ones moved towards positioning themselves in global markets. Most US firms followed product-proliferation strategies oriented towards their domestic market (with greater success than many European firms had because of the size of the domestic market) and experienced some increase in export activity. However, the latter effect resulted largely from a generally weakening dollar exchange value.

These six trends suggest that the textile mill products industries of both developed and developing countries face critical challenges in the 1980s:

(1) competition on the global and national levels will become even more intense;
(2) past corporate strategies may not be sufficient to guarantee success in the future; and
(3) increased government intervention in national textile complexes will probably occur.

The remainder of this section identifies some of the major, more general, factors that need to be taken into account by textile mill companies when formulating future strategies.

I *The worldwide textile mill products industry is becoming a global industry with national industries specializing (to the extent that government policy permits) in those sectors in which they enjoy comparative advantages.*

It has become increasingly clear that the 'shakeout', contraction and modernization of the European industries were part of a rationalization process that started shortly after the formation of the EC. Those industries that participated voluntarily in this rationalization process with the encouragement of their governments (notably the industries of West Germany and the Netherlands and the private sector of the Italian industry) have stabilized and are sufficiently competitive in specialized sectors on an international scale to survive further trade liberalization. Consequently, the governments of these industries can be expected to support further trade liberalization, probably in specific sectors. Those industries that did not participate in the rationalization process and that were comparatively more protected from regional and international competitive trends (notably the industries of France and the United Kingdom) as a result of government policy such as labor maintenance incentives have not become internationally competitive. They have not yet identified viable comparative advantages or become sufficiently specialized to survive further trade liberalization. Their governments can be expected to resist further liberalization in textiles by GATT.[2]

The major textile mill products industries of the Asia Pacific area (e.g. Japan, Taiwan, Hong Kong and South Korea) are well along in the implementation of their internationally oriented rationalization programs. In general, these programs recognize and accept the realities of international and domestic trends, particularly the continuing shift in comparative advantage in high-volume, low-cost textile and apparel products to lower-labor-cost developing countries and the escalation in domestic costs. With the close support of their governments, these industries are positioning themselves in high-value, low-volume segments of the world's textile markets. Japan and South Korea are also exploiting the comparative advantage of the developing countries through direct investments and contractual arrangements. These long-term programs will result in an intensification of competition in the differentiated markets sought after by European industries.

Primarily because of the size and diversity of its domestic market, the United States' textile mill products industry has lagged the European and Asia Pacific industries in positioning itself in world markets. However, some specialization has occurred and can be expected to continue in reaction to domestic and international market trends.

II   *The apparel industries of developed countries are increasingly at a distinct disadvantage* vis-à-vis *the apparel industries of developing countries and therefore pose a growing threat to the textile mill products industries of developed countries.*

Most of the apparel firms in the developed countries have not been able to respond competitively to the threat posed by the apparel industries of the developing countries. Developed countries' industries remain comprised of small, poorly resourced firms, and technological breakthroughs that would increase productivity sufficiently to offset the comparative advantage of low-wage industries have not materialized. As a result, the textile mill products industries of the developed countries are dependent on domestic apparel fabric markets that are increasingly vulnerable to foreign competition in the form of finished apparel and apparel accessories.

The textile mill products industries of the developed countries responded to this growing threat in different ways. While all of them responded by gaining the support of their governments for orderly market arrangements (e.g. MFA), their competitive reactions have been mixed. To secure markets for apparel fabrics and yarns, the Japanese and South Korean industries have by-passed (to some extent) their domestic apparel industries by investing in and contracting with apparel industries of developing countries – primarily in the Asia Pacific area. The West German and Dutch industries, utilizing a tariff provision that permits the export of *uncut* fabric for additional work (cutting and sewing) and the importation of finished apparel with duty paid only on the value-added overseas, have increasingly sought apparel manufacturers in other, lower-cost countries (notably Eastern Europe). The United States industry has been unable to take advantage of lower-cost, offshore apparel manufacturers, partly because of a dearth of international experience and partly due to the lack of a tariff provision similar to those utilized by European industries. The US tariff provision provides only for the exportation of *cut* fabric for additional work overseas. As a result, the US textile mill industry is still heavily dependent upon its domestic apparel industry.

III   *Demand for textile mill products (primarily apparel fabrics and yarns) is growing at a slower rate in developed countries than in other parts of the world.*

In addition to the threat posed by foreign apparel producers, the textile mill products industries of the developed countries are also faced with saturated domestic apparel markets. These markets are no longer growing at rates that exceed the growth rates of their populations. As a result, competition can be expected to intensify as firms seek market share at the expense of their domestic and foreign competitors.

The growth markets are increasingly to be found in other parts of the world, such as the centrally planned, Latin American and Near Eastern countries. These markets, however, are heavily protected.

IV   *International markets for textile mill products are increasingly being divided into two distinct markets: undifferentiated and differentiated yarns and fabrics.*

As noted in Chapter 8, the global market for apparel yarns and fabrics is being divided increasingly into two distinct markets requiring different strategies and competitive advantages. The first market is for basic yarns and fabrics, which can best be satisfied with an undifferentiated or mass-market strategy. Yet the comparative advantage for this type of strategy lies increasingly with the new emerging textile industries in developing countries. They have large pools of low-wage labor and ready access to modern production technology, and their outputs go to local, low-wage apparel industries that are strongly export-oriented.

The second market is for specialized yarns and fabrics. It has grown substantially since World War II, and is the combined result of textile mill products firms seeking to become dominant in specific market segments, and the growing sophistication of apparel markets in developed countries. The comparative advantage for this second market is with those industries that are closely linked to man-made fibers industries, can utilize advanced fabric forming and finishing technologies, have ready access to affluent markets and are experienced in marketing and international business, i.e. the industries of the developed countries.

Two additional and somewhat differentiated markets that are still in the process of being developed are the home furnishings and industrial goods markets. These markets are already quite substantial in the United States, and can be expected to grow sequentially first in Europe and then other parts of the world.[3] The industries of the developed countries have a distinct advantage over new emerging industries in these markets since the home furnishings market is a relatively small order-lot market, and the industrial goods markets require a close relationship between the textile mill products firm and a broad-based industrial sector to provide volume production.

V *Newly formed textile mill products industries follow a multi-stage 'industry' cycle as they develop.*
The experiences of Japan, South Korea and Taiwan suggest that the new emerging textile mill products industries of developing countries eventually lose most of their international advantage in the production of undifferentiated textile mill products. In many developing countries, the sequential and backward development of a textile complex (i.e. the development first of an apparel industry, then of a closely linked textile mill products industry, and finally of a man-made fibers industry) is part of an economic program to develop an industrial economy. As the industrialization program progresses, the internal competition for labor among industries results in the escalation of wages, thus reducing the country's comparative advantage in apparel manufactures. This in turn weakens the domestic market for textile mill products and strategic adjustment is required. In the cases of Japan, South Korea and Taiwan, this loss in comparative advantage to other Asia Pacific countries began to occur after approximately ten to

fifteen years. The time for eventual loss of comparative advantage is dependent upon the developing countries' ability to finance and support the technologies required of alternative industries, and on their ability to learn the manufacturing and marketing techniques of labor-intensive industries.

VI   *Technological innovation is increasingly available to the textile mill products industries of all nations but is concurrently placing increasing financial and training burdens on individual firms.*

Although the rate of technology innovation accelerated during the past two decades, the rate of technology diffusion also increased sharply, both domestically and internationally. These two trends place additional burdens on individual firms. Not only are they confronted with increased competition in the market place that requires new skills and management techniques, they must also find the financial resources necessary to purchase increasingly costly equipment and train their production workers in the use of this equipment. The problem is further accentuated because of the rapid obsolescence of the equipment.

VII   *Government intervention can be expected to increase in the near term, because of employment and foreign exchange issues.*

The textile mill products and apparel industries in virtually all countries provide employment for significant portions of their labor forces. In addition, the developing countries rely on these industries to generate the foreign exchange needed for their industrialization programs. These industries therefore are important both economically and politically to individual countries.

Global experiences and trends suggest that governments will continue to play important roles in molding and influencing the international competitiveness of the global textile mill products industry. Furthermore, in the past two decades four industry policy models appear to have been used by the governments of developed countries: (1) passive (protectionistic) policy; (2) internally focused structural-adjustment policy; (3) internationally focused structural-adjustment policy; and (4) internationalization policy. These policy models can be expected to influence government action for at least the next decade. The combination of policy models selected by a particular government is dependent on indigenous social, cultural, political and economic factors.

In general, a passive industry policy is a policy of providing a specific industry with protection from international competitive trends while other industry policies and programs take effect (e.g. tariffs, quotas, non-tariff barriers). While all governments adopted protectionistic policies for their textile mill products industries during the 1960s and 1970s, the United States government seemed to be the only government that did not couple this policy with one of the other policy types. Instead, it preferred to let internal, partially protected market forces bring about adjustment. It persistently opposed the concept of direct government intervention of the types undertaken by its counterparts in Europe and the Asia Pacific region. It was also reluctant to develop and implement comparable government-sponsored assistance programs for the retraining of workers displaced as a result of international shifts in comparative advantage.

An internally focused structural-adjustment policy is an industry-specific policy providing incentives and assistance programs designed to encourage the restructuring of the industry along predetermined lines to meet international competition in *domestic* markets, not *foreign* markets. The policy is generally coupled to a protective industry policy in order to provide the time necessary for the adjustment to take effect. The evidence presented in other chapters suggests, however, that the structural adjustment does not always result in an industry capable of competing in an unprotected domestic market. As a result, there is continuing pressure for the protective industry policy to become a permanent part of the government's overall policy for the targeted industry. The governments of France and the United Kingdom adopted such an industry policy during the 1960s and 1970s.

The internationally focused structural-adjustment policy is an industry-specific policy that provides incentives and assistance programs designed to encourage the restructuring of the industry to meet international competition in both *domestic* and *foreign* markets. Unlike the first two policy models, it recognizes international shifts in comparative advantage and provides for the transfer of displaced workers to other growth industries. In addition, its use of a protective industry policy is considered 'temporary', since competition in an eventually open international market place is of paramount importance. The governments of West Germany and the Netherlands adopted this industry policy during the 1970s. The Taiwanese government seems to have adopted this policy for the 1980s.

The internationalization industry policy has been adopted by the Japanese and South Korean governments. The policies, incentives and programs provided by these governments are designed to encourage and assist their industries to relocate labor-intensive production to developing countries with labor-cost advantages. Since these governments also use protective industry policies to protect their domestic markets, the industries will continue to be aggressive competitors in the markets of developed countries, to have access to the markets of developing countries, and to have protected domestic markets.

Future Responses

Global trends in the textile mill products industry indicate that textile mill companies can no longer develop corporate strategies that ignore, or that only tacitly accept, international developments. Future competitive strategies must be based on the industry's global environment, on trends in this environment and on a careful assessment of the firm's strengths and weaknesses.

Within the past two decades, the textile mill products industry has become global in scope, and includes national industries at different stages of growth, maturity and decline. National industries have adopted 'industry' strategies that emphasize comparative advantages while minimizing weaknesses. Governments have become inextricably involved in molding the competitive environment in which firms find themselves as a result of international trade agreements and domestic adjustment-assistance programs. Also, growth in demand for textile mill products is shifting from developed countries to developing countries and is being increasingly satisfied by local production.

Furthermore, the planning horizon selected for the strategic planning process has become more critical. The planning period needs to be long enough to include the analysis of long-term international trends, yet short enough to be of realistic and pragmatic value. West German and Japanese firms appear to have adopted ten-year planning cycles. Less internationally oriented firms (e.g. US firms) are still using two- or three-year cycles. Both planning cycles are useful. The intermediate planning cycle (two–three year) is certainly appropriate for addressing strategy decisions related to technological and fashion trends. The long-term planning cycle (ten-year) is more appropriate for corporate positioning decisions that require an assessment of future challenges and competitors and the development of resources to compete.

It is difficult to recommend corporate strategies that are equally appropriate for firms indigenous to several national industries. Firms have different capabilities and operate in different sub-markets. They are also strongly influenced by the corporate strategies developed by their immediate competitors, and are constrained to varying degrees by the structure of their indigenous industries and their national economic and political environments.

As a result, the following strategy alternatives are subdivided into two major groups by national characteristics. The first set of strategy alternatives is for firms in developing countries. The second set of strategy alternatives is for firms in developed countries. However, the alternatives within the two groups are general strategies and are not mutually exclusive. Firms should pursue as many of them as is feasible, appropriate and within their long-term mission, objectives and ability to generate necessary resources.

Strategy Options for Developing Countries
Developing countries have a distinct advantage in the manufacture of 'mass-market' textile mill products (e.g. high-volume, low-cost fabrics and yarns). They also have access to local, generally well-protected, high-growth apparel markets and to local apparel industries having a comparative advantage in the manufacture of 'mass-market' apparel and apparel accessories destined for developed countries (e.g. undergarments, children's wear, less fashion-sensitive shirts and blouses). However, the textile mill industries of developing countries are faced with strong and increasing protectionistic sentiments in the markets of the developed countries, with demands for more 'orderly' growth in their trade of textiles and apparel, and, in some foreign markets, with a poor-quality image. They also must be eventually responsive to wage escalations as other industries develop and compete for labor.

There are six general strategies that address these advantages and disadvantages.

(1) *Accelerate the transfer of textile mill manufacturing technology.*
   (a) At the corporate level this can be accomplished through an upgrading of equipment using internally generated capital, government loans or contractual arrangements or joint ventures with foreign firms. (An advantage of the third alternative is an expansion of product offerings.) Technology should probably be aimed at upgrading quality, increasing productivity and providing fabrics and yarns that meet the specifications and standards of foreign markets (e.g. width).
   (b) Trade associations can play vital roles in the transfer of technology. They can create technology information collection and dissemination centers and become catalysts in the formation of R&D projects.
   (c) Governments should investigate the feasibility of providing incentives designed to accelerate the acquisition of modern textile technology (e.g. loans and preferential exchange rates for the purchase of equipment, training programs and relief from joint-venture restrictions). They should also consider the development of joint technology research centers with other regional governments when

local market potentials are too small (e.g. South America, Central America).

(2)   *Increase market and marketing research efforts in foreign markets.*

    (a)   Individual firms need to increase their market and marketing research efforts in foreign markets to insure their outputs meet the needs of these markets. This can be done by establishing or expanding sales offices in major markets and developing information systems for monitoring and surveying these markets.

    (b)   Industry associations should become more actively involved in collecting and disseminating such market information. This information should be increasingly focused on sub-markets and be coordinated with the long-term plans of their members.

(3)   *Improve product quality and the quality image of the industry and individual firms.*

Long-term improvements in quality image cannot be achieved without real improvements in product quality. The two activities must be coordinated.

    (a)   Individual firms need to increase efforts at improving the quality of their product lines (commensurate with price) and possibly participate in cooperative image-building activities with their trade associations.

    (b)   Trade associations should undertake image-building activities in foreign markets. These activities should possibly include the apparel industry. However, the activities need to be closely tied to actual quality improvements.

(4)   *Forge close ties with apparel manufacturers and retailers.*

    (a)   Individual textile mill firms need to exploit the comparative advantage of their indigenous apparel industry by cooperating with and assisting their major buyers to improve quality, production and product (fabrics). They may also be in a position to enter into joint ventures, to provide loans and to assist in end-market research.

    (b)   Trade associations should investigate the feasibility of developing joint assistance programs with apparel producers' trade associations that focus on (1) the improvement of quality, (2) the development of market information, and (3) the development of management skills.

(5)   *Develop strategies for gaining market access to the markets of foreign countries.*

In addition to government-level negotiations, individual firms need to expend considerably more time on developing strategies for penetrating the markets of developed countries and other developing countries. This can be achieved with the assistance of textile mill firms in other countries through contractual arrangements that coordinate complementary products used for apparel (e.g. suiting and lining fabrics). As textile mill companies in developed countries become more specialized, many cooperative arrangements combining special and basic fabrics will probably arise.

(6) *Adopt intermediate- and long-term strategic planning processes.* The experiences of Japan, Hong Kong, Taiwan and South Korea suggest that the textile industries and governments of developing countries need to undertake intermediate- and long-term strategic planning that recognizes the eventual loss of comparative advantage. Possible long-term alternatives include:
   (a) Eventual overseas investments in other developing countries and contractual arrangements with firms in these countries:
   (b) Diversification into non-textile business; and
   (c) A gradual reduction in emphasis on apparel manufactures and exports and increasing emphasis on, first, home furnishings and then industrial goods.

Strategy Options for Developed Countries
Textile mill firms in the developed countries have an advantage in the acquisition of increasingly advanced technology and in influencing the future direction of technology innovation because of their proximity to textile machinery manufacturers. Larger and more progressive firms also have the managerial resources to develop the skills necessary for the development of and marketing of specialized fabrics and yarns. All firms have access to their respective affluent and sophisticated apparel, home furnishings and industrial markets, and to those apparel industries capable of manufacturing high-fashion apparel and apparel accessories. However, they face strong competition in basic fabrics and yarns because of the comparative advantages of developing countries, especially in labor costs. They also are faced with relatively slower market growth rates than in other markets, and those other growth markets are generally well protected.

The following eight general corporate strategy recommendations address these and other trends:

(1) *Place increased emphasis on specialized apparel fabrics and re-evaluate all apparel fabric offerings more frequently, using end-market research and market positioning techniques.*
Apparel output and hence fabric purchases will continue to

grow in the markets of the developed countries. However, they are not likely to grow at rates comparable to the demand for home furnishings and industrial fabrics.

This suggests that many of the future opportunities for national textile industries will be in non-apparel fabrics. And if apparel imports capture continually larger shares of domestic markets (which most experts agree will occur unless import restrictions are increased), the demand for many apparel fabrics will grow even more slowly and, in some cases, even decline. In the process, competition is expected to become more acute.

There will remain for the future a high, absolute level of local demand for most apparel, and there will remain a demand for certain quantities of select apparel fabrics, primarily for those fabrics used in higher-fashion and price-point apparel. Fabrics with good quality, comfort, aesthetic and easy care properties move in local market segments that textile mill firms can exploit and defend successfully.

In addition, the lack of international business sophistication of many apparel producers makes them unaware of, or unable to purchase, better-quality or lower-priced apparel fabric from abroad. Such firms will continue to buy most of their fabric locally, creating another market segment for local textile mill firms. Finally, the greater supply uncertainty of imports and greater customer service capabilities of local suppliers will also create defendable market segments.

(2) *Increase corporate focus on foreign markets and operations.*
The greatest future growth in demand for apparel fabrics (and perhaps all fabrics combined) is expected to occur *outside* the developed countries. Exponentially rising production and consumption of apparel in developing countries will create increased demand for apparel fabrics. Participation by textile firms in the developed countries in these high-growth foreign markets is therefore essential for many firms' growth, if not survival.

Some of this demand can be supplied by exports, but import-substitution policies of most developing countries, transportation costs and the volatility of exchange rates lessen this export potential. Therefore, to tap this foreign demand effectively, firms may need to invest in foreign production facilities or enter into joint ventures with foreign textile mill firms. Establishing foreign production facilities can permit better access to foreign markets. It can also create a 'corporate presence' in foreign markets that can then be used to help export other products (e.g. more specialized fabrics and yarns). Firms with strong brand-name lines, specialized fabric expertise and/or production technology have advantages that are attractive to textile firms in these markets.

(3) *Place increased effort on reducing production cost or enhancing product features.*

Reducing production costs permits more competitive pricing. For products that are basically undifferentiated and sold in the mass market (e.g. grey goods), it is a major way to compete successfully. The cost-reduction strategy requires the utilization of new production technology and know-how in the domestic market, or the movement of some production abroad to lower-cost countries. It also requires investment in human capital and working conditions (along the lines suggested below in Strategy 4).

On the other hand, enhancing product features (e.g. fabric quality, cleanability, durability, width) allows the firm to compete on *other than just a price basis*, and in specialized markets, even though pricing almost always remains important. With lower-priced textile mill products always threatened by foreign competitors and even domestic competitors, competing on a non-price basis can reduce competition and improve profitability and competitiveness. (As was mentioned earlier in this book, the Japanese have successfully followed this product-feature strategy, as have most of the more successful US and European firms.) The product-feature enhancement strategy requires the marketing (customer-oriented) orientation that will be described below in Strategy 5.

(4) *Increase investment in human capital and working conditions.*

Increased investment in new plant and equipment alone will probably not prove successful, and in some cases may even prove disastrous. Increased productivity, a key to increased competitiveness, requires more than just new machines. It also requires attention to the machine–operator interface, and the general attitude and skills of the workforce. If workers are not happy with their jobs (pay, benefits, working conditions and general treatment), they will not be productive or stay on the job. In addition, potentially productive workers will not seek jobs in the industry.

Specific recommendations include:

(a) Continue to invest in new equipment and processes that make textile plants a safer place to work.

(b) Recognize the implications of the changing demographics of the textile labor force and their related psychological needs, and accordingly change current industrial relations practices, e.g. more worker involvement in decision-making and planning (Williams, 1981; Barnett, 1981; DeNisi et al., 1981).

(c) Increase employee training at all levels of the firm. Concentrate particularly on: technical skills of production workers; management, marketing and financial skills of higher-level managers (including international aspects of these areas); and supervisory skills of middle managers.

(d) Improve the textile industry's public image as a safe, challenging and rewarding place to work for all levels of employees by implementing the above strategies and properly communicating these changes to the public.

(5) *Significantly increase the resources (time, money and personnel) devoted to marketing research and to developing marketing sophistication.*

The dynamics of competition and end-use markets are increasingly complex and more rapid. While this is most true for apparel fabrics, it is generally true for all fabrics. New applications for existing fabrics, new fiber combinations, new production technologies, new competitors and changing consumer needs and preferences constantly open up some markets and close others. Producers of textile mill products must better anticipate such changes if they are to increase their competitiveness. In short, the industries of the developed countries need more marketing sophistication. The evidence presented in this book indicates that the acquisition of this sophistication is essential for long-run viability. The following suggestions are directed at ways and means for textile companies to enhance their competitiveness by becoming more sophisticated marketers:

(a) Develop greater customer orientation rather than a product or production orientation. In other words, corporate activities should be based more on identifying and servicing customer needs rather than on what the company has production capability to do.

(b) Establish a formal marketing staff to provide both market and marketing research. As was also pointed out in Chapter 7, many textile firms do not have formal marketing staffs of any size, and concentrate on market research rather than on marketing research.

(c) Direct marketing strategies toward achieving long-term growth in well-defined market segments. For example, orient future activity not toward the entire home furnishings market, but toward specific price/quality segments within the home furnishings market.

(d) Develop better and more frequent methods of assessing how efficient and effective the firm's marketing efforts are, including its advertising, sales force, distribution and, if appropriate, merchandizing. Market information feedback is a critical yet often neglected function of textile company management and needs significant improvement.

(e) Establish a 'vice-president of marketing' position to co-ordinate all marketing activities and to elevate this activity to a level of importance commensurate with other functions thereby ensuring marketing policy impact at the highest level.

(6) *Increase emphasis on customer service.*

A major competitive advantage a firm can possess, particularly over foreign firms, is better customer service. Better service includes making modifications desired by customers in order lots, delivering, return policies, reorder provisions, quality levels, color, packaging, and so forth. Better service also requires working more closely with customers, which necessitates more time and effort. It can also encompass sharing marketing information with customers about new product plans, or joint plan development. While such modifications may increase the suppliers' cost, often the customer will be willing to pay a higher price for the better service, or will become a more dependable (captive) customer. Either result can provide the firm with a competitive edge in an increasingly competitive market. As was pointed out in Chapters 7 and 8, the Japanese firms have devoted considerable effort to this 'service' strategy, including providing equity capital and loans to their customers.

(7) *Initiate joint technology and marketing research efforts with firms that are their suppliers and/or customers, such as those in the fiber, equipment and apparel industries.*

Closer cooperation among firms in the major segments of the textile complex would mutually prove beneficial, particularly in the R&D and marketing research areas (possibly basic research and/or the identification of future research areas). In addition, cooperative efforts reduce the cost of such activities for each participant firm. The vertical integration of the Japanese complex currently provides such advantages for their firms. However, their ownership integration strategy would not have to be followed by firms of other countries if joint projects were undertaken instead.

While there may be some legal implications in some countries of cooperative efforts, there may also be a case for government sponsorship of such projects. Seeking such government sponsorship should also be considered a corporate strategy. There may also be some corporate risks involved in terms of sharing R&D and marketing research information. Yet the risks of not doing so may be even greater: namely, a decline in international competitiveness for a particular country's complex that would not be beneficial for any firm in the complex.

(8) *Implement better strategic planning and management.*
Virtually everything discussed in this book has shown the need for a strengthening of strategic planning and management and that many textile firms devote insufficient effort to them. While the day-to-day competitive pressures are significant, they will increase in the future if more effort today is not allocated to developing future strategy and the resources that will be needed to achieve it. Strengthened strategic planning will require a proper blending of all the previously discussed strategies in light of each firm's relative capabilities, its current market position and the trends in each market segment of the industry in which it expects to operate.

Conclusions

The challenges confronting the textile mill products industries of all countries are indicative of a global industry undergoing fundamental change. Technological innovation is accelerating, government intervention is increasing, production is becoming more capital intensive and growth in demand is shifting from the developed to the developing countries. Consequently, the adjustment strategies selected and implemented by national industries, governments and individual firms will be critical to their long-term competitiveness, even their survival.

Some industries and firms have responded competitively to these challenges, others have only reacted. It is still too early to pass judgement on the merits of the various adjustment strategies identified in this study. However, the experiences of France and the United Kingdom on the one hand, and those of West Germany, Italy, Japan, the Netherlands and Taiwan on the other, suggest that future strategies must be aimed at developing an international competitiveness, not just an internally focused domestic competitiveness. Even the US industry, which is unique because of its large domestic market, is beginning to show signs of lagging the more internationally oriented industries in its ability to remain internationally competitive.

However, the role that government has played in the success of particular industries to remain competitive is somewhat difficult to assess. The governments of Japan and Taiwan have been deeply involved in the adjustment processes of their textile industries. The governments of West Germany, Italy and the Netherlands, on the other hand, have preferred to let market forces and shifts in comparative advantage (to the extent permitted by the MFA) influence individual corporate adjustments. Their roles appear to have been to provide the time necessary for the adjustment to occur, and to assist in the transfer of displaced workers to other growth industries, particularly in the cases of West Germany and the Netherlands. It is probably safe to say that the two approaches reflect cultural and social differences between European and Asian countries. Notwithstanding these differences, a continuing 'shakeout' of the textile industries in developed countries can be expected, and this will place additional pressures on governments to participate actively in the transfer of workers to more profitable and internationally competitive industries.

The industries of the developing countries are faced with adjusting to competitive challenges that are somewhat different from those of the developed countries. They must contend with increasing protectionistic sentiments and, if the experiences of Japan and Taiwan can be generalized, they must eventually come to grips with a decline in their comparative advantage in the production of high-volume, low-cost textiles and apparel.

The strategy recommendations set forth in this chapter are general strategy recommendations. We believe that, if they are made the basis of more specific strategies that are tailored to the needs and resources of particular industries and firms, a more efficient and competitive global industry will be the result. And such an industry will be of ultimate benefit to the peoples of the world.

Notes

1 As noted in Chapter 8, the European industries' adjustments in the 1960s and 1970s resulted in national industries becoming specialized in those sectors of the EC textile industry in which they had comparative advantages. The result has been an EC textile industry with efficient national sub-parts.

2 See GATT (1982). This document notes that trade in textiles and clothing continues to be treated under an Agreement that is a major derogation from the General Agreement, and that it is necessary

> . . . to examine ways and means of, and to pursue measures aimed at, liberalizing trade in textiles and clothing, including the eventual application of the General Agreement, after the expiry of the 1981 Protocol extending the

Arrangement Regarding International Trade in Textiles [MFA], it being understood that in the interim the parties to the Arrangement shall adhere strictly to its rules.

3   See Wells (1968), pp. 1–6, for an explanation of the concept.

Appendix 1   Definition of the Textile Mill Products Industry

The definition of the textile industry used in this book is the one given by the US Office of Management and Budget (1972). This definition is synonymous with textile mill products. Quoted below is part of this definition for textile mill products:

Standard Industrial Classification
Major Group 22 (SIC 22)

This major group includes establishments engaged in performing any of the following operations: (1) preparation of fiber and subsequent manufacturing of yarn, thread, braids, twine, and cordage; (2) manufacturing broad woven fabrics, narrow woven fabric, knit fabric, and carpets and rugs from yarn; (3) dyeing and finishing fiber, yarn, fabric, and knit apparel; (4) coating, waterproofing, or otherwise treating fabric; (5) the integrated manufacture of knit apparel and other finished articles from yarn; and, (6) the manufacture of felt goods, lace goods, non-woven fabrics, and miscellaneous textiles.

Broad Woven Fabric Mills, Cotton – Group No. 221
Broad Woven Fabric Mills, Cotton – Industry No. 2211
    Establishments primarily engaged in weaving fabrics over 12 inches in width wholly or chiefly by weight of cotton.

These establishments manufacture many types of fabrics, including broadcloth, denims, duck, flannels, gauze, ginghams, muslin, percale, print cloths, shirting fabrics, towels and toweling, and yarn-dyed fabrics.

Broad Woven Fabric Mills, Man-Made Fiber and Silk – Group No. 222
Broad Woven Fabric Mills, Man-Made Fiber and Silk – Industry No. 2221
    Establishments primarily engaged in weaving fabrics over 12 inches in width, wholly or chiefly by weight of silk and man-made fibers including glass.

The fabrics produced in these establishments include automotive, bedspreads, draperies and drapery, pile, poplin, shirting, suiting, twills, underwear and velvets.

Broad Woven Fabric Mills, Wool (Including Dyeing and Finishing) – Group No. 223
Broad Woven Fabric Mills, Wool (Including Dyeing and Finishing) – Industry No. 2231
    Establishments primarily engaged in weaving fabrics over 12 inches in width, wholly or chiefly by weight of wool, mohair, or similar animal

fibers; those dyeing and finishing all woven wool fabrics or dyeing wool, tops or yarn; and those shrinking and sponging wool goods for the trade.

Mills in this category produce many fabrics including blankets and blanketings, felts, napping, overcoatings, raw stock dyeing and finishing, suitings, upholstery, worsted, and yarn bleaching, dyeing and finishing.

Narrow Fabrics and Other Smallwares Mills: Cotton, Wool, Silk and Man-Made Fiber – Group No. 224

Narrow Fabrics and Other Smallwares Mills: Cotton, Wool, Silk and Man-Made Fiber – Industry No. 2241

Establishments primarily engaged in weaving or braiding fabrics 12 inches or narrower in width of cotton, wool, silk, and man-made fibers, including glass fibers. Establishments primarily engaged in producing fabric covered elastic yarn or thread are also included in this industry.

Fabrics produced in these establishments include beltings, braids, cords, insulating tapes and braids, labels, laces, ribbons, webbing and zipper tape.

Knitting Mills – Group No. 225

This group includes three types of organizations which operate in the knitting mill industry: (1) the 'integrated' mill which purchases materials, produces textiles and related articles within the establishment, and sells the finishing products; (2) the 'contract' or 'commission' mill which processes materials owned by others; and (3) establishments commonly known as jobbers or converters of knit goods which perform the entrepreneurial functions of a manufacturing company, such as buying the raw material, designing and preparing samples, and assigning yarn to others for knitting products on their account.

Women's Full Length and Knee Length Hosiery – Industry No. 2251

Establishments primarily engaged in knitting, dyeing, or finishing women's and misses' full length and knee length hosiery, both seamless and full-fashioned, and panty hose.

Hosiery, Except Women's Full Length and Knee Length Hosiery – Industry No. 2252

Establishments primarily engaged in knitting, dyeing, or finishing hosiery except women's and misses' full length and knee length seamless and full-fashioned hosiery and panty hose.

Items included in this category are anklets and infants', children's, men's, boys' and girls' hosiery and socks.

Knit Outerwear Mills – Industry No. 2253

Establishments primarily engaged in knitting outerwear from knit fabric produced in the same establishment. Establishments primarily engaged in hand knitting outerwear for the trade are included in this industry.

For these establishments the fabrics listed include apparel, beachwear, blouses, dresses, jerseys and sweaters, shirts, slacks and suits.

Knit Underwear Mills – Industry No. 2254
Establishments primarily engaged in knitting underwear and nightwear from yarn, or in manufacturing underwear and nightwear from fabric produced in the same establishment.

Circular Knit Fabric Mills – Industry No. 2257
Establishments primarily engaged in knitting circular (tubular) fabric, or in dyeing or finishing circular (tubular) knit fabric.

Warp Knit Fabric Mills – Industry No. 2258
Establishments primarily engaged in knitting warp (flat fabric), or in dyeing or finishing warp (flat) knit fabric.

Fabrics produced by these mills include lace, mosquito netting, pile fabrics and tricot fabrics.

Knitting Mills, Not Elsewhere Classified – Industry No. 2259
Establishments primarily engaged in knitting gloves and other articles, not elsewhere classified.

In addition to gloves, the output of these mills includes bags and bagging, bedspreads, curtains, dishcloths, stockinette, towels and washcloths.

*Dyeing and Finishing Textiles, Except Wool Fabrics and Knit Goods –
Group No. 226*
Finishers of Broad Woven Fabrics of Cotton – Industry No. 2261
Establishments primarily engaged in finishing cotton broad woven fabrics, or finishing such fabrics on a commission basis.

These finishing operations include bleaching, dyeing, printing (roller, screen, flock, plisse), and other mechanical finishing such as preshrinking, calendering, and napping. This industry also includes the shrinking and sponging of cloth for the trade, and chemical finishing for water repellency, fire resistance, and mildew proofing.

Finishers of Broad Woven Fabrics of Man-Made Fiber and Silk – Industry No. 2262
Establishments primarily engaged in finishing purchased man-made fiber and silk broad woven fabrics or finishing such fabrics on a commission basis.

These finishing operations include bleaching, dyeing, printing (roller, screen, flock, plisse), and other mechanical finishing such as preshrinking, calendering, and napping.

Finishers of Textile, Not Elsewhere Classified – Industry No. 2269
Establishments primarily engaged in dyeing and finishing textiles, not elsewhere classified, such as bleaching, dyeing, printing, and finishing of raw stock, yarn, braided goods, and narrow fabrics, except wool and knit fabrics.

These establishments perform finishing operations on purchased textiles or on a commission basis.

Floor Covering Mills – Group No. 227
Woven Carpets and Rugs – Industry No. 2271
Establishments primarily engaged in weaving carpets and rugs from any textile yarn.

Important products of this industry include Axminster, Wilton, velvet and similar woven carpets and rugs; and woven automobile and aircraft floor coverings.

Tufted Carpets and Rugs – Industry No. 2272
Establishments primarily engaged in tufting carpets and rugs from any textile fiber.

Important products of this industry include tufted carpets, rugs, scatter rugs, and bathmats and bathmat sets except terry woven. Finishers of these products also are included in this industry.

Carpets and Rugs, Not Elsewhere Classified – Industry No. 2279
Establishments primarily engaged in manufacturing rugs, carpets, art squares, floor mattings, needle punch carpeting, and door mats and mattings from twisted paper, grasses, reeds, coir, sisal, jute or rags.

Yarn and Thread Mills – Group No. 228
Yarn Spinning Mills: Cotton Man-Made Fibers and Silk – Industry No. 2281
Establishments primarily engaged in spinning yarn wholly or chiefly by weight of cotton, man-made fibers, or silk.

Yarns produced by these mills include carded, combed, carpet, knitting nylon, polyester and weaving yarns.

Yarn Texturizing, Throwing, Twisting, and Winding Mills: Cotton, Man-Made Fibers and Silk – Industry No. 2282
Establishments primarily engaged in texturizing, throwing, twisting, winding, or spooling yarn wholly or chiefly by weight of cotton, man-made fibers or silk.

Yarn Mills, Wool, Including Carpet and Rug Yarn – Industry No. 2283
Establishments primarily engaged in spinning, twisting, winding, or spooling yarn (including carpet and rug yarn) wholly or chiefly by weight of wool, mohair, or similar animal fibers.

This industry's yarns include crochet, darning, knitting, thread and weaving yarns.

Thread Mills – Industry No. 2284
Establishments primarily engaged in manufacturing thread from natural or man-made fiber except flax (Industry 2299) and wool (Industry 2283)

Important products of this industry include sewing, crochet, darning, embroidery, tatting, hand knitting, and other handicraft threads.

Miscellaneous Textile Goods – Group No. 229
Felt Goods, Except Woven Felts and Hats – Industry No. 2291
Establishments primarily engaged in manufacturing pressed felt, regardless of fiber, by means of heat, moisture, and pressure; and, those making punched felt for rugs, cushions, and other products from hair, jute, wool, or other fibers by the needle loom process.

Listed for this industry are fifteen products including acoustic, automotive, carpet, insulation, pipe and boiler covering, and lining felts.

Lace Goods – Industry No. 2292
Establishments primarily engaged in manufacturing lace machine products, and those primarily engaged in dyeing and finishing of lace goods.

Important products in this industry include bed sets, covers, curtains, and curtain fabrics, and edgings, and netting lace.

Paddings and Upholstery Filling – Industry No. 2293
Establishments primarily engaged in manufacturing batting, padding, wadding, and filling for upholstery, pillows, quilts and apparel, from curled hair, cotton mill waste, moss, hemp tow, flax tow, kapok, and related materials.

Processed Waste and Recovered Fibers and Flock – Industry No. 2294
Establishments primarily engaged in processing textile mill waste for spinning, padding, batting, or other uses; in recovering textile fibers from clippings and rags; in cutting flock from waste, recovered fibers, or new fiber stock; and in manufacturing oakum and twisted jute packing.

Coated Fabrics, Not Rubberized – Industry No. 2295
Establishments primarily engaged in manufacturing coated and impregnated textiles, and in the special finishing of textiles, such as varnishing and waxing.

Tire Cord and Fabric – Industry No. 2296
Establishments primarily engaged in manufacturing cord and fabric for use in reinforcing rubber tires, industrial belting, fuel cells, and similar uses.

Nonwoven Fabrics – Industry No. 2297

Establishments primarily engaged in manufacturing non-woven fabrics (by bonding and/or interlocking of fibers) by mechanical, chemical, thermal or solvent means or by combinations thereof.

Cordage and Twine – Industry No. 2298

Establishments primarily engaged in manufacturing rope, cable, cordage, twine and related products from abaca (Manila), sisal, henequen, hemp, cotton, paper, jute, flax, man-made fibers including glass, and other fibers.

Textile Goods, Not Elsewhere Classified – Industry No. 2299

Establishments primarily engaged in manufacturing linen goods, jute goods except felt, and other textile goods, not elsewhere classified. Establishments primarily engaged in processing textile fibers to prepare them for spinning, such as wool scouring and carbonizing and combing and converting tow to top, are also classified here.

Important products in this industry include burlap, flax yarns and roving, wool and mohair hoils, rugbacking, towels and toweling (linen) and specialty yarns.

Appendix 2 Market Economies' Imports and Exports: Rankings, Shares and Totals by Three-Digit SITC

Table A2.1 *Market Economies' Imports: Rankings, Shares[a] and Totals[b]*

SITC 651 Yarn

Rank	1970		1971		1972		1973		1974		1975		1976		1977		1978		1979	
1	W. Germany		W. Germany		W. Germany		W. Germany		W. Germany		W. Germany		W. Germany		W. Germany		W. Germany		W. Germany	
	14.2		15.1		14.6		13.3		11.8		14.0		13.4		14.2		14.2		14.2	
	436.3		543.4		585.7		761.8		786.0		838.4		976.2		1100.7		1256.5		1541.3	
2	USA		USA		USA		Belg.–Lux.		Belg.–Lux.		Belg.–Lux.		Belg.–Lux.		Belg.–Lux.		UK		France	
	7.2		9.7		7.6		7.0		7.2		7.7		7.7		7.3		7.4		8.1	
	222.9		350.6		305.4		400.3		476.6		461.9		563.7		568.2		651.5		875.8	
3	Netherlands		Belg.–Lux.		Belg.–Lux.		Netherlands		UK		France		France		UK		Belg.–Lux.		UK	
	6.8		6.8		7.2		6.0		6.9		6.9		6.8		6.6		7.0		7.6	
	207.8		243.4		288.9		346.1		460.0		412.1		494.0		508.6		617.3		823.5	
4	Belg.–Lux.		Netherlands		Netherlands		France		France		UK		Hong Kong		France		France		Belg.–Lux.	
	6.1		6.0		6.2		5.8		6.5		6.1		6.0		6.4		6.8		7.0	
	186.9		217.1		248.8		331.5		429.6		367.8		435.8		495.5		599.6		761.0	
5	Hong Kong		UK		France		Hong Kong		Netherlands		Netherlands		UK		Netherlands		Hong Kong		Italy	
	4.9		5.4		5.8		5.5		6.1		5.8		5.8		5.5		5.7		7.0	
	151.4		195.4		232.9		316.1		403.1		349.5		423.7		428.3		507.8		758.9	
6	U.K.		France		UK		UK		Italy		Hong Kong		Italy		Hong Kong		Italy		Hong Kong	
	4.8		5.0		5.3		5.2		4.6		4.9		5.8		5.5		5.3		5.9	
	147.2		180.5		213.9		295.9		303.5		292.5		421.5		427.5		473.6		644.3	

	France	Hong Kong	Hong Kong	Italy	Hong Kong	Italy	Netherlands	Italy	Netherlands	Japan
7	France 4.5 139.6	Hong Kong 4.8 171.2	Hong Kong 4.8 193.8	Italy 4.7 267.9	Hong Kong 3.8 251.6	Italy 4.3 257.0	Netherlands 5.5 402.8	Italy 5.4 415.3	Netherlands 5.2 461.9	Japan 5.5 592.6
8	Italy 3.8 118.1	Austria 3.3 117.9	Italy 3.4 138.6	USA 4.6 261.9	Austria 3.0 200.8	Japan 3.3 197.5	Japan 3.6 259.5	USA 3.0 230.2	Japan 5.1 454.8	Netherlands 5.1 555.6
9	Austria 3.3 100.1	Italy 2.9 105.8	Austria 3.1 126.5	Japan 4.0 226.6	USA 2.9 192.6	Austria 3.0 176.9	Austria 2.8 206.1	Austria 2.9 225.4	USA 2.9 257.9	Austria 2.9 314.0
10	Sweden 3.0 91.4	Canada 2.9 105.3	Canada 2.8 113.9	Austria 3.1 179.7	Canada 2.6 175.9	Nigeria 2.8 167.7	USA 2.7 196.8	Nigeria 2.5 193.6	Austria 2.8 247.4	Canada 2.3 253.8

[a] Share is the first number appearing under each country name. It is the percentage of world imports taken by that country. The world is defined as market economies only.

[b] The second number under each country name is that country's total imports of that commodity during that year. These totals are expressed in US $m. and are valued on c.i.f. point of entry basis.

Source: United Nations, *Yearbook of International Trade Statistics*, New York, NY: UN, Vol. II, various issues 1970–1980.

Table A2.2 *Market Economies' Imports: Rankings, Shares[a] and Totals[b]*

SITC 652 Woven Cotton

Rank	1970	1971	1972	1973	1974	1975	1976	1977	1978	1979
1	USA	USA	USA	USA	USA	France	France	France	W. Germany	W. Germany
	10.3	9.4	11.1	9.6	9.1	9.9	10.5	10.0	10.1	11.4
	173.1	174.2	259.8	310.1	357.1	359.8	481.2	508.9	605.5	825.8
2	UK	UK	UK	Japan	W. Germany	W. Germany	W. Germany	W. Germany	France	France
	7.6	9.3	7.9	9.3	8.3	8.7	9.2	9.5	9.7	10.7
	128.3	171.4	185.2	303.7	323.7	315.5	423.6	483.6	585.2	770.8
3	W. Germany	W. Germany	W. Germany	UK	France	UK	USA	UK	UK	UK
	5.8	7.4	7.6	7.8	8.1	7.7	8.6	7.5	9.0	9.3
	97.3	137.0	179.0	253.4	317.0	278.3	394.3	381.9	541.4	671.9
4	Australia	Australia	France	France	UK	USA	UK	USA	USA	Italy
	5.6	5.6	7.2	7.1	7.8	6.1	7.5	7.0	7.5	7.7
	94.2	103.2	169.4	229.8	305.5	221.9	342.0	353.2	453.6	555.8
5	Italy	France	Australia	W. Germany	Australia	Hong Kong	Italy	Italy	Hong Kong	Hong Kong
	4.7	5.4	5.3	6.8	6.3	5.5	6.5	6.1	6.6	6.6
	79.9	99.2	125.2	219.6	247.0	201.1	297.0	311.2	394.6	480.0

6	Hong Kong 4.5 76.5	Hong Kong 5.0 93.0	Hong Kong 4.9 115.5	Australia 6.2 199.4	Italy 5.7 223.3	Italy 5.0 180.5	Hong Kong 6.0 276.2	Hong Kong 5.4 272.0	Italy 5.8 348.2	USA 5.6 401.9
7	France 4.2 70.1	Italy 3.9 72.5	Canada 4.5 105.7	Hong Kong 5.3 172.6	Hong Kong 4.4 171.1	Australia 4.4 161.3	Australia 4.6 212.2	Belg.–Lux. 4.4 220.8	Belg.–Lux. 4.3 256.1	Belg.–Lux. 4.1 299.5
8	Singapore 3.6 61.5	Canada 3.9 72.2	Japan 4.1 96.9	Italy 5.2 168.9	Netherlands 4.0 156.8	Netherlands 4.1 148.8	Netherlands 4.0 183.2	Iran 4.1 207.5	Australia 3.8 229.1	Japan 3.9 282.5
9	Canada 3.2 54.6	Belg.–Lux. 3.4 63.6	Netherlands 3.8 88.3	Belg.–Lux. 3.3 106.5	Belg.–Lux. 3.9 152.2	Belg.–Lux. 3.9 140.0	Belg.–Lux. 3.9 178.2	Australia 3.9 197.1	Netherlands 3.6 214.0	Netherlands 3.6 262.4
10	Netherlands 3.0 50.0	Netherlands 3.3 60.8	Belg.–Lux. 3.6 84.5	Netherlands 3.3 105.4	Japan 3.6 143.3	Canada 2.9 104.7	Canada 3.3 150.2	Netherlands 3.4 173.2	Japan 2.9 177.2	Australia 3.4 246.7

[a] Share is the first number appearing under each country name. It is the percentage of world imports taken by that country. The world is defined as market economies only.

[b] The second number under each country name is that country's total imports of that commodity during that year. These totals are expressed in US $m. and are valued on c.i.f. point of entry basis.

Source: United Nations, *Yearbook of International Trade Statistics,* New York, NY: UN, Vol. II, various issues 1970–1980.

Table A2.3 *Market Economies' Imports: Rankings, Shares[a], and Totals[b]*

SITC 653 Woven Non-Cotton

Rank	1970	1971	1972	1973	1974	1975	1976	1977	1978	1979
1	USA	USA	W. Germany	W. Germany	W. Germany	W. Germany	W. Germany	W. Germany	W. Germany	W. Germany
	13.1	14.1	12.7	12.5	11.6	12.9	11.2	12.3	12.5	11.9
	498.5	599.7	642.3	844.4	884.6	1009.4	970.0	1143.5	1439.9	1671.0
2	W. Germany	W. Germany	USA	USA	France	France	France	France	UK	UK
	11.6	12.0	12.5	9.0	7.0	7.2	7.1	7.4	7.7	8.2
	441.3	510.3	631.2	607.7	537.0	563.6	608.9	689.2	894.4	1149.6
3	Netherlands	Netherlands	France	France	USA	UK	USA	USA	France	France
	5.9	5.6	6.6	6.7	7.0	6.2	6.2	6.4	7.7	7.9
	223.2	238.8	331.2	456.1	535.5	482.2	531.2	594.3	890.2	1108.4
4	Hong Kong	France	UK	Japan	UK	USA	UK	UK	USA	Hong Kong
	5.1	5.5	5.6	6.1	6.2	5.7	5.3	6.3	7.3	6.2
	196.1	234.2	283.4	411.4	471.9	442.1	461.1	586.6	839.3	874.1
5	France	Hong Kong	Netherlands	UK	Japan	Netherlands	Hong Kong	Hong Kong	Hong Kong	USA
	5.0	5.4	5.4	5.6	5.7	5.1	5.2	5.2	5.7	5.7
	191.1	230.3	270.6	378.2	438.6	396.4	450.3	482.2	661.6	801.1

6	Canada 4.9 186.4	UK 5.3 226.8	Hong Kong 5.0 253.6	Netherlands 5.1 344.8	Netherlands 5.1 390.5	Belg.–Lux. 4.5 349.3	Netherlands 4.7 407.9	Netherlands 4.5 417.6	Japan 5.2 602.0	Japan 5.3 753.1
7	UK 4.7 179.5	Canada 5.0 214.0	Canada 5.0 252.6	Hong Kong 4.8 322.4	Hong Kong 4.5 343.4	Japan 4.5 349.1	Japan 4.6 398.1	Japan 4.5 414.4	Netherlands 4.6 534.3	Netherlands 4.3 605.1
8	Belg.–Lux. 3.8 144.3	Belg.–Lux. 4.1 174.8	Belg.–Lux. 4.1 207.5	Belg.–Lux. 4.5 307.5	Belg.–Lux. 4.4 340.4	Hong Kong 4.1 318.8	Canada 4.1 351.1	Belg.–Lux. 3.9 364.7	Belg.–Lux. 3.9 450.1	Belg.–Lux. 3.7 518.8
9	Singapore 3.7 141.8	Singapore 3.8 161.2	Singapore 3.3 169.8	Canada 3.8 256.8	Canada 3.9 297.1	Canada 3.6 277.4	Belg.–Lux. 4.0 346.0	Canada 3.7 339.9	Canada 3.3 376.3	Italy 3.8 534.1
10	Italy 3.2 121.6	Italy 2.6 109.8	Japan 3.1 154.4	Italy 3.5 239.0	Italy 3.1 241.1	Italy 2.6 199.2	Iran 3.2 276.2	Italy 3.3 307.8	Saudi Arabia 3.1 357.3	Canada 3.6 510.9

[a] Share is the first number appearing under each country name. It is the percentage of world imports taken by that country. The world is defined as market economies only.

[b] The second number under each country name is that country's total imports of that commodity during that year. These totals are expressed in US $m. and are valued on c.i.f. point of entry basis.

Source: United Nations, *Yearbook of International Trade Statistics*. New York, NY: UN, Vol. II, various issues 1970–1980.

Table A2.4 Market Economies' Imports: Rankings, Shares[a] and Totals[b]

SITC 654 Lace, Ribbon, Etc.

Rank	1970		1971		1972		1973		1974		1975		1976		1977		1978		1979[c]	
1	W. Germany		W. Germany		W. Germany		W. Germany		W. Germany		W. Germany		W. Germany		W. Germany		W. Germany		W. Germany	
	14.7	41.8	16.8	49.2	15.6	52.5	12.8	57.8	11.0	55.6	10.7	53.4	10.6	61.4	11.9	79.5	11.8	105.1	11.0	129.9
2	USA		USA		USA		Japan		UK		UK		UK		UK		UK		UK	
	7.3	20.7	8.5	24.9	8.1	27.3	9.4	42.2	7.3	37.0	8.6	43.1	8.9	51.6	8.7	58.0	9.8	87.8	8.3	97.0
3	Italy		Canada		UK		UK		Canada		France		France		Saudi Arabia		Japan		Saudi Arabia	
	6.5	18.5	6.7	19.8	7.5	25.1	7.3	33.0	6.4	32.3	5.7	28.6	5.8	33.9	6.0	40.2	5.8	52.1	7.4	86.4
4	Hong Kong		UK		Canada		Canada		Japan		Canada		Japan		France		Saudi Arabia		France	
	5.8	16.5	5.9	17.4	6.9	23.3	6.1	27.2	6.2	31.4	5.6	28.0	5.7	33.0	5.6	37.5	5.8	52.1	5.5	64.4
5	Canada		Singapore		France		USA		Italy		Singapore		Canada		Italy		France		Japan	
	5.7	16.1	5.2	15.2	4.8	16.2	5.7	25.9	5.9	29.9	5.1	25.6	5.5	31.9	4.9	32.9	4.9	44.0	5.4	63.8

6	UK 5.4 15.3	Italy 4.5 13.1	Italy 4.6 15.3	Italy 4.9 22.2	France 5.2 26.3	Japan 4.8 24.1	Italy 4.9 28.6	Canada 4.8 32.0	Italy 4.9 43.4	Italy 5.1 59.5
7	Japan 3.8 10.6	Hong Kong 4.2 12.2	Japan 4.3 14.5	France 4.9 22.0	USA 5.0 25.6	Italy 4.8 24.1	USA 4.6 27.1	USA 4.4 29.4	Canada 4.4 39.7	Canada 4.1 48.5
8	France 3.7 10.6	France 4.1 12.0	Belg.–Lux. 3.8 12.9	Belg.–Lux. 3.8 17.2	Singapore 4.7 23.8	USA 3.9 19.6	Singapore 4.4 25.4	Japan 4.3 28.6	USA 4.2 37.9	Benin 4.0 47.5
9	Singapore 3.6 10.2	Belg.–Lux. 3.5 10.4	Hong Kong 3.8 12.6	Singapore 3.8 17.0	Belg.–Lux. 3.8 19.8	Yug. 3.6 18.1	Hong Kong 3.6 20.7	Singapore 3.7 25.0	Hong Kong 3.2 28.8	USA 3.8 44.4
10	Australia 3.4 9.7	Japan 3.3 9.8	Singapore 3.3 11.2	Hong Kong 2.9 13.2	Saudi Arabia 2.8 14.4	Belg.–Lux. 3.4 16.7	Saudi Arabia 3.5 20.6	Hong Kong 3.0 20.3	Singapore 2.8 25.2	Hong Kong 3.6 42.7

[a] Share is the first number appearing under each country name. It is the percentage of world imports taken by that country. The world is defined as market economies only.

[b] The second number under each country name is that country's total imports of that commodity during that year. These totals are expressed in US $m. and are valued on c.i.f. point of entry basis.

[c] Estimated.

Source: United Nations, *Yearbook of International Trade Statistics*, New York, NY: UN, Vol. II, various issues 1970–1980.

Table A2.5 *Market Economies' Imports: Rankings, Shares[a], and Totals[b]*

SITC 655 Special Products

Rank	1970		1971		1972		1973		1974		1975		1976		1977		1978		1979[c]	
1	W. Germany		W. Germany		W. Germany		W. Germany		USA		W. Germany		W. Germany		W. Germany		W. Germany		W. Germany	
	10.6		11.5		12.3		11.4		11.6		9.8		10.1		11.2		12.0		12.8	
	109.9		133.2		163.1		206.8		284.4		226.9		248.7		320.6		402.2		532.3	
2	USA		USA		USA		USA		W. Germany		USA		USA		France		France		France	
	8.9		9.1		9.3		8.7		9.3		9.3		8.7		8.4		8.9		9.0	
	92.3		104.9		123.6		158.4		226.8		215.7		214.3		240.9		298.6		374.8	
3	Canada		Canada		France		France		Canada		France		France		USA		USA		USA	
	6.6		6.7		7.5		8.7		8.0		8.6		8.7		7.9		7.4		7.6	
	68.4		77.9		99.1		156.8		195.2		199.6		213.3		225.0		247.9		314.3	
4	Netherlands		France		Canada		Canada		France		Canada		Canada		Canada		UK		UK	
	6.6		6.7		6.8		6.7		7.8		7.2		6.1		5.8		6.1		6.6	
	68.1		77.5		90.7		120.5		192.0		167.0		150.8		164.3		204.0		274.8	
5	France		Netherlands		UK		UK		UK		Netherlands		Netherlands		UK		Canada		Canada	
	6.1		5.8		5.7		6.2		5.1		4.9		4.8		5.3		5.8		5.5	
	63.3		66.7		75.9		112.6		125.6		114.2		118.1		150.2		194.3		229.4	

Rank										
6	UK 5.6 57.7	UK 5.7 66.4	Netherlands 5.6 73.8	Netherlands 5.6 100.6	Netherlands 5.1 124.6	UK 4.9 112.9	UK 4.8 117.7	Netherlands 4.6 132.1	Netherlands 4.9 163.3	Italy 4.7 195.4
7	Italy 4.5 46.6	Belg.–Lux. 4.6 53.7	Italy 4.5 59.2	Italy 5.0 90.8	Italy 4.7 115.5	Italy 4.2 98.4	Italy 4.4 106.9	Italy 4.2 119.4	Italy 4.0 132.1	Netherlands 4.5 185.0
8	Belg.–Lux. 4.4 45.2	Italy 4.2 49.0	Belg.–Lux. 4.2 55.8	Belg.–Lux. 4.1 74.8	Belg.–Lux. 3.9 96.6	Belg.–Lux. 3.8 88.3	Belg.–Lux. 3.7 90.9	Belg.–Lux. 3.9 112.1	Belg.–Lux. 3.8 127.9	Belg.–Lux. 3.9 160.1
9	Sweden 4.1 43.0	Sweden 3.7 42.3	Sweden 3.5 46.9	Sweden 3.2 58.2	Sweden 3.1 75.9	Sweden 3.4 77.8	Sweden 3.4 83.6	Sweden 3.1 88.1	Sweden 2.9 97.2	Sweden 3.1 127.2
10	Switzerland 3.0 31.5	Hong Kong 3.2 36.9	Switzerland 3.2 42.3	Switzerland 3.0 54.5	Switzerland 2.9 71.7	Hong Kong 2.6 60.7	Hong Kong 3.4 83.6	Hong Kong 2.8 80.6	Hong Kong 2.8 94.3	Hong Kong 2.8 117.5

[a] Share is the first number appearing under each country name. It is the percentage of world imports taken by that country. The world is defined as market economies only.

[b] The second number under each country name is that country's total imports of that commodity during that year. These totals are expressed in US $m. and are valued on c.i.f. point of entry basis.

[c] Preliminary figures.

Source: United Nations, *Yearbook of International Trade Statistics*, New York, NY: UN, Vol. II, various issues 1970–1980.

Table A2.6 *Market Economies' Imports: Rankings, Shares[a] and Totals[b]*

SITC 656 Miscellaneous NES

Rank	1970	1971	1972	1973	1974	1975	1976	1977	1978	1979[c]
1	USA	USA	USA	W. Germany	W. Germany	W. Germany	W. Germany	W. Germany	W. Germany	W. Germany
	9.9	9.3	9.3	9.3	8.6	9.5	9.3	9.0	9.0	9.4
	66.1	68.1	87.9	119.3	140.5	162.8	186.5	214.1	258.6	322.5
2	W. Germany	W. Germany	W. Germany	USA	USA	France	France	USA	USA	France
	7.4	8.7	9.2	7.3	6.9	6.9	7.3	7.5	7.4	7.7
	49.4	63.8	87.0	93.1	113.6	118.1	145.9	179.2	214.1	265.3
3	Canada	UK	UK	UK	UK	UK	USA	France	France	UK
	6.0	7.9	7.2	6.5	6.3	6.7	7.3	6.5	6.7	7.3
	40.2	58.2	67.4	82.7	103.4	115.6	145.4	155.2	191.9	248.6
4	Netherlands	Canada	Canada	Canada	Australia	USA	Netherlands	Saudi Arabia	Netherlands	USA
	6.0	5.5	6.3	5.6	6.0	5.7	5.6	5.7	6.2	7.1
	40.2	40.8	59.6	71.3	98.2	98.3	112.9	136.6	178.7	241.7
5	UK	Netherlands	Netherlands	Netherlands	Japan	Netherlands	UK	Netherlands	Saudi Arabia	Netherlands
	5.6	5.4	5.7	5.5	5.6	5.5	5.6	5.3	5.9	5.5
	37.4	39.9	53.3	70.6	93.7	94.9	112.7	125.5	169.1	189.5

6	Australia 4.9 / 32.7	France 4.9 / 36.6	France 5.4 / 50.7	France 5.2 / 67.0	France 5.5 / 90.5	Canada 4.9 / 84.6	Canada 5.6 / 111.3	UK 4.7 / 112.5	UK 5.7 / 164.6	Hong Kong 4.7 / 161.6
7	France 4.6 / 30.9	Australia 4.5 / 32.9	Australia 3.8 / 35.7	Japan 4.9 / 63.4	Netherlands 5.5 / 90.3	Hong Kong 3.9 / 67.3	Hong Kong 4.2 / 83.8	Canada 4.4 / 104.3	Hong Kong 4.4 / 127.7	Saudi Arabia 4.4 / 151.6
8	Hong Kong 3.0 / 22.1	Hong Kong 3.7 / 27.0	Hong Kong 3.5 / 32.5	Hong Kong 4.5 / 57.7	Canada 5.4 / 89.0	Sweden 3.4 / 59.2	Saudi Arabia 3.8 / 76.8	Hong Kong 4.2 / 99.3	Belg.–Lux. 4.1 / 118.4	Belg.–Lux. 3.9 / 134.1
9	Sweden 3.2 / 21.6	Sweden 2.8 / 20.5	Sweden 2.9 / 27.6	Australia 4.0 / 50.6	Hong Kong 3.2 / 52.3	Belg.–Lux. 3.4 / 59.0	Belg.–Lux. 3.5 / 70.5	Belg.–Lux. 3.7 / 89.5	Canada 3.5 / 100.8	Japan 3.7 / 126.6
10	Italy 2.6 / 17.4	Italy 2.6 / 19.1	Italy 2.8 / 27.0	Italy 3.1 / 40.8	Belg.–Lux. 3.2 / 52.0	Australia 3.3 / 56.5	Australia 3.4 / 68.8	Kuwait 3.5 / 84.2	Japan 2.7 / 78.8	Canada 3.3 / 113.8

[a] Share is the first number appearing under each country name. It is the percentage of world imports taken by that country. The world is defined as market economies only.

[b] The second number under each country name is that country's total imports of that commodity during that year. These totals are expressed in US $m. and are valued on c.i.f. point of entry basis.

[c] Preliminary figures.

Source: United Nations, *Yearbook of International Trade Statistics*, New York, NY: UN, Vol. II, various issues 1970–1980.

Table A2.7 *Market Economies' Imports: Rankings, Shares[a] and Totals[b]*

SITC 657 Floor Covering

Rank	1970	1971	1972	1973	1974	1975	1976	1977	1978	1979
1	W. Germany	W. Germany	W. Germany	W. Germany	W. Germany	W. Germany	W. Germany	W. Germany	W. Germany	W. Germany
	29.2	34.1	32.6	29.3	25.0	28.0	27.0	28.1	29.1	30.6
	252.0	353.3	419.9	535.1	520.6	590.5	682.0	829.5	1079.5	1336.4
2	Netherlands	Netherlands	France	France	France	France	France	France	France	France
	8.1	6.9	7.1	7.7	8.6	9.4	9.1	8.2	8.1	8.7
	69.9	71.7	91.8	140.0	179.6	198.4	230.4	241.1	299.8	381.5
3	USA	USA	USA	USA	Netherlands	Netherlands	Netherlands	Netherlands	Netherlands	USA
	7.1	6.6	7.1	6.7	7.0	6.8	6.8	6.4	7.0	7.2
	61.7	68.8	91.2	122.7	145.5	143.7	171.7	187.6	258.9	313.2
4	France	France	Netherlands	Netherlands	Switzerland	UK	USA	USA	USA	UK
	6.8	6.6	7.0	6.7	5.9	5.3	5.8	6.1	6.7	6.9
	58.4	68.8	90.1	121.8	124.0	112.8	146.1	178.7	248.1	302.6
5	UK	UK	UK	Switzerland	USA	Switzerland	UK	UK	UK	Netherlands
	5.8	5.4	5.6	6.2	5.7	5.1	5.0	5.2	6.0	6.1
	49.9	55.5	72.4	112.4	119.8	107.3	125.9	152.8	222.3	265.3

6	Sweden 5.4 46.7	Switzerland 5.2 53.5	Switzerland 5.5 71.2	UK 5.8 105.6	UK 5.2 108.9	Sweden 5.1 106.6	Sweden 4.6 117.0	Saudi Arabia 4.6 135.0	Saudi Arabia 4.9 181.5	Switzerland 4.8 208.8
7	Switzerland 5.2 44.9	Sweden 5.0 52.1	Sweden 4.6 58.9	Italy 4.2 77.5	Australia 4.9 102.7	USA 5.0 106.0	Switzerland 4.5 112.9	Switzerland 4.2 124.4	Switzerland 4.4 162.7	Belg.-Lux. 4.2 182.6
8	Australia 4.0 34.4	Belg.-Lux. 3.6 37.1	Italy 3.6 46.1	Sweden 3.9 71.0	Belg.-Lux. 4.6 95.5	Belg.-Lux. 4.1 86.1	Belg.-Lux. 3.9 97.3	Belg.-Lux. 4.1 120.0	Belg.-Lux. 4.4 162.4	Saudi Arabia[c] 4.1 178.3
9	Canada 3.3 28.3	Australia 3.5 36.5	Belg.-Lux. 3.5 45.3	Belg.-Lux. 3.7 67.9	Sweden 4.5 93.0	Canada 3.1 66.1	Saudi Arabia 3.6 87.9	Sweden 3.6 106.1	Sweden 3.0 111.3	Sweden 3.0 129.8
10	Belg.-Lux. 3.1 26.6	Italy 3.0 30.8	Canada 2.9 37.9	Australia 3.5 63.4	Italy 4.3 91.5	Italy 2.9 62.0	Australia 3.4 85.4	Austria 3.1 91.7	Austria 2.7 100.0	Japan 2.8 120.5

[a] Share is the first number appearing under each country name. It is the percentage of world imports taken by that country. The world is defined as market economies only.

[b] The second number under each country name is that country's total imports of that commodity during that year. These totals are expressed in US $m. and are valued on c.i.f. point of entry basis.

[c] Estimated.

Source: United Nations, *Yearbook of International Trade Statistics*, New York, NY: UN, Vol. II, various issues 1970–1980.

Table A2.8 *Market Economies' Exports: Rankings, Shares[a] and Totals[b]*

SITC 651 Yarn

Rank	1970	1971	1972	1973	1974	1975	1976	1977	1978	1979[c]
1	W. Germany 16.48	W. Germany 17.06	W. Germany 15.63	W. Germany 18.02	W. Germany 17.63	W. Germany 16.29	W. Germany 16.76	W. Germany 14.95	W. Germany 15.20	W. Germany 15.13
	542.1	646.7	668.6	1101.3	1286.6	1030.0	1246.6	1208.8	1384.4	1665.7
2	Japan 12.92	Japan 14.16	Japan 11.96	France 9.79	Japan 11.08	France 9.35	France 9.26	Japan 10.07	France 9.37	France 9.05
	425.8	536.8	511.5	598.3	808.8	590.9	689.2	814.5	853.3	996.1
3	France 10.00	France 9.42	France 9.40	Japan 9.48	France 8.94	Japan 9.28	Japan 8.42	France 9.85	Italy 8.60	Italy 8.48
	329.6	357.0	402.2	579.6	652.1	586.6	626.2	796.1	782.6	934.2
4	UK 8.52	Italy 8.68	Italy 9.02	UK 7.60	Italy 7.72	Italy 8.29	Italy 7.11	Italy 7.43	Japan 8.37	UK 7.65
	280.7	328.9	385.7	464.3	563.6	524.0	528.7	601.0	761.9	842.0
5	Italy 7.79	UK 8.26	UK 8.10	Italy 7.50	UK 7.61	Netherlands 7.37	Belg.–Lux. 6.92	UK 7.10	UK 7.33	Japan 7.01
	256.9	313.0	346.7	458.4	555.6	465.7	514.6	574.1	667.5	772.2

6 Belg.–Lux. 7.67 252.9	Netherlands 8.06 305.5	Netherlands 7.76 332.0	Netherlands 7.37 450.2	Netherlands 7.12 519.9	UK 7.09 448.3	UK 6.90 513.0	Belg.–Lux. 6.90 558.2	Belg.–Lux. 6.23 566.9	Netherlands 5.94 654.0
7 Netherlands 7.63 251.6	Belg.–Lux. 7.09 268.9	Belg.–Lux. 7.32 312.9	Belg.–Lux. 6.65 406.6	Belg.–Lux. 6.09 444.5	Belg.–Lux. 6.75 426.7	Netherlands 6.82 507.4	Netherlands 6.29 508.7	Netherlands 5.93 539.6	Belg.–Lux. 5.90 649.8
8 USA 4.43 145.9	Switzerland 4.00 151.6	Switzerland 4.17 178.3	USA 4.51 275.4	USA 5.61 409.6	USA 4.75 300.0	USA 5.07 377.4	USA 5.12 413.7	USA 4.04 367.9	USA 5.62 618.4
9 Switzerland 3.99 131.4	Pakistan 3.57 135.3	Pakistan 3.32 142.0	Pakistan 3.75 229.7	Switzerland 3.58 261.5	Switzerland 4.05 256.2	Switzerland 4.02 299.0	Switzerland 3.89 314.7	Switzerland 4.01 365.2	Switzerland 4.15 457.5
10 Egypt 2.50 82.5	Pakistan 2.20 83.5	USA 3.29 140.8	Switzerland 3.68 225.0	Egypt 2.29 167.1	Korea 3.24 205.0	Korea 3.99 296.9	Korea 3.10 250.4	Korea 3.71 337.7	Korea 4.03 443.7

[a] Share is the first number appearing under each country name. It is the percentage of world exports taken by that country. The world is defined as market economies only.

[b] The second number under each country name is that country's total exports of that commodity during that year. These totals are expressed in US $m. and are valued on f.o.b. point of departure basis.

[c] Preliminary figures.

Source: United Nations, *Yearbook of International Trade Statistics*, New York, NY: UN, Vol. II, various issues, 1970–1980.

Table A2.9 *Market Economies' Exports: Rankings, Shares[a] and Totals[b]*

SITC 652 Woven Cotton

Rank	1970	1971	1972	1973	1974	1975	1976	1977	1978	1979[c]
1	Japan	Japan	Japan	Hong Kong	USA	USA	W. Germany	W. Germany	W. Germany	W. Germany
	13.06	11.98	11.30	9.55	11.40	12.00	12.12	12.00	12.91	13.77
	187.6	195.2	231.1	268.6	386.3	378.5	501.8	556.1	674.8	898.9
2	Hong Kong	W. Germany	USA	USA	W. Germany	W. Germany	USA	USA	France	USA
	10.51	9.04	10.02	9.38	10.34	11.15	12.10	9.51	9.75	9.64
	150.9	147.2	204.9	263.8	350.9	351.7	500.9	440.7	509.8	629.0
3	USA	Hong Kong	W. Germany	W. Germany	Hong Kong	Japan	Hong Kong	Japan	USA	France
	7.85	9.03	9.48	9.26	8.96	8.24	9.43	8.94	8.19	9.63
	112.8	147.1	193.8	260.5	303.8	259.8	390.6	414.1	428.0	628.5
4	W. Germany	USA	Hong Kong	India	France	Hong Kong	Japan	France	Hong Kong	Hong Kong
	7.36	8.43	7.69	7.80	7.84	8.09	7.79	8.21	7.57	8.09
	105.7	137.3	157.4	219.6	265.8	255.3	322.4	380.4	395.5	528.2
5	France	France	France	France	Japan	France	France	Hong Kong	Japan	Italy
	7.09	7.32	7.28	7.45	7.10	7.65	7.34	7.31	7.13	7.15
	101.8	119.3	148.9	209.7	240.8	241.5	303.9	338.9	372.5	466.3

6	India 6.85 98.3	India 6.23 101.6	India 6.32 129.4	Japan 6.93 195.1	India 7.02 238.1	Netherlands 5.72 180.4	India 6.63 274.5	India 6.50 301.2	Italy 7.09 370.4	Netherlands 5.15 335.9
7	Netherlands 5.52 79.3	Netherlands 5.87 95.7	Netherlands 5.55 113.5	Pakistan 5.20 147.4	Netherlands 5.48 185.7	India 5.10 160.8	Netherlands 5.41 224.0	Italy 5.33 247.1	Netherlands 5.45 284.6	Japan 5.10 332.9
8	UK 4.47 64.2	Pakistan 4.33 70.5	Italy 4.70 96.2	Netherlands 5.06 142.4	Belg.–Lux. 4.32 146.6	Italy 4.93 155.4	Italy 4.58 189.4	Netherlands 5.30 245.4	Switzerland 5.30 276.9	Switzerland 4.81 314.1
9	Pakistan 4.09 58.7	UK 4.28 69.7	Belg.–Lux. 4.43 90.6	Belg.–Lux. 4.15 116.7	Pakistan 3.92 133.0	Pakistan 4.18 131.7	Belg.–Lux. 4.06 168.1	Belg.–Lux. 4.18 193.8	Belg.–Lux. 4.54 237.2	Belg.–Lux. 4.73 308.7
10	Belg.–Lux. 3.64 52.3	Italy 4.19 68.3	Pakistan 4.14 84.7	Switzerland 3.73 104.9	Italy 3.80 128.8	Belg.–Lux. 4.04 127.5	Switzerland 3.58 148.3	Switzerland 4.09 189.6	India 4.37 228.4	India 4.37 285.2

[a] Share is the first number appearing under each country name. It is the percentage of world exports taken by that country. The world is defined as market economies only.

[b] The second number under each country name is that country's total exports of that commodity during that year. These totals are expressed in US $m. and are valued on f.o.b. point of departure basis.

[c] Preliminary figures.

Source: United Nations, *Yearbook of International Trade Statistics*, New York, NY: UN, Vol. II, various issues 1970–1980.

Table A2.10 *Market Economies' Exports: Rankings, Shares[a] and Totals[b]*

SITC 653 Woven Non-Cotton

Rank	1970	1971	1972	1973	1974	1975	1976	1977	1978	1979[c]
1	Japan	Japan	Japan	Japan	Japan	Japan	Japan	Japan	Japan	Japan
	23.69	24.22	22.01	19.75	20.66	21.60	22.67	21.43	19.02	17.32
	940.1	1117.3	1185.8	1379.0	1703.2	1738.1	1952.3	2012.0	2209.6	2408.7
2	W. Germany	W. Germany	W. Germany	W. Germany	W. Germany	W. Germany	W. Germany	W. Germany	W. Germany	Italy
	12.98	13.99	12.95	14.41	14.04	14.13	14.52	14.68	14.64	15.26
	514.8	645.5	697.5	1005.9	1157.8	1136.9	1250.3	1378.5	1701.5	2121.9
3	Italy	Italy	Italy	Italy	Italy	Italy	Italy	Italy	Italy	W. Germany
	11.46	10.89	11.93	11.34	10.51	12.46	11.87	13.23	14.64	14.58
	454.7	502.2	642.6	792.1	866.5	1002.9	1022.1	1241.8	1700.5	2028.3
4	UK	UK	UK	Belg.–Lux.	France	France	Belg.–Lux.	UK	South Korea	France
	9.23	8.42	7.37	7.36	6.91	7.20	6.28	6.47	6.67	6.40
	366.1	388.6	396.8	513.7	569.3	579.3	540.8	607.3	775.0	890.8
5	Belg.–Lux.	France	Belg.–Lux.	France	Belg.–Lux.	Belg.–Lux.	France	France	France	South Korea
	6.83	6.81	7.15	7.26	6.88	6.94	5.97	6.14	6.17	6.27
	271.1	314.2	385.2	506.8	567.4	558.2	513.9	576.4	717.4	872.5

#										
6	France 6.74 267.3	Belg.-Lux. 6.53 301.4	France 7.00 377.2	UK 6.97 486.5	UK 6.74 555.8	UK 6.09 490.2	UK 5.60 482.5	Belg.-Lux. 5.90 553.7	UK 6.07 705.4	UK 5.90 820.5
7	Netherlands 5.09 201.8	India 5.53 255.2	Netherlands 5.01 269.9	Netherlands 5.16 360.4	USA 5.06 417.5	Netherlands 5.27 424.3	South Korea 5.03 433.4	South Korea 4.93 462.8	Belg.-Lux. 5.51 639.8	USA 5.49 764.2
8	India 4.77 189.1	Netherlands 5.28 243.7	India 4.91 264.7	USA 4.10 287.5	Netherlands 5.04 415.5	USA 4.86 390.9	USA 4.99 429.5	USA 4.35 408.0	USA 4.26 495.0	Belg.-Lux. 5.22 726.4
9	USA 3.89 154.4	USA 3.16 145.9	USA 3.23 174.0	India 3.49 244.5	India 3.40 280.1	South Korea 3.38 271.8	Netherlands 4.94 425.3	Netherlands 4.32 405.5	Netherlands 4.16 483.2	Netherlands 3.80 528.9
10	Pakistan 3.03 120.3	Switzerland 2.19 100.9	Bangladesh 2.95 159.0	South Korea 3.05 213.6	South Korea 2.50 205.8	India 2.38 191.2	India 2.20 189.8	Switzerland 2.26 212.0	Switzerland 2.24 259.9	Hong Kong 2.13 296.2

[a] Share is the first number appearing under each country name. It is the percentage of world exports taken by that country. The world is defined as market economies only.

[b] The second number under each country name is that country's total exports of that commodity during that year. These totals are expressed in US $m. and are valued on f.o.b. point of departure basis.

[c] Preliminary figures.

Source: United Nations, *Yearbook of International Trade Statistics*, New York, NY: UN, Vol. II, various issues 1970–1980.

Table A2.11 *Market Economies' Exports: Rankings, Shares[a] and Totals[b]*

SITC 654 Lace, Ribbon, Etc.

Rank	1970	1971	1972	1973	1974	1975	1976	1977	1978	1979[c]
1	France	France	France	France	France	Austria	Austria	Austria	Austria	Austria
	20.89	20.12	19.59	18.42	15.79	17.56	16.76	15.99	16.09	15.05
	56.5	57.3	64.0	78.4	77.5	95.7	108.7	116.3	152.6	166.7
2	Switzerland	Austria	Austria	Austria	Austria	France	France	France	France	France
	14.95	13.94	14.68	14.69	14.51	14.52	12.55	12.55	12.62	12.81
	40.4	39.7	48.0	62.5	71.2	79.1	81.4	91.2	119.7	142.0
3	Austria	Switzerland	Switzerland	Switzerland	Switzerland	Switzerland	Switzerland	Japan	Switzerland	Switzerland
	13.70	12.78	12.03	13.38	13.21	12.13	11.82	12.00	12.07	11.86
	37.0	36.4	39.3	56.9	64.8	66.1	76.7	87.3	114.4	131.3
4	Japan	W. Germany	W. Germany	W. Germany	W. Germany	Japan	South Korea	Switzerland	South Korea	South Korea
	11.50	10.52	10.01	9.72	9.78	9.30	10.47	11.34	11.93	11.04
	31.1	29.9	32.7	41.4	48.0	50.7	67.9	82.5	113.1	122.3
5	W. Germany	Japan	Japan	Japan	Japan	W. Germany	Japan	South Korea	Japan	W. Germany
	8.68	10.50	9.19	8.26	8.03	8.27	10.42	11.30	9.74	8.92
	23.5	29.9	30.0	35.1	39.4	45.1	67.6	82.1	92.3	98.8

6	UK 7.02 / 19.0	UK 6.74 / 19.2	USA 6.96 / 22.7	USA 6.03 / 25.7	USA 6.82 / 33.4	South Korea 7.68 / 41.8	W. Germany 8.71 / 56.5	W. Germany 8.78 / 63.8	W. Germany 8.56 / 81.1	Japan 8.51 / 94.2
7	USA 5.61 / 15.2	USA 6.31 / 18.0	UK 6.16 / 20.1	UK 5.65 / 24.1	UK 6.10 / 29.9	UK 6.15 / 33.5	USA 5.55 / 36.0	USA 5.46 / 39.7	USA 6.14 / 58.2	USA 5.87 / 65.0
8	Italy 3.43 / 9.3	Italy 3.73 / 10.6	Italy 3.57 / 11.7	South Korea 5.12 / 21.8	South Korea 5.39 / 26.5	USA 5.92 / 32.3	UK 5.22 / 33.9	UK 4.71 / 34.2	UK 4.73 / 44.9	UK 5.75 / 63.8
9	Belg.–Lux. 2.55 / 6.9	Belg.–Lux. 2.61 / 7.4	Belg.–Lux. 3.18 / 10.4	Belg.–Lux. 3.23 / 13.7	Belg.–Lux. 3.26 / 16.0	Belg.–Lux. 2.97 / 16.2	Belg.–Lux. 3.01 / 19.5	Italy 3.19 / 23.2	Italy 3.49 / 33.1	Italy 4.14 / 45.9
10	Netherlands 1.50 / 4.1	Netherlands 1.81 / 5.2	South Korea 2.42 / 7.9	Italy 2.90 / 12.3	Italy 2.95 / 14.5	Italy 2.78 / 15.1	Italy 2.94 / 19.1	Belg.–Lux. 2.91 / 21.2	Belg.–Lux. 2.23 / 21.1	Belg.–Lux. 2.36 / 26.1

[a] Share is the first number appearing under each country name. It is the percentage of world exports taken by that country. The world is defined as market economies only.

[b] The second number under each country name is that country's total exports of that commodity during that year. These totals are expressed in US $m. and are valued on f.o.b. point of departure basis.

[c] Preliminary figures.

Source: United Nations, *Yearbook of International Trade Statistics*, New York, NY: UN, Vol. II, various issues 1970–1980.

Table A2.12 Market Economies' Exports: Rankings, Shares[a] and Totals[b]

SITC 655 Special Products

Rank	1970	1971	1972	1973	1974	1975	1976	1977	1978	1979[c]
1	W. Germany	W. Germany	W. Germany	W. Germany	W. Germany	W. Germany	W. Germany	W. Germany	W. Germany	W. Germany
	21.30	20.97	20.08	21.53	20.31	18.44	18.88	18.84	18.40	18.04
	205.6	236.0	268.7	403.2	501.7	426.2	456.4	515.8	624.3	758.0
2	France	USA	France	France	USA	Belg.–Lux.	USA	Belg.–Lux.	USA	USA
	9.97	9.37	9.60	9.34	9.33	10.00	10.25	10.20	13.22	13.15
	96.2	105.4	128.5	175.0	230.5	231.0	247.9	279.2	448.3	552.5
3	USA	France	Japan	Japan	Belg.–Lux.	Japan	Belg–Lux.	Japan	Belg.–Lux.	Belg.–Lux.
	9.35	9.33	9.14	9.20	8.41	8.75	10.15	9.32	8.78	8.50
	90.2	105.0	122.2	172.4	207.6	202.3	245.5	255.3	297.9	357.2
4	UK	Belg.–Lux.	USA	USA	France	USA	Japan	USA	Japan	Italy
	8.62	8.93	9.03	9.05	8.37	8.71	9.57	9.29	7.86	8.03
	83.2	100.5	120.8	169.5	206.7	201.2	231.5	254.2	266.7	337.2
5	Belg.–Lux.	Netherlands	Belg.–Lux.	Netherlands	Netherlands	France	France	France	Italy	France
	8.53	8.54	8.77	8.81	8.26	8.36	8.18	7.81	7.51	7.46
	82.3	96.1	117.3	165.1	204.0	193.1	197.7	213.9	254.9	313.4

6	Netherlands 8.00 77.2	UK 8.38 94.3	Netherlands 8.70 116.4	Belg.–Lux. 8.32 155.9	Japan 7.87 194.4	Netherlands 8.09 186.8	Netherlands 7.79 188.5	Netherlands 7.56 207.0	Netherlands 7.42 251.5	Netherlands 7.05 296.0
7	Japan 7.47 72.1	Japan 7.58 85.3	UK 7.58 101.4	UK 6.73 126.0	UK 6.88 169.8	UK 7.39 170.7	UK 6.54 158.2	UK 6.83 186.9	France 7.30 247.5	UK 6.77 284.4
8	Italy 5.61 54.2	Italy 5.31 59.8	Italy 5.16 69.0	Italy 5.08 95.1	Italy 4.61 113.9	Italy 5.47 126.5	Italy 5.71 138.0	Italy 6.56 179.6	UK 6.60 223.9	Japan 6.66 279.8
9	Switzerland 3.20 30.9	Switzerland 3.05 34.4	Switzerland 3.21 42.9	Switzerland 3.42 64.1	Switzerland 3.65 90.2	Switzerland 3.87 89.4	Switzerland 3.33 80.4	Switzerland 3.20 87.7	Switzerland 3.25 110.3	Switzerland 3.00 126.0
10	Canada 2.80 27.1	Canada 2.70 30.6	Canada 2.93 39.2	Sweden 2.38 44.6	Portugal 2.68 66.2	Sweden 2.41 55.8	Sweden 2.42 58.4	Sweden 2.46 67.2	South Korea 2.29 77.6	South Korea 2.46 103.4

[a] Share is the first number appearing under each country name. It is the percentage of world exports taken by that country. The world is defined as market economies only.
[b] The second number under each country name is that country's total exports of that commodity during that year. These totals are expressed in US $m. and are valued on f.o.b. point of departure basis.
[c] Preliminary figures for 1979.

Source: United Nations, Yearbook of International Trade Statistics, New York, NY: UN, Vol. II, various issues 1970–1980.

Table A2.13 Market Economies' Exports: Rankings, Shares[a] and Totals[b]

SITC 656 Miscellaneous NES

Rank	1970	1971	1972	1973	1974	1975	1976	1977	1978	1979[c]
1	India	India	India	India	India	USA	USA	USA	USA	USA
	13.71	14.34	15.38	11.70	12.33	11.63	11.98	11.25	9.97	11.03
	91.1	108.3	137.8	136.0	191.5	186.1	214.5	242.9	250.9	329.6
2	Pakistan	Japan	Hong Kong	USA	USA	India	India	India	India	Hong Kong
	9.09	8.37	7.97	9.14	11.83	9.42	7.75	8.25	7.78	7.59
	60.5	63.2	71.9	106.2	183.7	150.7	136.7	178.2	195.7	226.7
3	Japan	Hong Kong	USA	France	Hong Kong	Belg.–Lux.	Hong Kong	W. Germany	W. Germany	W. Germany
	8.17	8.33	7.95	7.24	6.59	6.63	6.99	7.00	7.44	7.04
	54.3	62.9	71.7	84.2	102.4	106.1	125.2	151.2	187.1	210.1
4	USA	USA	Japan	Belg.–Lux.	France	Hong Kong	W. Germany	Italy	Hong Kong	India
	8.07	7.75	7.74	7.23	6.39	6.55	6.95	6.68	6.28	6.67
	53.6	58.5	69.8	84.1	99.3	104.7	124.5	144.3	158.0	199.2
5	Hong Kong	France	France	Hong Kong	Belg.–Lux.	France	Belg.–Lux.	Hong Kong	Belg.–Lux.	Italy
	7.32	6.74	7.19	7.05	6.32	6.41	6.44	6.23	6.20	6.43
	48.6	50.8	64.8	82.0	98.2	102.6	115.3	134.5	155.9	192.0
6	France	Belg.–Lux.	Belg.–Lux.	W. Germany	W. Germany	W. Germany	Italy	Belg.–Lux.	Italy	Belg.–Lux.
	6.72	6.69	7.04	5.93	6.23	5.96	5.95	6.09	6.19	6.00
	44.6	50.5	63.5	68.9	96.8	95.4	106.6	131.5	155.6	179.2

7	Belg.–Lux. 6.57 43.7	Italy 5.71 43.1	Italy 5.39 48.6	Portugal 5.40 62.8	Portugal 4.83 75.0	Italy 5.81 92.9	France 5.70 102.0	France 5.58 120.5	France 5.56 139.8	Portugal 5.91 176.4
8	Italy 5.71 37.9	Pakistan 5.17 39.0	W. Germany 5.34 48.1	Japan 4.48 52.1	Italy 4.53 70.3	UK 4.86 77.7	UK 4.88 87.3	UK 5.31 114.7	UK 5.52 138.8	UK 5.70 170.2
9	UK 5.59 37.2	UK 5.11 38.6	Portugal 4.33 39.0	Italy 4.47 51.9	UK 4.33 67.3	Portugal 4.76 76.2	Bangladesh 4.65 83.4	South Korea 4.33 93.5	Bangladesh 4.90 123.3	France 5.34 159.5
10	W. Germany 4.87 32.3	W. Germany 5.02 37.9	UK 4.29 38.7	Bangladesh[d] 4.30 50.0	Pakistan 3.56 55.4	Bangladesh 4.08 65.3	Portugal 3.70 66.2	Spain 4.01 86.6	Portugal 4.74 119.1	Spain 4.44 132.9

[a] Share is the first number appearing under each country name. It is the percentage of world exports taken by that country. The world is defined as market economies only.

[b] The second number under each country name is that country's total exports of that commodity during that year. These totals are expressed in US $m. and are valued on f.o.b. point of departure basis.

[c] Preliminary figures.

[d] Estimate.

Source: United Nations, *Yearbook of International Trade Statistics,* New York, NY: UN, Vol. II, various issues 1970–1980.

Table A2.14 Market Economies' Exports: Rankings, Shares[a] and Totals[b]

SITC 657 Floor Covering

Rank	1970	1971	1972	1973	1974	1975	1976	1977	1978	1979[c]
1	Belg.-Lux.	Belg.-Lux.	Belg.-Lux.	Belg.-Lux.	Belg.-Lux.	Belg.-Lux.	Belg.-Lux.	Belg.-Lux.	Belg.-Lux.	Belg.-Lux.
	24.20	25.12	25.05	24.60	23.98	24.91	24.76	22.29	22.43	21.64
	186.4	232.7	293.1	397.3	453.6	480.2	540.0	643.9	805.4	914.5
2	UK	UK	UK	UK	UK	UK	UK	Iran	Iran	Iran
	13.25	12.32	11.69	12.42	13.07	11.56	12.37	12.04	13.17	13.67
	102.1	114.1	136.7	200.6	247.2	222.8	272.6	347.9	473.0	577.5
3	W. Germany	W. Germany	W. Germany	W. Germany	W. Germany	W. Germany	W. Germany	UK	UK	UK
	8.88	8.87	8.97	9.67	9.21	8.86	8.83	11.11	9.42	8.29
	68.4	82.1	104.9	156.2	174.2	170.7	212.8	321.1	338.4	350.5
4	Netherlands	Iran	Netherlands	Netherlands	USA	USA	USA	W. Germany	W. Germany	W. Germany
	8.14	8.21	8.09	7.85	8.40	8.13	6.87	7.95	7.98	7.62
	62.7	76.1	94.6	126.7	158.9	156.7	186.2	229.6	286.7	321.9
5	Iran	Netherlands	Iran	USA	Netherlands	Netherlands	Netherlands	USA	Netherlands	Netherlands
	7.04	7.95	7.87	7.21	7.45	6.51	6.35	6.18	6.03	6.43
	54.3	73.6	92.0	116.5	140.9	125.4	138.6	178.7	216.6	271.8

6 USA 5.15 39.7	USA 4.35 40.3	USA 4.85 56.7	Iran 6.55 105.8	Iran 6.24 118.0	Iran 5.58 107.7	Iran 5.00 112.6	Netherlands 5.71 165.1	USA 5.60 201.2	USA 6.31 266.7
7 Japan 4.33 33.4	Japan 3.72 34.5	Denmark 3.37 39.4	Denmark 3.15 50.9	Denmark 3.25 61.5	Denmark 3.87 74.6	India 4.33 83.0	India 3.91 112.9	India 5.20 186.8	India 5.70 240.8
8 France 3.49 26.9	France 3.35 31.0	Japan 3.09 36.1	India 2.69 43.4	Pakistan 3.03 57.6	Pakistan 3.33 64.1	Pakistan 3.65 95.5	Pakistan 3.76 108.8	Pakistan 4.20 150.7	Pakistan 4.56 196.8
9 India 3.13 24.1	Denmark 3.06 28.4	India 3.05 35.7	France 2.40 38.7	India 2.82 53.4	India 3.11 60.0	Denmark 3.51 84.0	Denmark 3.16 91.3	Denmark 3.04 109.3	Denmark 3.07 129.6
10 Denmark 3.09 23.8	India 2.79 25.8	France 2.86 33.4	Japan 2.29 36.9	France 2.29 43.3	France 2.48 47.7	Japan 2.61 55.6	Japan 2.34 67.7	Japan 2.07 74.4	Morocco 1.85 78.2

a Share is the first number appearing under each country name. It is the percentage of world exports taken by that country. The world is defined as market economies only.

b The second number under each country name is that country's total exports of that commodity during that year. These totals are expressed in US $m. and are valued on f.o.b. point of departure basis.

c Preliminary figures.

Source: United Nations, *Yearbook of International Trade Statistics*, New York, NY: UN, Vol. II, various issues 1970–1980.

Appendix 3 US Regulations Affecting the Textile Industry

This list was developed by expanding a 1977 US Department of Commerce publication, *Federal Regulation, Policy, Ruling, Etc.*, with the assistance of the Advisory Board and several textile company lawyers.

FEDERAL REGULATION, POLICY, RULING, ETC.	*AGENCY*
Agricultural Adjustment Act of 1935 Section 32 – Percentage of cotton product duties appropriated for promotion of cotton products	Department of Agriculture
Agricultural Adjustment Act of 1938 Section 22 – Establishment of Quota on Cotton	Department of Agriculture
Agricultural Adjustment Act of 1956 Section 204 – Authority to negotiate	Committee for International Trade Administration
Antidumping Act (1921)	Department of Treasury
Armed Service Procurement Regulation Buy America Act Appropriation Act Restrictions	Department of Defense
Arrangement Regarding International Trade in Textiles (MFA)	Committee for International Trade Administration
Care Labeling of Textile Wearing Apparel (1972)	Federal Trade Commission
Care Labeling Regulation (currently pending)	Federal Trade Commission
Clean Air Act (1971) Existing Sources Standard New Sources Standard (proposed)	Environmental Protection Agency
Comprehensive Environmental Response, Compensation and Liability Act of 1980	Environmental Protection Agency

Consolidated Permit Regulations	Environmental Protection Agency
Consumer Product Safety Act (1972)	Consumer Product Safety Commission

General: Prohibition of consumer products which present an unreasonable risk of injury associated with the product

Specific: Flammable Fabrics Act (1953)	Consumer Product Safety Commission
Standard for Flammability of Clothing Textiles (CS 191–53)	Consumer Product Safety Commission
Standard for Flammability of Children's Sleepwear: sizes 0–6X (FF 3–71)	Consumer Product Safety Commission
Standard for the Surface Flammability of Carpets and Rugs (FF 1–70)	Consumer Product Safety Commission
Standard for the Surface Flammability of Small Carpets and Rugs (FF 2–70)	Consumer Product Safety Commission
Standard for the Flammability of Children's Sleepwear: sizes 7–14 (FF 5–74)	Consumer Product Safety Commission
Davis-Bacon Act	Department of Labor
Effluent Guidelines	Environmental Protection Agency
Equal Employment Opportunity	Department of Labor
Hazardous Waste Regulations	Environmental Protection Agency
Federal Water Pollution Control Act (1972) Effluent Guidelines (1974) Toxic Standard	Environmental Protection Agency
Flammability Floor Covering Standard	Health, Education, & Welfare
Fur Products Labeling Act (1961)	Federal Trade Commission
General Agreement on Tariffs and Trade (GATT)	Various

Guide for Down Fillings (Voluntary)	Federal Trade Commission
HUD Carpet Certification Program	Housing and Urban Development
National Energy Conservation Policy Act	Department of Energy
Natural Gas Policy Act (1978) 　Fuel Use Act 　Incremental Pricing	Department of Energy
National Wool Act of 1954 　Percentage of wool products duties 　appropriated for promotion of wool 　products	Department of Agriculture
Occupational Safety and Health Act (1970)	Occupational Safety and Health Administration
General: General industry safety and health 　　　　　　standards 　Specific: Occupational Exposure to Cotton 　　　　　　Dust Standard (1978) 　　　　　　Occupational Noise Exposure 　　　　　　Standard and Proposed 　　　　　　Regulation (1974) 　　　　　　Toxic and Hazardous Substances 　　　　　　Exposure Standard and 　　　　　　Proposed OSHA Carcinogen 　　　　　　Regulation	
Public Utility Regulatory Policies Act (1978)	Department of Energy
Resource Conservation and Recovery Act (1976)	Environmental Protection Agency
Robinson-Patman Act, the Clayton Act and other antitrust legislation. 　Prohibition of actions that have an 　anti-competitive effect, e.g. monopoly, 　price discrimination, cartels, mergers in 　certain cases, agreements, etc.	Federal Trade Commission
Superfund Regulations	Environmental Protection Agency
Tariff Act of 1930 　Countervailing Duties 　Unfair Import Practices	Various Department of Treasury Department of Treasury

Tariff Classification Act of 1962	International Trade Commission
Toxic Substances Control Act (1976)	Environmental Protection Agency
Trade Act of 1974	Various
Trade Adjustment Assistance for Workers	Department of Labor
Trade Adjustment Assistance for Firms	Department of Commerce
Trade Agreements Act (1979)	
Trade Expansion Act 1962	Various
Vinson-Trammel Act	Department of Treasury
Walsh-Healey Act	Department of Labor
Wool Products Labeling Act (1939)	Federal Trade Commission

Appendix 4 Summary of Major US Regulatory Issues as of Mid-1981

Care Labeling. In 1981, the Federal Trade Commission (FTC) approved an amendment greatly expanding the number of different textile items covered in the 1972 trade regulation rule on care labeling. The new amendment requires items such as draperies, linens and carpets to attach labels that contain, among other things, information on the care of the textile product. The industry believes the amended rule to be unnecessary, unjustified and expensive to abide by.

Clean Air Act. The Environmental Protection Agency (EPA) regulations on air-quality standards are viewed as unrealistic, too inflexible and very costly. The industry recommends that the regulations be eased in those areas of the country not having the greatest air pollution problems. The industry would also like to avoid any additional controls regarding the use of its coal-fired industrial-size boilers.

Consolidated Permit Regulations. The EPA regulations currently require textile companies to obtain numerous permits prior to construction and frequently to conduct over 100 different priority pollution tests after the mill is in operation. If one permit is delayed, the entire project is held up. This vulnerability has 'permitted' activists to disrupt building progress through temporary legal skirmishes over minor technicalities related to only one of the many permits. After the one point is resolved, another permit is challenged and delayed. The industry would like to have the entire regulatory process reconsidered and, if not eliminated, at least consolidated so that all the permits (and challenges) would be considered at one time. It would also like to eliminate the 65 pollution tests currently required, as it has been determined that the industry does not produce those pollutants.

Davis-Bacon Act. The act requires the payment of 'minimum wages' for government construction anywhere in the country. As this increases the cost of construction, the industry would like to have the requirement of 'minimum wages' abolished or have the wage levels reduced.

Effluent Guidelines. The EPA has many regulations related to effluent emissions, pre-treatment and new source performance standards. The industry feels that many of these are overly stringent and deserve reconsideration. Attempts should be made to justify the need for a regulation, which should not be imposed without regard to costs. Specifically, the American Textile Manufacturers Institute (ATMI) recommends that:

(1) the Clean Water Act be amended to drop BPT (Best Practicable Technology) when there is no demonstrated need;

(2) new source performance standards be no more restrictive than limits for existing sources;

(3) color limitations be dropped;

(4) Best Conventional Technology cost test should be recalculated by omitting plant size as a factor.

Equal Employment Opportunity. While the industry accepts the objectives of equal employment opportunities and is opposed to sexual or racial discrimination, it feels that current regulations are too vague and place the companies on the defensive. Regulations are being interpreted as if the company is guilty (when charged) until it can prove itself innocent. Furthermore, in order to bid on governmental projects, a company must accept a great deal of red tape. Companies also find themselves on the defensive when they are judged guilty instead of the offending employee. The industry would like to have the regulations more clearly written, would like to have claimants required to 'show cause' for suits before firms need to respond, and would like to have more emphasis placed on guilty individuals unless it can be shown that the company somehow encouraged illegal behavior.

Hazardous Waste Regulations. The EPA has numerous requirements for the treatment of 'hazardous wastes'. The industry believes that the definitions and regulations are sometimes improper and of no value. ATMI specifically recommends:

(1) the elimination of the regulation of recycled materials (currently being incorrectly labeled by the government as 'waste');

(2) the elimination of several improper testing and monitoring requirements; and

(3) the development of a classification system to regulate wastes according to their degree of hazardousness (no such system currently exists and all 'hazardous wastes' must be treated as if equally dangerous).

Industrial Revenue Bonds. The Treasury Department has proposed rules that would severely limit the ability of small companies to take advantage of the industrial revenue bond provisions of the tax code. The industry opposes these proposed changes.

National Energy Conservation Policy Act. The Department of Energy (DOE) currently requires reports regarding energy use even though all textile firms already meet the targets set. These reports are viewed by the industry as unnecessary red tape, which should no longer be required.

Natural Gas Policy Act. This 1978 act permits the suppliers of natural gas to charge industrial users more than others. Those firms unable to switch to another energy source are therefore at a disadvantage. The textile industry recommends that all users pay the same price for natural gas.

Occupational Safety and Health Act. Occupational Safety and Health Administration standards for both cotton dust and noise exposure are considered to be too high by the textile industry. The industry wants cost-benefit studies to be conducted to establish the appropriate standards.

Powerplant and Industrial Fuel Use Act. The Department of Energy is responsible for enforcing a complex set of rules that direct industrial fuel users to switch from oil and natural gas to coal or some other alternative fuel. Since deregulation seems to have eliminated the need for many of these time-delaying and expensive provisions, the industry would like to have them repealed.

Public Utility Regulatory Policies Act. Titles I and III of this 1978 act require the Department of Energy to create standards and guidelines for electric and gas utilities that must often be adopted by all state regulatory commissions. The textile industry feels that this seriously jeopardizes the ability of state agencies and local utilities to meet the needs and conditions unique to a particular geographical area. It therefore recommends the repeal of Titles I and III.

Superfund Regulations. The EPA is charged with enforcing regulations pertaining to waste spills. However, confusion exists regarding the definitions of a 'reportable quantity'. The industry would like to have this 'cleaned up' and also recommends that the EPA direct more of its attention to the abandoned waste disposal sites.

Toxic Substances Control Act. The EPA has set standards controlling the use of new chemical substances that may be too exacting for achievement without impeding technological innovation. ATMI believes that these standards are too high and discriminate against the smaller businesses, which cannot afford the high testing costs.

Tris Reimbursement. This issue concerns the economic losses suffered by the ban on the use of the chemical Tris. ATMI favors a governmental payment for the losses incurred as a result of the Tris ban.

Vinson-Trammel Act. This act severely constrains profits arising from certain military contracts. ATMI suggests the repeal of this act.

Walsh-Healey Act. An amendment has been proposed to allow Federal contractors the option of instituting a four-day work week. ATMI supports legislation that would grant more flexibility concerning these matters than is currently provided under the law.

Appendix 5   US Trade Adjustment Assistance

The Secretary of Commerce certifies that a firm is eligible for assistance and the Secretary of Labor certifies workers as eligible for benefits if they determine:

(1) that a significant number or proportion of workers in a particular firm or sub-division have become totally or partially separated, or are so threatened;

(2) that sales or production, or both, of such firm or sub-division have decreased absolutely;

(3) that increases in imports of articles like or directly in competition with articles produced by such workers 'contribute importantly' to a total or partial separation or threat thereof, and to a decline in sales or production.

If a firm is found eligible to apply for adjustment assistance it will receive technical or financial assistance or both from the Economic Development Administration.

Economic Development Administration technical assistance may be furnished by Federal agencies or through private individuals, firms, and institutions. When furnished through private sources, not more than 75 per cent of the cost may be borne by the United States.

A loan guarantee shall not exceed 90 per cent of the loan balance. Guaranteed loans are limited to $3 million and shall have interest rates no higher than the maximum established for guaranteed loans made under the Small Business Act.

Direct loans shall not amount to more than $1 million for any one firm. The interest rate shall be determined by taking into consideration the cost of borrowing to the United States, plus an added amount to cover administrative cost and possible loss under the program.

If a worker is found eligible to apply for adjustment assistance he may receive weekly payments which, when added to State Unemployment Insurance payments to which a worker is entitled, equal 70 per cent of the average weekly wage before his employment was disrupted by import competition.

The maximum allowance that a worker can receive can be no greater than the national average weekly wage in manufacturing. A worker may receive such allowances for up to fifty-two weeks, unless the worker exceeds sixty years of age, in which case he may receive an additional twenty-six weeks of allowances.

The program also assists workers to regain satisfactory employment through the use of a full range of manpower services and, if needed, job search and relocation allowances.

[GATT, 1980, pp. 185 and 186]

Appendix 6 Brief Summary of Textile Measures Taken so far in Japan

	Old textile law	New textile law	Structural improvement under the special textile law	Interim special measures for the textile industry	Measures for unregistered looms taken under the special measures law	Structural improvement effected under the renewed new textile law
Purpose	With a view to contributing to the normal development of exports, the rationalization of the textile industry will be sought by regulating the installation of textile production facilities.	With a view to enabling the nation's textile mills to withstand free competition, installation of textile facilities is regulated for the time being and normalization of exports is encouraged.	With a view to achieving economy of scale to the extent necessary for strengthening its competitive position, projects will be undertaken to improve its industry structure through the modernization of facilities and corporate mergers.	Relief given to textile manufacturers who are affected by the self-regulation of exports to the United States and by the enforcement of regulations pursuant to bilateral agreements concluded by the government.	Elimination of the existence of unregistered looms and financial stability of textile manufacturers.	With a view to effectively coping with the growing competition from developing countries and meeting diversifying domestic demand and strengthening its international competitive position, projects for structural improvement will be undertaken through the development of knowledge intensive technologies.

Authority	Law on Extraordinary Measures for Textile Industry Facilities.	Law on Extraordinary Measures for Textile Industry Facilities, etc. (Law No. 103 of 1964)	Law on Extraordinary Measures for Structural Improvement of Specific Textile Industries (Law No. 82 of 1967)	Cabinet decisions of: (1) 21 May 1971 (2) 17 December 1971 (3) 20 October 1972	Law concerning Special Cases of Loom Registration pursuant to Orders Issued under the Law concerning the Organization Structure of Small and Medium Enterprise Organizations (Law No. 74 of 1973)	Law on Extraordinary Measures for Structural Improvement of the Textile Industries (Amendment to 1974)
Period	June 1956 – September 1964	1 October 1964 – September 1970	16 August 1967 – 30 June 1974	Fiscal 1971 – Fiscal 1973	1 November 1973 – 30 June 1978	30 June 1974 – 30 June 1984
Industry groups covered	Spinning, weaving and dyeing	Spinning, dyeing and finishing	Specified spinning (cotton, staple fiber and synthetic fiber); specified weaving (cotton, staple fiber and silk and rayon); knitting, specified dyeing (looms dyeing and finishing)	Textile manufacturers affected by the regulation referred to above	Clothes manufacturers (cotton, staple fiber, silk, rayon, woolen, hemp and towel clothes manufacturers)	All textile industries

Source: Information compiled by Tran Van Tho, International Business Information K.K., Tokyo, Japan.

Appendix 7 Content and Standards for Financial Aid to the Japanese Textile Industry

This information was compiled by Tran Van Tho, International Business Information K.K., Tokyo, Japan.

I Financing by the Association for the Development of Small–Medium Sized Enterprises.

Provides favorable terms to new companies which are established by designated associations, enterprise associations, cooperative associations or by small–medium enterprises.

Terms: interest: 2.6%/year, for within 70% of financing required (60% from the state, 10% from the prefecture).
Period: the time required to develop new merchandise.

Equipment investment: within 16 years (3 year deferral).
Operation capital: within 7 years (3 year deferral).
Equipment leasing: within 12 years (2 year deferral).
Modernization of equipment, etc.: within 12 years (2 year deferral).

Standards: the following conditions must be fulfilled, in addition to the rules, regulations and laws of the Law for the Development of Small–Medium Sized Enterprises:

(A) Development of new merchandise: investment in the following enterprises:

    (1) To establish a product development center (equipment capital financing), for designated associations, joint ventures, enterprise associations, etc.
        (a) For the purchase of land, buildings and laboratories by designated associations.
        (b) For the purchase of same by joint ventures and enterprise associations.
        However, financing not allowed for joint ventures and dummy companies of large corporations.
        Further, financing for the following family firms and joint ventures not allowed (the same applies for loans from the Small–Medium Enterprise Development Association):

        (1) Where the entrepreneur owns more than 50% of the shares or provided more than 50% of the capital for a joint venture,

(2) where an employee has provided more than 50% of capital or owns more than 50% of stock, or where there is a relationship between one who has provided 50% of capital or owns 50% of stock and the company concerned.

(B) For purchase of equipment for R&D, for operations employing personnel and technicals for R&D (operating capital): financing to designated associations, joint ventures, enterprises.

(1) R&D
(2) design
(3) systems development
(4) information gathering, research
(5) education, training
(6) testing
(7) other
    (a) Equipment leasing financing: equipment leasing which is carried out by designated associations, in order to implement R&D for new products (equipment financing capital), for designated associations.
    (Exceptions as above.)
    (b) Modernization of equipment: for purchase of land, buildings, laboratories by designated associations. For purchase of same by joint ventures, etc.

II Financing by Small–Medium Enterprise Financing Bank.

Financing by the Association for Development of Small–Medium Enterprises is limited to the above-mentioned associations. Aid is given to *individual* small–medium enterprises which want to reform their organizations.

Terms: interest: 7.65%/year (limited to about $720,000).
Period: within 10 years (2 year deferral).

Standards: the following standards in addition to the laws and regulations of the Small–Medium Enterprise Financing Bank Law:

(A) Development of new merchandise: purchase of land, buildings, laboratories for new products development centers.
(B) Modernization of equipment: purchase of land, buildings and machinery in order to modernize equipment.

III Financing by the Japan Development Bank.

Financing for those not covered by the above items.

Terms: interest: 7.65%/year, up to 50% of required financing.
Period: within 10 years (2 years deferral).

Standards: in addition to the Japan Development Bank Law, the following standards must be observed:

(A)   Development of new merchandise: purchase of land, buildings, laboratories for new products development centers.

(B)   Modernization of equipment: purchase of equipment, buildings for production, and buildings for transport and storage of materials and products.

This financing is directed at enterprises above a certain level in size (or groups of small enterprises).
When new equipment is installed, old equipment must be discarded.

Appendix 8   Interview Guide

There are two parts to this interview guide: (1) general observations on the global and domestic threats and opportunities confronting the textile mill products industry during the next five–ten years; and (2) the corporate objectives and strategies the interviewed companies are planning for the next three–five years.

General Observations

1 What do you believe are the major threats confronting the textile mill products industry and your company within the next 5–10 years?
  a Technology
  b Government policies and actions (domestic and foreign)
  c Foreign competition
  d Trends in concentration of the industry (growth in the size of companies)
  e Inputs (resource availability and costs)
    1 fibers
    2 yarns
    3 non-fiber inputs
  f Demographic changes affecting end-markets and labor pool
  g Markets (domestic and foreign)
    1 apparel markets
    2 home furnishings market
    3 industrial markets
  h Other potential threats (for example, the replacement of fabrics with paper products)

2 What do you believe are the major opportunities for the textile mill products industry and your company within the next 5–10 years?
  a Technology
  b Government policies and actions (domestic and foreign)
  c Foreign markets
    1 apparel markets
    2 home furnishings market
    3 industrial markets
    4 other markets
  d Domestic markets
    1 apparel markets
    2 home furnishings market
    3 industrial markets
    4 other markets
  e Demographic changes affecting end-markets

3   What should the textile mill products industry be doing to remain viable during the next 5–10 years?

4   What role would you like to see the government take to assist the textile mill products industry (new policies, new programs, deregulation, deletion of old policies, etc.)?

5   What role would you like to see your trade association perform?

Corporate Objectives and Strategies

The following questions should be phrased to cover the past several years and the next 3 to 5 years. There are seven areas of the company's activities that are of primary interest.

1   Marketing objectives and strategies
   a   Market share objectives
      1   apparel market (domestic and foreign)
      2   home furnishings market (domestic and foreign)
      3   industrial uses (domestic and foreign)
   b   Product-line changes and additions
   c   New markets (domestic and foreign)
   d   Promotional objectives
      1   size of sales force
      2   advertising budget
      3   sales offices and/or branches (domestic and foreign)
   e   Pricing strategies
      1   price levels
      2   gross margin concerns
   f   Market research objectives
   g   Product development objectives
      1   existing markets
      2   new markets
   h   Forward integration plans

2   Supplier objectives and strategies
   a   Backward integration plans
   b   Supplier objectives (for example, reduce dependency)
      1   fibers
      2   yarns
      3   domestic versus foreign
   c   Supplier mix

3   Production objectives and strategies
   a   Quality standards
   b   Research and development objectives
   c   Research and development budgets
   d   Equipment and technology (for example, modernization)

   e Capital/labor ratios
   f Location plans
   g Offshore production

4 Physical distribution and logistics objectives and strategies
   a Material handling
   b Warehousing
   c Inventory objectives
   d Transportation and shipping
   e Order processing

5 Management and organization objectives and strategies
   a Management development strategies (skills, training, development)
      1 production
      2 marketing
      3 finance
      4 planning
      5 research and development
   b Ownership policies and objectives (for example, joint ventures)
   c Management–labor relations
   d Organizational structure and changes
   e Diversification plans (thoughts on moving into new industries)

6 Financial objectives and strategies
   a Capitalization objectives and strategies
   b Working capital objectives
   c Financial control changes
   d Financial criteria
      1 ROI
      2 payback period
      3 other criteria

7 External relations objectives and strategies
   a Relations with government
   b Relations with trade associations
   c Relations with communities in which firm operates
   d Relations with major buyer industries

8 Planning approach used by firm (strategic)
   a Planning horizons (time)
   b Location of planning activity
   c Departments and plants involved in planning activity
   d Methods used for decisions
      1 industry averages
      2 portfolio analysis
      3 business position assessment
      4 PIMS (Profit Impact of Market Strategy)

References

American Apparel Manufacturers Association, Apparel Political Education Committee (1980), *Apparel Trade Under 807*, Arlington Va: American Apparel Manufacturers Association.

American Textile Manufacturers Institute (1978), 'Older but better', Economic Memo No. 18, Washington, DC, May/June.

Arbeitgeberkreis Gesamttextil (1981), *Lohne und Arbeitskosten der Testilindustrie: Internationaler Vergleich*, Frankfurt a/M: Arbeitgeberkreis Gesamttextil.

Arpan, Jeffrey S., Barry, Mary and Tho, Tran Van (1981), 'The fiber, fabric, and apparel complex in the Asia Pacific: the patterns and textures of competition and the shape of things to come', paper prepared for the University of Washington Conference on 'International Transfer of Resources: Strategic Company Responses in the Dynamic Asia Pacific Environment', Montreal, October 1982.

Arpan, Jeffrey, S., Barry, Mary and Tho, Tran Van (forthcoming), 'The textile complex in the Pacific Basin', in R. Moxon, T. Roehl and J. F. Truitt (eds), *International Business Strategies in the Asia Pacific Area*, Greenwich, Conn.: JAI Press.

Arpan, Jeffrey S., de la Torre, Jose, Toyne, Brian, *et al.* (1982), *The US Apparel Industry: International Challenge/Domestic Response*, Atlanta, Ga: Business Publishing Division of the College of Business Administration, Georgia State University, Research Monograph No. 88.

Barnett, Andy H. (1981), *Projections of Employment and Demographic Characteristics for the Textile Labor Force in the Year 1990*, Columbia, SC: University of South Carolina, College of Business Administration, Division of Research. 'The big textile picture for 1991' (1980), *Textile Industries*, Atlanta, Ga: Smith Publishing Co., July.

Breitenacher, Michael (1981), *Textilindustrie: Strukturwandlungen und Entwicklungsperspektiven für die achtziger Jahre*, Ifo-Institut für Wirtschaftsforschung, Berlin: Duncker & Humblot.

Business Statistics Office (1980), *1978 Report on the Census of Production*, PA 1002, Business Monitor, London: HMSO.

Comitextil (1979), *Bulletin*, No. 3, Brussels.

Commission of the European Communities (1981), *Commission Communication to the Council on the Situation and Prospects of the Textile and Clothing Industries in the Community*, COM(81)388 final, Annex IX, Brussels: the Commission.

COMPUSTAT® Data Base Services, New York, NY: Standard & Poors Inc.

Council on Wage and Price Stability (1978), *A Study of the Textile and Apparel Industry*, Washington, DC: US Government Printing Office.

DeNisi, Angelo S., Meglino, Bruce M. and Youngblood, Stuart A. (1981),

Employee Attitude Study, Columbia, SC: University of South Carolina, College of Business Administration, Division of Research.

Eurostat (1981), *Structure and Activity of Industry, 1976*, Luxembourg: Statistical Office of the EC.

Federal Reserve Bulletin, Washington, DC: Publication Services, Board of Governors of the Federal Reserve System, various issues.
Federtessile (1980), *Il Settore tessile e abbigliamento in Italia*, Milan: Franco Angeli Editore.
Fryer, J. S., Barnett, A. H., DeNisi, A. S., Meglino, B. M., Williams, C. G. and Youngblood, S. A. (1981), *The Textile Labor Force in the 1980s*, Columbia, SC: University of South Carolina, College of Business Administration, Division of Research, April.

GATT (1980), 'Report by the Working Group on Adjustment Measures', unpublished paper, Geneva: General Agreement on Tariffs and Trade, Textile Committee, 7 October.
GATT (1982), 'Ministerial Declaration', Ministerial Meeting, Thirty-Eighth Session, Geneva: General Agreement on Tariffs and Trade, 24–29 November.

INDA (1978), *Guide to Non-Woven Fabrics*, New York, NY: The Association of the Non-Woven Fabrics Industry.
International Cotton Advisory Committee (1980), *Quarterly Bulletin*, Washington, DC: October.
International Monetary Fund (1981), *International Financial Statistics Yearbook*, Washington, DC: IMF.

Kotler, Philip (1980), *Marketing Management: Analysis, Planning, and Control*, 4th edn, Englewood Cliffs, NJ:: Prentice-Hall.
Kurth, Wolfgang (1980), 'Textiles and Clothing: A National and International Issue', International Symposium on Industrial Policies for the Eighties, Madrid, May, mimeo.

Maizels, Alfred (1963), *Industrial Growth and World Trade*, Cambridge, England: Cambridge University Press.
Ministero dell'Industria, del Commercio e dell'Artigianato (1979), *Programma finalizzato: sistema della moda*, Rome.

OECD (1963–82), *Textile Industry in OECD Countries*, Paris: Organization for Economic Cooperation and Development, bienially.
OECD (1980–2), *Indicators of Industrial Activity*, Paris: Organization for Economic Cooperation and Development, quarterly.

Puchala, Donald and Zupnick, Elliot (1982), 'Adjustments to changing world trade: the NICs, the OECD and textiles', unpublished paper, New York, NY: Columbia University.

Shepherd, Geoffrey (1981), *Textile-Industry Adjustment in Developed Countries*, Thames Essay, No. 30, London: Trade Policy Research Centre.

Suehiro, Alcina (1980), *Comparative Advantage of Textile Industries in Asia* (a progress report), Tokyo: Institute of Developing Economies.

'Taiwan plan projects smaller, more efficient textile industry' (1981), *Business Asia*, 20 March.

Tanzer, Andrew (1981), 'Government sets 10-year plan for textile industry', *The Journal of Commerce*, October.

Textile Council (1969), *Cotton and Allied Textiles*, Vol. 2, Manchester: Textile Council.

Textile Hi-Lights, Atlanta, Ga.: McGraw Hill/Washington, DC: American Textile Manufacturers Institute, various issues.

Textile Organon (1960–82), Roseland, NJ: Textile Economics Bureau Inc., various issues.

'Textiles – Current Analysis' (1980), *Industry Survey*, New York, NY: Standard & Poors, 10 December.

'Textiles – Basic Analysis' (1980), *Industry Survey*, New York, NY: Standard & Poors, 17 July.

Textilwirtschaft, Frankfurt, monthly.

Torre, Jose de la, with Bacchetta, Michel (1979), *Decline and Adjustment: European Policies Toward Their Clothing Industries*, Fontainebleau, France: European Institute of Business Administration, June.

Toyne, Brian *et al.* (1983), *The US Textile Mill Products Industry: International Challenges and Strategies for the Future*, Columbia, SC: University of South Carolina Press.

United Nations (1960–82), *Monthly Bulletin of Statistics*, New York, NY: UN.

United Nations (1960–82), *Demographic Yearbook*, New York, NY: UN.

United Nations (1964–81), *Yearbook of Industrial Statistics*, New York, NY: UN.

United Nations (1966–82), *Yearbook of International Trade Statistics*, New York, NY: UN.

United Nations (1971), *Foreign Trade Statistics of Asia and the Pacific*, Series A, New York, NY: UN.

United Nations Commission on Trade and Development (1980), *Handbook of International Trade and Development Statistics*, Geneva: UNCTAD.

US Bureau of the Census (1981), *County Business Patterns*, Washington, DC: US Government Printing Office.

US Bureau of the Census (1978), *Statistical Abstract of the US 1978*, Washington, DC: US Government Printing Office.

US Department of Commerce (1964–82), *Annual Survey of Manufacturers*, Washington, DC: US Government Printing Office.

US Department of Commerce (1964–82), *US Foreign Trade: Exports*, Washington, DC: US Government Printing Office.

US Department of Commerce (1964–82), *US Foreign Trade: Imports*, Washington, DC: US Government Printing Office.

US Department of Commerce (1979–82), *Country Market Survey, Textiles*, various countries, International Marketing Series, Washington, DC: US Government Printing Office.

US Department of Commerce (1964–82), *US Exports/Domestic Merchandise, SIC-Based Products by World Areas*, Washington, DC: US Government Printing Office.

US Department of Commerce (1964–82), *US Imports/Consumption and General, SIC-Based Products by World Areas*, Washington, DC: US Government Printing Office.

US Department of Commerce (1977), *Federal Regulation, Policy, Ruling, etc.*, Washington, DC: US Government Printing Office.

US Department of Commerce (1980), *Foreign Export Credit Insurance Programs*, Washington, DC: US Government Printing Office.

US Department of Commerce, Office of Textiles and Apparel (1981a), *Foreign Regulations Affecting United States Textile/Apparel Exports*, Washington, DC: US Government Printing Office, August.

US Department of Commerce (1981b), *1977 Census of Manufacturers: Concentration Ratios in Manufacturing*, Washington, DC: US Government Printing Office, September.

US Department of Commerce (1981c), *A Study of the Feasibility of Export Trading Companies to Promote Increased Exports by the US Textile and Apparel Companies*, 4 vols, Washington, DC: US Government Printing Office, 16 February.

US Department of Commerce (1982), *International Economic Indicators*, Washington, DC: US Government Printing Office.

US Department of Commerce (1982), *Survey of Current Business*, Washington, DC: US Government Printing Office, March.

US Department of Labor, Bureau of Labor Statistics (1979), *Employment and Earnings, United States, 1909–1978*, Bulletin No. 1313–11, Washington, DC: US Government Printing Office.

US International Trade Commission (1981), *Publication 1131*, Washington, DC: USITC, May.

US Office of Management and Budget (1972), *Standard Industrial Classification Manual*, Washington, DC: US Government Printing Office.

US Tariff Commission (1980), *Economic Factors Affecting the Use of Item 807 and 806.30 of the Tariff Schedules of the United States*, TC Publication 339, Washington, DC: US Government Printing Office, September.

Vaugn, Edward A. (1964), 'An evaluation of the effects of various management strategies on profits relative to the cotton broad woven goods economic cycle', Masters thesis Charlottesville, Va.: Institute of Textile Technology, June.

Weiss, Leonard (1961), *Economics and American Industry*, New York, NY: Wiley.

Wells, Louis T. (1968), 'A product life cycle for international trade?' *Journal of Marketing*, July.

Werner Associates Inc. (n.d.), *Commentary on Hourly Labour Costs in the Primary Textile Industry Winter 78–79*, Brussels.
Werner Associates Inc. (n.d.), *Spinning and Weaving Labour Cost Comparisons Summer 1981*, Brussels.
Werner Associates Inc. (1981), *Newsletter*, New York/Brussels, June.
Williams, C. Glyn (1981), *An Analysis of the Textile Labor Force with Implications for the 1980s*, Columbia, SC: University of South Carolina, College of Business Administration, Division of Research.
World Bank (1980), *World Bank Atlas*, Washington, DC: The World Bank.

Yamazawa, Ippei (1981), 'Sen-i Sangyo no Kozo Chosei to Yunyu Seisaku', *The Hitotsubashi Review*, Tokyo, vol. 85, no. 5, May.

Index